Democracy and Redistribution

When do countries democratize? What facilitates the survival of authoritarian regimes? What determines the occurrence of revolutions, often leading to left-wing dictatorships, such as the Soviet regime? Although a large literature has developed since Aristotle through contemporary political science to answer these questions, we still lack a convincing understanding of the process of political development. Employing analytical tools borrowed from game theory, Carles Boix offers a complete theory of political transitions, in which political regimes ultimately hinge on the nature of economic assets, their distribution among individuals, and the balance of power among different social groups. Supported by detailed historical work and extensive statistical analysis that goes back to the mid-nineteenth century, this book shows, among many other things, why democracy triumphed in nineteenth-century agrarian Norway, Switzerland and the Northeastern United States yet failed in countries with a powerful land-owning class. It accounts for the spread of democracy in the developed world while clarifying why authoritarianism prevails in wealthy oil nations and explains the distribution of revolutionary outbursts and regime shifts in the world in the last two centuries. To round off its exploration of the nature of political regimes, the book offers as well an assessment of the distributive and governance consequences of democracies and dictatorships.

Carles Boix is professor of political science at Princeton University. His research and teaching interests include comparative political economy and comparative politics. His book *Political Parties, Growth and Equality* (Cambridge, 1998) won the 1999 American Political Science Association Best Book Award in political economy.

Cambridge Studies in Comparative Politics

General Editor
Margaret Levi   *University of Washington, Seattle*

Assistant General Editor
Stephen Hanson   *University of Washington, Seattle*

Associate Editors
Robert H. Bates   *Harvard University*
Peter Hall   *Harvard University*
Peter Lange   *Duke University*
Helen Milner   *Columbia University*
Frances Rosenbluth   *Yale University*
Susan Stokes   *University of Chicago*
Sidney Tarrow   *Cornell University*

Other Books in the Series

Lisa Baldez, *Why Women Protest*
Stefano Bartolini, *The Political Mobilization of the European Left, 1860–1980: The Class Cleavage*
Carles Boix, *Political Parties, Growth and Equality: Conservative and Social Democratic Economic Strategies in the World Economy*
Catherine Boone, *Merchant Capital and the Roots of State Power in Senegal, 1930–1985*
Michael Bratton and Nicolas van de Walle, *Democratic Experiments in Africa: Regime Transitions in Comparative Perspective*
Valerie Bunce, *Leaving Socialism and Leaving the State: The End of Yugoslavia, the Soviet Union and Czechoslovakia*
Ruth Berins Collier, *Paths Toward Democracy: The Working Class and Elites in Western Europe and South America*
Donatella della Porta, *Social Movements, Political Violence, and the State*
Gerald Easter, *Reconstructing the State: Personal Networks ad Elite Identity*
Robert J. Franzese, Jr., *Macroeconomic Policies of Developed Democracies*

Continued on the page following the index.

A l'Alícia
"...more than reason." (*Much Ado about Nothing*, V, 4)

Democracy and Redistribution

CARLES BOIX

Princeton University

CAMBRIDGE
UNIVERSITY PRESS

CAMBRIDGE UNIVERSITY PRESS
Cambridge, New York, Melbourne, Madrid, Cape Town, Singapore, São Paulo

Cambridge University Press
32 Avenue of the Americas, New York, NY 10013-2473, USA

www.cambridge.org
Information on this title:www.cambridge.org/9780521825603

First published 2003
Reprinted 2005, 2006, 2007

Printed in the United States of America

A catalog record for this publication is available from the British Library

Library of Congress Cataloging in Publication Data

Boix, Carles.
Democracy and redistribution / Carles Boix.
   p.   cm. – (Cambridge studies in comparative politics)
Includes bibliographical references and index.
ISBN 0-521-82560-1 – ISBN 0-521-53267-1 (pb.)
1. Democratization.   2. Political development.   3. Economic development.
I. Title.   II. Series.
JC423.B6255   2003
3209.6–dc21   2002041689

ISBN 978-0-521-82560-3 hardback
ISBN 978-0-521-53267-9 paperback

Contents

Figures

List of Figures

Tables

List of Tables

Acknowledgments

This book has benefited from comments by Alícia Adserà, James Alt, Delia Boylan, Jeff Campbell, Matt Cleary, Gösta Esping-Andersen, Lloyd Gruber, Jonathan Guryon, David Laitin, José María Maravall, Luis Medina, Susan Pratt, Adam Przeworski, Ignacio Sánchez-Cuenca, Carey Shugart, Duncan Snidal, James Snyder, Andy Sobel, Susan Stokes, Lora Viola, Michael Wallerstein, Lisa Wedeen and Christa van Wijnbergen. I also thank participants in seminars at Fundación Juan March, Madrid; Washington University; the University of Chicago; Harvard-MIT Positive Political Economy Workshop; McGill University; Kellogg Institute for International Studies, Notre Dame University; UCLA; Ohio State University; CIDE, Ciudad de México; Stanford University; and Yale University. My deepest gratitude goes, however, to Luis Garicano, with whom I wrote the baseline model described in Chapter 1. Finally, I wish to acknowledge the financial support of the Franke Institute for the Humanities at the University of Chicago. The Institute freed me from teaching in the academic year 1999–2000 under the assumption I would be writing on a different project: I hope that, despite my change of plans, the result is worth their investment.

Introduction

Under what conditions are stable democracies adopted? What facilitates the survival of authoritarian regimes? What determines the occurrence of sudden revolutionary explosions, often leading to expropriation and left-wing dictatorships, such as the Soviet revolution? And, finally, what are the distributional consequences of different political regimes?

To answer these long-standing questions, a large theoretical literature has developed since Aristotle through Marx and Weber. In the last fifty years this body of work has been joined by a vast array of empirical studies in modern political science. Econometric studies have found democracy to be inextricably linked to economic development. In turn, different strands of more historical research have alternatively associated the existence of democratic regimes with either the destruction of the agrarian world, the formation of cross-class coalitions or the growing strength of the working class. Finally, under the renewed influence of neoinstutionalism, several scholars have claimed that a stable democracy can prosper only when sustained by a particular set of constitutional rules and embedded in certain social norms and practices.

Yet for all the extensive treatment that the causes and the consequences of the process of democratization have received, we still lack a convincing theory of political development and transitions. Take, to start with, the well-known positive correlation between democracy and economic development – uncovered by Lipset in 1959, replicated by numerous studies in the following decades, and confirmed by Przeworski and Limongi's sophisticated analysis of the world sample of nations in the period from 1950 to 1990. Excluding Duverger's law on the effect of single-member districts on party systems, it may be the strongest empirical generalization

1

we have in comparative politics to date. But even cursory analysis reveals at least three important weaknesses.

First, we do not know how well that correlation travels back to the period preceding World War II – in fact, it probably does not, since most nineteenth-century democracies thrived in countries that, by today's standards, we would consider relatively poor. Second, it is unclear how the level of per capita income, or, more generally, the extent of economic development, may explain the reverse side of the introduction of democratic regimes, that is, the occurrence of political violence and revolutionary explosions as well as the emergence of various types of right-wing and left-wing dictatorships across countries. Finally, and above all, the correlation between development and democracy is still in need of a full-fledged description of the causal mechanisms through which democratic (and authoritarian) regimes are established. It is true that several explanations have been developed to account for the relationship between economic modernization and political democratization. Still, they remain incomplete. None of them has characterized either the preferences that different political actors, be they individuals or social groups, harbor toward different political regimes or the strategies that the former engage in to bring the latter about. In other words, they have not employed analytical microfoundations to develop a theory of regime change. Consequently, the scholarly literature cannot explain with precision the conditions under which different political systems emerge and break down.

The refusal to employ analytical tools to build a theory of political transitions has not remained circumscribed to modernization theory. As will be detailed in the first section of this introduction, this theoretical strategy has been fairly common to all the scholars working on the issue of regime transitions. And this is what, in most likelihood, has led the most influential surveys of democratization literature, such as Huntington's *The Third Wave*, to abandon any unified causal theory and to present the emergence of current democracies as the result of multiple and alternative causal paths.[1]

With the deficiencies of the literature on democratization in mind, this book develops, and systematically tests, a unified model that derives the distribution of different political regimes, that is, the occurrence of

---

[1] See Huntington (1991). To some extent, Dahl (1971) takes a similar theoretical stance, discussing democratization as the result of a laundry list of diverse economic, cultural and chronological factors.

democracies, right-wing authoritarian regimes and revolutions leading to civil wars and communist or left-wing dictatorships, from a set of simple yet reasonable assumptions about the preferences and resources of social actors or individuals in a given country: the domestic distribution of economic assets, that is, the degree of economic equality; the nature of those economic assets, broadly determined by their mobility; and, finally, the distribution of political resources (to repress or outmaneuver any opponents) among individuals. In turn, the political logic of distributive conflict that underlies the choice of political regimes is employed to explain the redistributive consequences of each political regime.

As I examine in a more extended manner later in this introduction, and then fully in Chapters 1 through 4, democracy prevails when either economic equality or capital mobility are high in a given country. On the one hand, economic equality promotes democracy. As the distribution of assets and income becomes more balanced among individuals, the redistributive impact of democracy diminishes and the probability of a peaceful transition from an authoritarian regime to universal suffrage increases. On the other hand, a decline in the specificity of capital, that is, a reduction in the cost of moving capital away from its country of origin, curbs the redistributive pressures from non–capital holders. As capital becomes more mobile, democratic governments must curb taxes – if the taxes were too high, capital would escape abroad. Accordingly, the extent of political conflict among capital holders and nonholders diminishes, and the likelihood of democracy rises.

By contrast, authoritarianism predominates in those countries in which both the level of inequality and the lack of capital mobility are high. In highly unequal societies, the redistributive demands of the worse-off citizens on the wealthy are particularly intense. As a result, the latter have a strong incentive to oppose the introduction of democracy, which would enable the majority of the population to impose heavy taxes on them. The prevalence of highly immobile types of capital exacerbates the authoritarian solution. Unable to shift assets abroad to escape the threat of high taxes, capital owners grow more resolute in their efforts to block democracy.

Whether or not the adoption of an authoritarian regime is stable, that is, unaffected by political conflict, depends on the political resources of the contending parties. If the lower classes are demobilized or the ruling elite has strong repressive capabilities, there is a peaceful and durable authoritarian regime. However, if the organizational capacity of the poor rises, the likelihood of revolutionary explosions and civil wars escalates. If the poor win, they proceed to expropriate the assets of the wealthy and establish a left-wing dictatorship.

The redistributive consequences of each political regime are logically at odds with each other. In right-wing authoritarian regimes, transfers are practically zero (with taxes limited to financing and sustaining defense, police and administrative services). In democracies, the public sector grows steadily, pushed by both redistributive demands and, as I will elaborate later, pressures to reduce the volatility of business cycles and economic risks. In revolutionary regimes, the nationalization of private assets leads first to the introduction of central planning and socialism and, devoid of transparent mechanisms of political accountability, very often to widespread corruption and economic stagnation.

In the rest of this introduction I proceed as follows. In the first section, I examine the state of current theoretical and empirical debates over democratization and political development in general. There I detail the contributions and weaknesses of three broad types of research: modernization theory, the sociological approach to regime choice and rational-choice models. In discussing them, I gradually suggest a way to weave some of their components together to build a theoretically more compelling and empirically more satisfactory model of political transitions. In the second section, I offer an overview of the argument of the book. In the third section, I detail how the book is organized.

The Theoretical and Empirical Debate

Within the vast literature on political development and political transitions, we can distinguish three broad strands of research: political modernization, the sociological literature on regime formation and, more recently, the notion of democracy as a political and institutional equilibrium.[2]

To make sense of the empirically robust association between the frequency of democracy and the level of economic development (Lipset 1959; Jackman 1973; Bollen 1979; Burkhart and Lewis-Beck 1994; Przeworski and Limongi 1997), the literature on political modernization has offered three explanations of the emergence of democracy.[3] In the first account, the

---

[2] For an excellent survey of the first two strands of work, see Rueschemeyer, Stephens and Stephens (1992), Chap. 2.

[3] Although here I make an effort to distinguish them analytically, they often are lumped together in modernization writings.

predominance of democratic institutions in developed countries has been attributed to a functional match between democracy and social modernization. Since a market economy is sustained by a free flow of information within an organizational environment based on predominantly horizontal networks, this explanation holds that markets can prosper only when they are embedded in a political framework characterized by the recognition of constitutional liberties and democratic practices (Cutright 1963; indirectly, Lerner 1958). Accordingly, developed economies and political democracies should emerge and survive together, at least in the long run.

Mostly due to the lack of precision about the causal direction in that functionalist model, a second explanation, in part overlapping with the first one, emphasizes the extension of pluralistic values associated with the process of economic development. Here both rising education levels and the formation of an autonomous labor force (a labor force composed of employees increasingly required to make their own decisions in the production process) generate a public opinion that willingly tolerates the existing multiplicity of values and opinions and that embraces liberal democracy as the legitimate mechanism to settle its disagreements.[4]

Even though the idea that the extension of toleration reinforces or even causes democracy seems an eminently plausible one, to avoid turning it into a purely tautological concept, we need to ascertain what makes the practice of toleration relatively easier or less costly for the citizens of developed societies.[5] The decline in the costs of toleration, triggered by or associated with the process of economic development, has been alternatively attributed to either a shift in religious and cultural values or a change in the structure of material or economic relations. The link between religious practices and political democratization seems a tenuous one. Democracy was established in most developed countries well before most of them underwent a widespread process of secularization in the 1960s. Likewise, as I show in Chapters 2 and 3, there is no evidence that certain religions, such as Protestantism, with its imputed emphasis on individual autonomy, are more conducive to democracy than others.[6]

---

[4] This is the explanation emphasized in Lipset (1959: 79–80). It is also present in Dahl (1971), Bollen (1979) and Inglehart (1997: Chap. 6).

[5] This is readily acknowledged by Dahl (1971: 14–16). By contrast, the sources and operation of a tolerant attitude in politics remain much more ambiguous among other scholars, such as Inkeles (1966) or Lerner (1958).

[6] In Chapter 2, I show that a higher level of religious fragmentation reduces the likelihood of a democratic breakdown. This result actually reinforces the idea that the success of democracy

By stressing the transformation of the economic and social structure, the third theoretical account within the modernization school seems to supply a more convincing explanation for the fall in the costs of toleration that comes with economic development. As articulated by Lipset, the process of economic modernization results in both a reduction in the level of income inequality, which is a source of political conflict and fosters the adoption of authoritarian solutions, and the growth of a broad middle class, who then acts as a moderating political force (Lipset 1959: 83–84). But even in this case, in which there is an embryonic reference to the presence of certain actors and their interests, the theoretical account is cast in imprecise terms. One must concur with Rueschemeyer, Stephens and Stephens when, after summarizing the modernization literature, they conclude that the causal mechanisms linking economic development and the presence of a democratic regime still "remain, in effect, in a black box" (1992: 29). More precisely, the insufficiencies of the literature of political modernization stem from its lack of attention to a central theoretical link: political agency. Scholars working in this tradition have hardly depicted the actors that intervene in the choice of political regimes, the reasons that motivate their actions, and the political strategies they employ to secure their goals.

Devoid of a clear theoretical backbone, modernization theory has failed to provide a reasonable answer to at least three main issues in the process of political development. First, the occurrence of widespread political violence over time and the revolutionary waves of the last two centuries have never found an easy accommodation within modernization theory – why conflict should occur at certain income levels but not at others remains unclear. The emergence of communist regimes has been treated as a deviant outcome that must be explained through variables, such as the distribution of land and the emergence of guerrillas, which automatically fall outside of a crude linear theory of modernization. Second, modernization theory has fallen short of accounting for the short-term dynamics in the process of transition to (or away from) democracy – an issue that seems especially relevant for the segment of semideveloped economies, where democratic consolidation has been particularly elusive. Finally, the theoretical frailty of modernization literature has had important empirical consequences. If the level of per capita income directly predicts the likelihood of democracy (or, if Przeworski and Limongi are right, the likelihood

is related to a balanced distribution of power among different social groups rather than to the attitudinal traits of the groups.

of democratic breakdown), then one cannot explain the presence of (at least partially) democratic episodes in societies that predate the phenomenon of economic modernization: some Greek city-states, the attempts made during the last period of the Roman Republic, several cities and territories (such as the mountainous Swiss cantons) in the late Middle Ages, and the agrarian democracies of the early nineteenth century (the Northeastern states in the United States, Iceland, Norway or Switzerland).[7] Conversely, if the level of per capita income merely proxies for a set of more direct causes, such as a changing distribution of income or a growing middle class, then we must specify those causes and develop the proper empirical tests to understand what shapes the choice of political regimes.

In contrast to the theory of political modernization, the language of political agency has played a central role in the sociological theories of democratization. In his path-breaking work on regime change, Moore (1966) stressed, on the one hand, the particular balance between peasants and landlords, and, on the other, the interaction between the landlords and the commercial bourgeoisie as the key factors shaping the historical paths leading to democracy, fascism and communism in the mid-twentieth century. Luebbert (1991) later applied the same preoccupation with the role of social actors and classes to conclude that a cross-class coalition institutionalized through a pact between liberal and social democratic parties accounted for the triumph of democracy in several interwar democracies. Finally, Rueschemeyer, Stephens and Stephens (1992) associated the occurrence of a democratic regime with the strength of the working class.[8] There is no doubt that these authors probe more deeply into the causes of democracy than do the most quantitatively oriented researchers of the modernization literature. But they still sidestep the issue of explicitly modeling the preferences and incentives of actors engaged in struggles over the determination of the political regime. As a result, they offer another type of correlation analysis – one with fewer observations than modernization theory yet with a more sophisticated elaboration of the causes leading to the choice of political regimes than the one advanced by quantitative researchers.

Triggered by the democratic transitions of the 1970s and the 1980s, the third and last strand of research on the causes of democratization has veered away from both the statistical research and the sociological work

---

[7] For a similar critique, see Dahl (1971: 69).

[8] For a critical review of this literature, see Kitschelt (1992).

just reviewed. In what may be considered the foundational work of this type of analysis, O'Donnell and Schmitter (1986) insist on describing a democratic outcome as the result of a highly contingent pact among previously contending groups. Defining the latter in terms of their position toward the introduction of a democratic solution, the authors consciously suppress any direct reference to the groups' material interests or social status. Democracy is seen as a negotiated solution among the moderate forces of both the regime and antiregime elites.

Although first cast in non-game-theoretical terms, this approach to the problem of democratization rapidly received formal treatment. Employing the tools of game theory, democracy was then defined as an institutional equilibrium, that is, as a stable outcome that results from the strategic choices that different individuals or parties in contention make to maximize their own welfare (Przeworski 1991: 26–34; Weingast 1997). This venue of analysis formalized an insight partly intuited by some authors of the first wave of democratization studies. As stressed by Dahl (1971: 14–16), in the choice of political regimes all political actors assess the net benefits of tolerating a democratic regime, which implies the chance of losing the election, being in opposition and bearing the costs of the policies approved by the contending sector, against the utility of permanently excluding the opposing block through an authoritarian government. As the costs of toleration decline, that is, as the difference between their welfare under an authoritarian regime and in a democratic system diminishes, political actors increasingly favor a democratic regime. Similarly, as the costs of exclusion augment, that is, as the price of repressing the opposition goes up, democracy becomes a more acceptable alternative. In short, whenever all sides have no incentive to pursue an exclusionary strategy, democracy is established. Conversely, if any of them prefers to pursue an authoritarian path, political violence and ultimately a dictatorship prevail.

The insights generated by the application of game-theory tools to the study of democratic transitions play a crucial role in this book. Still, the existing formal characterization of a democratic equilibrium remains incomplete in two senses, and these must be addressed if we wish to solve the theoretical and empirical puzzles posed by the process of political development. First, the literature of democracy as an equilibrium does not specify the conditions under which the costs of rejecting or accepting a democratic outcome vary for the individuals participating in the political game; in other words, it does not describe what shapes their welfare function. Second, and in a related manner, it remains substantially ambiguous about who count, as actors in the process of establishing a political regime.[9] For both reasons, that approach does not describe the conditions under which democracy may or may not be out of equilibrium – that is, it cannot explain why democracies succeed in some instances yet fail in others. Thus, for example, it cannot account either for the breakdown of democracy in Spain in 1936 or for its stability after 1976. To use the title of the memoirs of Gil Robles, the leader of the largest right-wing political party in Spain at the time, "peace was not possible" in 1936 (Gil Robles 1978). By contrast, as Alexander (2002) shows, in the 1970s most conservative Spanish politicians judged their country's transition to democracy to be unavoidable and hardly threatening. We must conclude that for democracy to have become a dominant strategy for all parties involved, the underlying conditions in which Spanish elites operated had to have changed in the historical interval.

Notice that the same problem haunts the nonformal conception of democracy as a political pact among elites. According to the most recent literature on democratic consolidation, a successful political transition hinges on the ability of political elites, who often have learned from dramatic past conflicts, to negotiate broad, encompassing agreements and to craft the proper constitutional framework.[10] Yet no political elite operates in a vacuum. Since politicians are always accountable to their principal, be it the voters or a certain social sector or political organization, they risk being displaced by a new set of representatives if they do not meet the interests and demands of their supporters – unless they have a monopoly over representation. Hence, the survival of any political pact cannot be understood without reference to its broader social implications. For an elite pact to be robust its consequences must fall within the boundaries of what is acceptable to the public. To put it differently, a too strict concept of democracy as an equilibrium in which political actors strike pacts regardless of the environment in which they operate and the preferences they represent does violence to the well-known correlation between democratic stability and economic development. Thus, to build a satisfactory theory of political transitions, we need to specify the actors that play the game as well as their preferences and political resources. And, to do so, we need to rely in part

---

[9] In Przeworski (1991: 26–34), for example, the actors are alternatively political parties, unions, the military, the bourgeoisie or even a coalition of some of these groups.

[10] See, for example, Gunther (1992), Linz (1993) and Linz and Valenzuela (1994). Notice that this insight about the learning "abilities" of political leaders goes counter to the empirical finding of Londregan and Poole (1990) that coups breed coups.

9

on the lessons developed by the sociological tradition of democratization literature.

In the next section I examine how these two main theoretical building blocks, that is, the game-theoretical treatment of the process of regime choice and the economic and social characterization of the players of the game, can be combined into a general theory of political transitions and regime change. I also describe how this approach generates insights that both accommodate and enrich the existing empirical research that has related the emergence of democracy and the process of economic development.

The Argument of the Book

To build a theory of political transitions and regime choice, this book starts with the observation that a political regime is a mechanism employed to aggregate individual preferences about the ideal distribution of assets among those individuals governed by this institutional mechanism. In a democracy, all individuals vote (or may vote). In a dictatorship, only the preferences of part of society are taken into account to decide the final allocation of assets.

Since each political regime has different redistributive consequences, every individual supports the political arrangement that maximizes his welfare, or, more specifically, his final disposable income. The political strategy of each individual varies with the amount and type of economic assets he controls, always constrained by the costs he has to bear to achieve his preferred outcome. Those political costs derive from either excluding part of the population from voting or, conversely, trying to overturn the restrictions imposed by an authoritarian regime.

Economic Equality

Given this simple set-up, the book predicts, in the first place, that increasing levels of economic equality bolster the chances of democracy. As the distribution of income becomes more equal among individuals, redistributive pressures from the poorest social sectors on the well-off voters diminish. Accordingly, the relative costs of tolerating a mass democracy decline for the holders of the most productive assets. In other words, since the tax they will pay in a democratic regime finally becomes smaller than the costs of repression that they would have to bear to exclude the majority of citizens, they accept the introduction of a system of universal suffrage.

The relationship between income distribution and the type of political regime can be traced back to Aristotle, for whom a well-functioning polity could take place only in cities devoid of extreme inequalities. Still, this book makes two contributions to this literature. In the first place, it formalizes the conditions under which income inequality affects the choice of political regime. The only analytical model relating democratization and equality has been recently developed by Acemoglu and Robinson (2000).[11] Yet, contrary to this book, they argue that because it is easier for the elite to credibly commit to future democracy than to future low taxes, the rich are more likely to introduce democracy when inequality is highest.[12] Since it is not obvious why democracy rather than a commitment to more redistribution in the future is harder for the elite to reverse, higher levels of inequality should generate more authoritarianism and lower taxes altogether. This simple intuition is borne out by the empirical analysis I present in Chapters 2 and 3. In the second place, this book engages in a systematic empirical test of the impact of income distribution on the chances of establishing a democracy. Muller (1988) in a direct manner and Lipset (1959) and Moore (1966) indirectly have offered empirical studies partly underlining the negative relationship between economic inequality and political democracy. But no scholar relating the rate of democratic success to the distribution of material resources has ever shown in a convincing manner the empirical validity of those claims. This has probably been due to the lack of broad and reliable data sets of income inequality until very recently. In the book I calculate the yearly probability of democratic transition and democratic breakdown as a function of income distribution in the period from 1950 to 1990, using direct data on income inequality provided in Deininger and Squire (1996). A second panel containing observations from the mid-nineteenth century to the late twentieth century measures the effect of inequality on regime transitions indirectly through the distribution of rural property and the level of human capital. The statistical analysis shows that democratization and, particularly, democratic consolidation have been systematically bolstered by high levels of income equality

---

[11] For a survey of the literature on democratization and inequality, see Landa and Kapstein (2001).

[12] In a second formal model, however, Acemoglu and Robinson (2001) reverse the conclusion and sustain that equality promotes democracy.

and a fair distribution of property in the countryside across the world in the last two centuries. These results are also confirmed by the historical study I undertake on the development of political institutions in the states of the United States and in the cantons of Switzerland during the last centuries.

Capital Mobility

In addition to showing the impact of inequality on the choice of political institutions, this book predicts that a decline in the extent to which capital can be either taxed or expropriated as a result of its characteristics also fosters the emergence of a democratic regime. As the mobility of capital increases, tax rates necessarily decline since otherwise capital holders would have an incentive to transfer their assets abroad. Similarly, when capital can be easily hidden from the state or when it becomes of a kind that can be used only by its owner, the temptation to confiscate it also declines. As the redistributive pressures from non–capital holders decline, curbed by an increasingly mobile capital, political conflict diminishes and the likelihood of democracy rises.[13] The recent transition to democracy in South Africa is an excellent case in point: whereas opposition to democracy ran high among the Afrikaner farming communities, it barely existed among the English-speaking financial and industrial elites, who could easily (and actually did) move their capital abroad (Wood 2000).[14]

As I develop more extensively in Chapters 1 through 3, by taking into account the type of economic assets, that is, the extent to which the assets are mobile or difficult to tax, we can make important empirical progress on at least two fronts. First, it clarifies why economies with a large proportion of fixed assets, such as the oil countries, remain authoritarian, despite having extremely high levels of per capita income (thus defying the predictions of modernization theory). Second, and more generally, it explains why economic development is associated with the triumph of democracy. The positive effect of economic development on democracy in part traces the declining levels of inequality in industrial societies. But

---

[13] This insight is related to Montesquieu's concerns about the ways in which tyrants could be restrained by mobile capital.

[14] As also noted by Wood (2000), the South African prospects for democratization improved as a segment of the Afrikaner community gradually moved from farming to industrial and financial activities in the postwar period, that is, from holding fixed assets to investing in mobile capital.

the correlation between the two is due to the transformation that capital experiences with economic modernization. Economic modernization implies, first, a shift from an economy based on fixed assets, such as land, to an economic system based on a highly mobile capital. It is also associated with the accumulation of human capital, which is generally harder to expropriate than physical capital. Naturally, as the ease with which capitalists can escape taxation goes up, their support for an authoritarian solution declines.

Political Mobilization and Political Violence

Besides the distribution and types of economic assets, political regimes are as well a function of the balance of power (that is, the distribution of political resources) among the parties in contention. As the least well-off overcome their collective action problems, that is, as they mobilize and organize in unions and political parties, the repression costs incurred by the wealthy rise. In other words, keeping the current levels of income inequality and capital mobility constant, a shift in the balance of power generates a change in the political institutions in place.

As extensively developed in Chapter 1, in economies with either relatively moderate levels of economic inequality or highly mobile assets, the political mobilization of the lower or working classes (or, similarly, a weakening of the governing elites as a result of external wars, the loss of external territories or the collapse of their foreign allies) should precipitate the introduction of a democratic regime. The relative costs of repression (compared to the tax losses due to democracy) rise to a point at which it is rational for the authoritarian elite to give way to democracy. This partly explains the sweeping and peaceful democratization of Western Europe after the First World War and the democratization wave in East Asia that followed the collapse of the Soviet Union.

In economies where inequality is high and capital is mostly immobile, that is, in societies in which the poor would benefit substantially from expropriating all assets, the same process of political mobilization triggers instead political violence, sometimes in the form of civil wars and revolutions. To understand the intuition behind this result, consider the most recent models developed in international-relations theory to account for the outbreak of wars. States would never go to war (and endure its destructiveness) if they had complete information about the capabilities of the contending parties and thus full knowledge about the final outcome of a conflagration

(Fearon 1995). They would always rather settle their grievances through bargaining. A similar insight can be applied to domestic politics. As is the case for interstate conflicts, domestic political agents have no incentive to pay the extra costs of war if they know the outcome of war ex ante. If the well-off know that they cannot repress the poor successfully, they should begin by proclaiming a democracy. Similarly, if the poor realize that any attempt at revolution will be finally defeated, they will have to accept an authoritarian regime. This result changes, however, if the parties in contention have some uncertainty about the actual balance of power in society. A growing belief among the poor that they may have a real chance of victory makes the expected gains that follow a successful revolution outweigh the costs of engaging in political violence and therefore opens up the way to revolutionary action (again, in unequal, fixed-asset areas). In this way, this book has the ability to theoretically integrate the great revolutionary explosions of the past, such as the Russian and Chinese revolutions, as well as what we may call the "Angola" or "Sierra Leone" puzzle, that is, the intolerable persistence of domestic war in certain areas of the globe today.

Economic Growth and Trade

The basic model of this book is structured as a static game played by one generation of individuals during a given period of history, independently of how the game was played by a previous generation or will be played in the future. To overcome this simplification, the book considers as well how a more sophisticated understanding of the economy may change the results of the basic model. Three results are here worth noting. First, economic growth acts as a valuable but never as a sufficient condition to secure a democratic outcome. If lowering taxes can generate a higher growth rate in the future, the poor may have an incentive to commit to lower levels of redistribution. This in turn may reduce the opposition of the well-off to democracy. Still, the possibility of introducing democracy hinges on the organizational capacity of the poor to credibly commit to abide by their programmatic promises once democracy is actually introduced. In short, strong left-wing parties and unions may be instrumental to the success of democracy. Second, social mobility, which acts as an equalizing force, increases the chances of a democratic outcome. Finally, trade is shown to have a conditional impact on democratization. In countries where the poor are the abundant factor relative to the rest of the world, trade liberalization raises their income, equalizes conditions and, other things beings equal, boosts the chances of democracy. Conversely, if the poor are the scarce factor, trade openness depresses their wages, intensifies social conflict and endangers democracy.

Democracy as an Equilibrium and the Role of Constitutions

In dealing with the conditions that make democracies possible, democratization literature has a puzzling character. On the one hand, the sociological strand of the literature has not traditionally examined the impact that different sorts of constitutional arrangements may have on the process of democratic consolidation. On the other hand, neoinstitutionalist models, which have been built precisely with the goal of determining the impact of institutional arrangements, have done so without taking into account preexisting economic and social conditions – that is, they have looked at institutions as if they were operating in a social vacuum.

We will achieve a proper understanding of economic and institutional factors only if we assess them in a fully specified model that includes both. The basic model of this book meets this requirement. By assuming a given distribution of preferences (and a corresponding set of political strategies), we can employ the model to assess the real impact of different constitutional arrangements once we hold constant noninstitutional conditions. Contrary to the received wisdom, I show that changing the constitutional framework of a country has a small impact on the stability of a democratic regime. Generally speaking, constitutions do not sustain democratic equilibria because the latter result simply from the fact that no actor has any incentive to deviate from a democracy-compliance strategy. And, in turn, that strategy is the result of the economic parameters and the balance of power of political actors. When a society is sufficiently equal or when capital is sufficiently mobile, democracy prevails regardless of the rules (parliamentarism, plurality rule, and so on) employed. When a society is acutely unequal, no constitutional rule can sustain democracy: if it secures redistribution in favor of the least well-off, it will be contested by the rich; if it blocks the redistributive outcome preferred by the poor, it is simply a form of authoritarianism. Within that general result, I find, however, two interesting exceptions – both of which have to do with the idea that certain types of institutions may shape the distribution of political resources among individuals. First, in asset-specific countries, that is, in countries where capital is hardly mobile, presidentialism may be worse than parliamentarism because it makes it easier for the president, who concentrates many powers, to confiscate assets and then establish a dictatorship. Second, the decentralization of political decisions into smaller and more economically homogeneous territories may reduce the level of political conflict and bolster the chances of democracy.

Politicians and States as Rent Appropriators

For the sake of simplicity, the basic theoretical model of this book starts by assuming that both citizens and their representatives share in the same interests and pursue identical political strategies. Conservative politicians and the military intervene to sustain the property rights of capitalists. Liberal parliamentarians maneuver to expand the representation of the middle classes. Trade union organizers and left-wing party bureaucrats fight to maximize the welfare of labor. As a result, the struggle over the nature of the political constitution (and the corresponding decision over taxes and transfers) takes place at the "societal" level. That is, the model is mostly about "horizontal" conflict among different social sectors (or social types of individuals).

As established in Chapters 2 and 3, such a streamlined model turns out to have considerable explanatory power. Nevertheless, we know that politics also includes a "vertical" dimension of conflict between electors and politicians, or, in other words, between social actors and state elites. Although policy makers ultimately depend on the support of certain social groups, they have some autonomy to pursue their own goals, to forge coalitions and, if they so wish, to appropriate some rents and assets for themselves. Accordingly, once the social conditions behind the choice of regimes have been modeled, we need to assess the extent to which politicians and state elites, now acting as independent agents, can shape the causes and consequences of different political systems. In Chapter 6, I show that, by limiting the level of rent seeking, well-functioning democracies are close to "self-sustaining" regimes – it is very difficult for politicians to shift the distribution of assets in a way that undermines the structural conditions that prompted the transition to democracy to start with.[15] By contrast, in dictatorships politicians can reshape society to their advantage – although the extent to which they do varies with the internal distribution of power in the authoritarian regime. Finally, the insights derived from this discussion are applied to describe the

---

[15] This principal-agent model, in which politicians can exploit their electors, is also applied, in Chapter 4, to explore the effects of presidentialism on democratic stability.

conditions that have led to differences in the level of inequality and capital mobility across the world over time.

Plan of the Book

This book is organized as follows. Chapter 1 presents the baseline model in two steps. It first describes the distributional consequences of different political regimes. It does so by employing the well-known positive theory of taxation developed by, among others, Meltzer and Richards (1981). It then examines how these different outcomes inform the strategies of different actors toward the choice of the voting mechanism itself, and it solves, for different levels of inequality and different mixes of assets in the economy, the different political equilibria that will occur. Although the bulk of Chapter 1 is devoted to a simple game in which there are only two actors, it also discusses the choice of political regimes with three actors (an upper class, a middle class and a lower class) and explores how a variation in the types of assets within each class can be employed to build a sector-based (rather than a class-based) model of politics.

The following two chapters test the predictions the model makes about the distribution of different types of political regimes and the likelihood of political conflict. Chapter 2 provides econometric evidence employing two data bases for the periods 1950 to 1990 and 1850 to 1980. To observe the interests and strategies of different actors and how, in line with the game-theoretic model of the book, these lead to different political regimes, Chapter 3 engages in deeper historical analysis. As already mentioned, it analyzes the evolution of constitutional regimes and suffrage requirements within two confederate states: Switzerland from the fifteenth century until the 1874 constitutional reform and the United States through the first third of the twentieth century. At least three reasons make the choice of these countries compelling. First, both Switzerland and the United States have shown an extraordinary degree of variation across time and territory. Second, the empirical validity of the theory is strengthened by showing that it applies to the political evolution of subnational units, in addition to the cross-national variation examined statistically. Third, since the quasi-insular character of the United States and the neutrality status of Switzerland make these countries relatively immune to the strategies of a single world power, we can assume that their regime outcomes were shaped mainly by their own internal conditions.

Chapter 4 examines several extensions of the model of Chapter 1 in two ways. In its first half, it deals with the impact of economic growth (and the role of commitment institutions among the lower classes), the effect of social mobility and trade openness. In its second half, Chapter 4 grapples with the impact that different sorts of constitutional arrangements may have on the likelihood of sustaining democracy: the choice of electoral regimes, the introduction of presidentialism, federalism and secession.

Chapter 5 examines the distributive consequences of democracy and representation. It does so by testing how the size of the public sector evolves in response to a change in the political system across the world. By showing that democracy indeed reshapes the role of the state in the economy, the results of Chapter 5 corroborate the assumptions that underlie the theoretical model of this book. That is, they confirm that redistributive struggles are at the heart of the choice of political regimes.

Finally, Chapter 6 introduces the possibility of conflict between citizens or public opinion, conceived as a principal, and politicians, understood as the citizens' agents. The first section examines the extent to which politicians may deviate from serving the interests of their representatives conditional on the type of political regime and the existing distribution and nature of assets. As already indicated, democracies are mechanisms that are relatively successful in constraining the expropriatory temptations of politicians. By contrast, authoritarian regimes, in shielding the rulers against the protest of citizens, generate much higher levels of corruption and rent appropriation. This insight gives us the basis to model the cyclical political dynamics that lie behind left-wing dictatorships in very asset-specific environments. In so doing, it shows why a recurrent pattern of revolutions, followed by very stable "left-wing" tyrannies in the hands of exploitative cliques, which are then assaulted once more by new revolutionary groups, is so pervasive in certain African, Latin American and Middle Eastern nations. The second part of the chapter applies the idea of a "vertical" conflict between politicians and the population to explore the questions of economic reform and development. After showing that rapid domestic reforms, such as in the distribution of agrarian property, can hardly transform the underlying economic structure of unequal societies to open the way to democratization, the last section reflects on the long-run political and economic conditions behind the origins of inequality and the transformation of fixed-asset societies into economies abundant in mobile capital.

1

A Theory of Political Transitions

De toutes nos forces, nous étions tournés vers les biens matériels...

—François Mauriac, *Le nœud de vipères*

As argued in the introduction to this book, the discipline of comparative politics is still in need of an analytical model that, departing from simple assumptions about the preferences and strategies of political actors, spells out the different social and political conditions that result in the establishment of either democratic constitutions, right-wing authoritarian regimes or left-wing dictatorships.

In this chapter I build a formal theory of the choice of political regimes in two steps. In the first section, I formally model an economy in which the population varies along two dimensions – the level of capital endowment of each individual, and the extent to which capital is mobile and can actually be taxed – and discuss the distributional consequences that different political regimes have on different types of individuals.

In the second section, I take up the question of how and with what results those different redistributive consequences inform the strategies that different political actors, diverse in terms of their level of income, capital mobility and political resources, follow to determine the system of government. This section shows that a democratic outcome becomes possible when the inequality of conditions among individuals, and therefore the intensity of redistributive demands, falls to the point that an authoritarian strategy to block redistribution ceases to be attractive to the well-off. It reveals as well that the likelihood of democracy increases when the mobility of capital goes up. As capital mobility rises, taxes in a democracy decline – if

19

they did not, capital would move abroad. Accordingly, democracy becomes cheaper than authoritarianism to the holders of assets.

Besides the distribution and nature of economic assets, the choice of political regime is affected by the political and organizational resources of the parties in contention. Thus, for example, as the poor become mobilized in the form of left-wing mass parties, the costs of repression increase for the rich. As discussed at length in the second section and in the concluding paragraphs of the third, a change in the balance of power among political groups has different consequences depending on the underlying economic conditions. For low or medium levels of income inequality and asset specificity, the political strengthening of the lower classes speeds up the introduction of democracy. By contrast, for high levels of inequality and asset specificity, where the costs of democratization are too high for the rich, the mobilization of the poor increases the likelihood of revolutionary explosions and civil wars.

Following the formal argumentation of the first two sections, the third section discusses how the interaction of the level of income inequality and the mobility (or nonspecificity) of capital accommodates, in a manner that is both simple and powerful, the occurrence of democratic events in this century and in previous historical periods. The model clarifies why quasi-democratic structures prevailed in classical Athens and in certain commercial European cities of the late Middle and early Modern Ages. It explains why democracy was embraced early in the predominantly agrarian economies of Norway, of some Alpine valleys and of several Northeastern states in the United States whereas it failed to take root in countries where a powerful landowning class faced a mass of laborers. The model matches the well-known finding that democracy is well correlated with per capita income while reconciling this correlation to the fact that authoritarianism prevails among the very wealthy set of oil producers. It provides an explanation for the higher rate of occurrence of democratic regimes in small countries and under particular configurations of the international system. And it accounts for the distribution and wavelike pattern of the revolutionary outbursts and regime shifts that have often occurred in the world in the last centuries – such as the revolutions of 1830 and 1848 in Europe, the collapse of absolutist monarchies after World War I, the decolonization movement of the 1950s and 1960s and the recent democratization wave of the late twentieth century.

Finally, the fourth section enriches the theoretical structure of the chapter – thus far based on the analysis of the strategic interaction of two actors, a wealthy elite and a lower class – by examining the political dynamics that follow from having three social agents – an upper class, a middle class and the poor. Again, the growing equality of conditions among individuals as well as the mobility of capital precipitate the historical transitions from aristocratic or monarchical regimes to systems of limited democracy and, then, to universal suffrage. Still, this more complex model has two added benefits. First, it allows us to show how the triumph of universal suffrage required the strengthening and equalization of the working class vis-à-vis the other classes – in other words, it shows that the middle class rarely constitutes a "natural" ally of the lower classes. Second, it accommodates, in a rather straightforward manner, by varying the level of asset specificity across sectors, the phenomenon of cross-class coalitions (such as the rural-urban cleavage of several nineteenth-century European countries) that cannot be easily explained if we use only a single dimension based on income distribution.

The Initial Distribution of Assets and the Demand for Redistribution

In this section, I describe the components that underpin the model – the structure of the economy, with two types of individuals, poor and rich – and the types of political regimes, democratic, right-wing authoritarian and communist.[1]

Before I provide details of the model, two key features need to be underlined. First, the model is based on the plausible assumptions that the poor cannot commit to lower the level of taxation (to sustain a democratic outcome) and the rich cannot avoid revolutions by promising to redistribute in the future. As emphasized in the introduction to this book, at stake is power itself (and the capacity to allocate assets that comes with power). This logically precludes the use of mechanisms to commit to solutions that deviate from the interests of the agents. In other words, since none of the parties can credibly believe that the other side would restrain itself against its own optimal solution (in terms of resources and goals), each party accordingly acts in the same way and pursues its own advantage.

---

[1] The first two sections ("The Initial Distribution of Assets and the Demand for Redistribution" and "The Choice of Political Regime") have been coauthored with Luis Garicano. In what follows, I adhere as much as possible to the notational conventions of Persson and Tabellini (2000), particularly in taxation isssues.

Second, we can think of the model described here as a game played by a generation of agents, poor and rich, during a given period of history (the period in which they live). At the beginning of the period, they take the economic and political variables in their country (inequality, asset specificity, political resources in the hands of each class) as given and settle on the political regime under which they will be governed. As this period ends, a new generation decides again on the political institutions in place. By assumption, each generation is independent from either preceding or following generations: its members do not care about the wealth they leave to their successors or the political system the next generation will inherit. As a result, no generation has any mechanism to commit to a different equilibrium than the one described by the model. I relax these very strict conditions in various ways – allowing for a change in the level and distribution of assets within a generational period (through either growth or social mobility) and entertaining the possibility of intergenerational linkages – later in Chapter 4.

Preferences, Technology and Endowments

To explore the conditions that determine the choice of political regime, consider a simple economy with two types of individuals, poor and wealthy.

The poor, who constitute the majority, that is, are a share $\alpha > \frac{1}{2}$ of the population, hold together a total capital stock K_p. The remaining minority of wealthy individuals, who are a share $1 - \alpha$ of the population, hold an aggregate capital stock K_w. The economy-wide stock of capital is then $K_p + K_w = K$. For notational convenience, the aggregate share of capital of each group can be represented as $k_j = K_j/K$, so that $k_p + k_w = 1$. As a result, the capital held by each poor citizen is $k_p^i = k_p/\alpha$. In turn, the capital held by each wealthy individual is $k_w^i = k_w/(1 - \alpha)$. By definition, $k_p^i < k_w^i$. As the share of capital held by the wealthy k_w increases, inequality increases.

Capital endowment determines individual income through a production function with constant returns to scale, so that output can be normalized to $y_j = k_j$, $j = w, p$.

Finally, capital can be thought of as being somewhat specific to the country in which it is being used. The extent to which an asset is specific is measured by its productivity at home relative to its productivity abroad. Whenever capital is moved abroad, it loses a share σ of its value. More exactly, capital k, which at home would produce $y = k$, produces abroad $y^a = k(1 - \sigma)$. Thus, the more specific the capital, that is, the larger σ, the less attractive the option of moving capital abroad becomes to its owners.

Initial Distribution of Assets

The degree of specificity varies across types of capital: it is practically complete for land, yet extremely low for money or generic skills.

The preferences are given by indirect utility functions linear in income under risk neutrality, so that $U_{jt} = Ey_{jt} - c_{jt}$, where c_{jt} are the costs of the political system. I ignore the expectations operator for notational simplicity.

Political Systems

Political life can take place under one of the following states: authoritarianism, communism, democracy or revolutionary war. In an authoritarian or right-wing dictatorship, the wealthy repress the poor, excluding them from the decision-making process. In a communist or left-wing dictatorship, the poor rule after expropriating all the wealthy's capital. In a democracy, property is preserved and everybody votes on the tax rate. Finally, in war, both parties incur the costs of war and the wealth that they obtain depends on the ultimate outcome. As discussed in detail in the following section on the choice of political regime, ex ante there is some uncertainty about the outcome of the war.

Democracy and Redistribution   Consider first how the tax rate is set in a democracy. Following the standard practice in the political economy literature (Meltzer and Richards 1981; Persson and Tabellini 2000), the state taxes economic agents with a linear tax τ on their income y and then distributes the resulting revenue equally among all individuals. As a result, each individual pays τk_j and then receives τk_a, or, more simply, τ since k_a, the average capital per person, is equal to 1.[2] The tax generates some welfare losses that for the sake of simplicity may be represented by the quadratic function $\frac{\tau^2}{2}$.

Assume that the tax rate is set by simple majority rule. The median voter, who is a poor individual, will set taxes to maximize his income, that is, his initial income, which is a function of his capital endowment, and the net transfer received from the government, taking into account the welfare losses of taxation:

$$\max_{\tau}(1 - \tau)\frac{k_p}{\alpha} + \tau - \frac{\tau^2}{2} \tag{1}$$

---

[2] Average per capita income is

$$k_a = \alpha\frac{k_p}{\alpha} + (1 - \alpha)\frac{(1 - k_p)}{(1 - \alpha)} = 1.$$

23

In maximizing net transfers, the median voter will always be subject to the wealthy choosing not to move their income abroad – that is, he will make sure that the after-tax income of the wealthy is equal to or higher than their income abroad. Assume, for notational simplicity, that the timing of the political process is such that each individual wealthy voter can choose to move her income abroad and still receive a transfer.[3] Then the constraint can be expressed as:

$$(1 - \tau)k_w^i \geq (1 - \sigma)k_w^i \qquad (2)$$

Solving this optimization problem, the tax will be:

$$\tau^* = \min\left\{1 - k_p^i, \sigma\right\} \qquad (3)$$

That is, the median voter will choose a tax rate equal to the smaller of two parameters: the level of specificity of the wealth (σ) and the difference between the average capital in the economy and the capital owned by the median voter, who, again, is a poor individual. (The after-tax income of the citizens that results from this maximization can be denoted by $\widehat{y}_j^i$. Note, in particular, that $\widehat{y}_w^i$ is the maximum of the two values generated by setting $\tau^* = 1 - k_p^i$ or $\tau^* = \sigma$.) The interpretation of this result is straightforward. Consider first the case in which the specificity of capital is high: σ is close to 1, so that the wealthy lose a substantial part of their income if they move their wealth abroad. Accordingly, the wealthy cannot credibly threaten with their exit in response to heavy taxes, and the level of the tax rate is not constrained by capital mobility. The optimal tax for the median voter is determined simply by the level of income inequality, that is, by the difference between the average capital and the capital of the poor. The smaller the share of the wealth controlled by the poor k_p, that is, the more unequal the income distribution, the higher the tax rate and the resulting distribution will be.

As the level of specificity of capital declines (and σ approaches 0) the tax rate becomes constrained by the possibility that the wealthy will move their capital abroad. Even if income inequality is high, and the corresponding redistributive pressure strong, the poor cannot set a high tax rate because,

---

[3] This is a Nash equilibrium assumption: the deviation by each voter, in deciding to carry her capital abroad, takes the transfers in the economy as given. Altering this assumption so that exiting the country must be done before obtaining transfers slightly complicates the algebra but does not change any of the analysis that follows.

under those circumstances, the rich would just leave the country. In short, capital mobility, like equality of conditions, results in low taxation.

Mobility, the Costs of Tax Monitoring and the Sensitivity of Income to Taxes It is important to stress that, for the sake of simplicity, I am just modeling (and discussing) the constraining effects that an increase in capital mobility may have on the tax rate (and, as we shall see, on the choice of political regime). But the idea and the consequences of capital mobility can be extended in two additional ways.

On the one hand, the concept of capital mobility can be expanded to encompass the degree to which capital can be easily taxed, that is, the extent to which the tax authority can monitor any given asset and its returns. A fully "taxable" asset is one that cannot be hidden for tax purposes and therefore yields the expected tax return. A nontaxable asset is one whose income flow is difficult to monitor and whose owner can easily escape from the tax-enforcement authority – this is the case, for example, of certain professional skills, the provision of consulting services or the transactions of small shopkeepers. Although mobility and "taxability" tend to go together, they may not always coincide. A mobile asset is by definition a nontaxable asset. But the opposite is not necessarily true. Individuals with assets that are not extremely mobile may still be able to avoid taxes without any risk of being caught.[4] A change in the extent to which an asset can be monitored and taxed has the same consequences as a shift in the degree of mobility. As the former declines, that is, as the after-tax or after-confiscation returns drop relative to their "real" tax value, the tax rate should fall and hence the redistributive threat of democracy should too.

On the other hand, a similar point applies if we replace the level of asset specificity with the sensitivity of income to tax – that is, by the rate at which economic agents shift resources from work and investment into leisure. Given a positive rate of substitution, total output and total tax revenue will eventually decline at a certain tax rate – in fact to 0 for a tax of 100 percent. Notice too that the more sensitive that taxpayers are to taxation (that is, the

---

[4] As pointed out by Adam Smith "there are . . . two different circumstances which render the interest of money a much less proper subject of direct taxation that the rent of land. First, the quantity and value which any man possesses can never be a secret, and can always be ascertained with great exactness. But the whole amount of the capital stock he possesses is almost always a secret . . . Secondly, land is a subject which cannot be removed, whereas stock easily may" (Smith [1981]: 848).

faster they stop deploying their capital in response to a tax hike) the more constrained voters will be in raising taxes. In other words, for high levels of income elasticity to taxes, taxation will be low and democracy will be easier to introduce.[5]

Right-Wing Authoritarianism and the Use of Repression   In a right-wing authoritarian regime the poor are excluded from the decision-making process. Since the median voter is now a wealthy voter who sees no point in transferring income to herself, no redistribution takes place.

The imposition of such a regime requires the exercise of repression by the rich. The cost that the wealthy incur to exclude the poor can be denoted by ρ. Given that the tax is 0, the wealthy's income is $k_w^i - \rho_i$. In turn, each poor person has an income k_p^i.

The cost of repression varies with the organizational and technical means at the disposal of both the wealthy and the poor. For the sake of simplicity, we can model the costs of repression as falling into two possible situations: either low (ρ_l) or high (ρ_h), with $\rho_l < \rho_h$. These two types of repression costs describe the success rate of the rich in suppressing any revolt. The cost of repression is said to be low whenever the wealthy efficiently suppress any revolt by the poor. By contrast, whenever the rich fail to suppress a revolution of the poor, the costs of repression can be thought of as high.

To enumerate a few examples, the costs of repression are low whenever the poor are completely demobilized, the wealthy have extremely sophisticated mechanisms of control or the country's geography makes the suppression of political protest and violence relatively easy. By contrast, whenever the lower classes overcome their collective action problems and organize in political parties and trade unions or when they live in highly mountainous terrain, which breeds the formation of guerrilla movements, the costs of repression become high.[6]

---

[5] I take this up again in Appendix 1.2 (paragraph 1) to offer a different (yet probably complementary) explanation of the emergence of democracy from the account developed in the main text.

[6] I do not model here the parameters that determine the level of repression costs; rather, I take them as given. Again, as discussed in a variegated literature on social mobilization and political conflict, repression costs are likely to be a function of population shares, the economic resources of each class, the extent to which individual actors have overcome any collective action problems, landscape, international aid and so on. See, for example, Olson (1965), Tilly (1978) and Tarrow (1994).

Civil War, Revolution and Expropriation   The repression that accompanies an authoritarian regime does not always remain uncontested. On the contrary, the poor may choose to revolt in response to the wealthy's decision to repress them.[7] As already mentioned, the outcome of that revolutionary explosion and of the ensuing war between the two classes will be a function of the resources of the parties or, in other words, of the repression cost borne by the rich. If the repression technology of the rich is efficient, they will eventually put down the revolution and reassert their rule. If the cost the wealthy incur in a civil war in which they are successful is ϖ, then their income will be $y_w^{war} = k_w - \varpi$.[8] In turn, the poor will lose their assets, and their income will become $y_p = 0$.

If the poor win the revolutionary war, they impose a communist regime in which the wealth of the rich that is country specific, and cannot therefore be moved away, is confiscated. The poor incur, when winning a civil war, a cost of war ϖ. Thus the income of the victorious class of poor will be $y_p^{war} = k_p + \sigma k_w - \varpi$.

The Choice of Political Regime

Having laid out a stylized model to highlight the distributional consequences of different levels of income inequality and asset specificity, it is now possible to explore the conditions that determine the selection of the political regime. I do so through a game of imperfect information.

Information Structure and Political Conflict

The question of revolutionary action and civil conflict, with which I closed the preceding section, constitutes, as is the case for interstate wars, a puzzling phenomenon from a theoretical point of view. If the parties at odds with each other are rational, that is, if they are interested in maximizing their income, and if they can anticipate the balance of forces involved, they should settle for the outcome that war would bring about without incurring the costs of war. In other words, since war destroys resources, and absent any disagreements about who is likely to win, both the poor and the wealthy would rather avoid it. Either the poor would threaten revolution and the

---

[7] The model assumes that in expectation the poor are always better off under democracy than under a revolutionary outcome.

[8] I assume throughout that when the rich have an efficient repressive technology, they prefer winning a war to accepting democracy.

wealthy would concede democracy, or the wealthy would repress the poor, who would then give up any attempt to revolt.[9]

To account for the emergence of political violence and war, I follow here the most recent literature on international relations, according to which wars take place when the parties in conflict have different views on how likely they are to win.[10] With some informational asymmetry across parties about the resources of the opposition, both sides may decide that it is to their respective advantage to maintain or seize power through violent means. This may naturally lead to an outbreak of political violence.

To capture this environment of uncertainty, I assume that the wealthy are able to fully observe the cost of repression, as it enters their consumption. By contrast, this cost remains unobservable to the poor. Thus the latter need to estimate the likelihood that they will succeed in a civil war before embarking on a revolution. In turn, the rich have to decide, depending on the likelihood that the poor will eventually revolt, whether to use their repressive technology or to voluntarily give up their power and move to a democracy. It is when the poor underestimate the repressive technology of the wealthy while the wealthy play down the organizational capacity of the poor that we witness a revolutionary explosion followed by war.

The Role of Information and the Timing of Political Transitions. The introduction of information in the study of political change has an added benefit beyond its main task of offering an explanation for violence. From the discussion just developed, it follows that, given a certain context of uncertainty, changes in the distribution of information across classes and social sectors about their corresponding political resources should trigger sudden shifts in political regimes as well as bouts of political conflict, revolutions and unexpected coups. This probably matches well with (and accounts for) our current empirical observations about the short-term dynamics of political transitions.

The recent literature on democratization has shown that events such as defeats in war, the death of the dictator or internal struggles in the ruling elite, which are exogenous to the structural conditions that determine

---

[9] In technical terms, absent informational asymmetries, the subgame perfect equilibria of the game do not involve civil war.

[10] See Fearon (1995) for a survey of alternative views in international relations on the rationality of actors going to war. The most recent theoretical contributions to the study of political transitions, such as Acemoglu and Robinson (2000, 2001), have ignored informational asymmetries and, as a consequence, cannot account, for example, for the most predominant political outcome of sub-Saharan Africa.

the medium-run stability of political regimes (in this book, inequality and country specificity of wealth), play a key role in democratic transitions (O'Donnell and Schmitter 1986) and revolutionary episodes (Kuran 1991). To some scholars, this empirical observation (that "nonstructural" factors lead to transitions to democracy) radically questions previous models emphasizing the role of long-run variables, such as inequality or class composition, in the prospects of democratization.[11] To other scholars, it requires combining an exogenous theory of democratization (where a set of events, happening randomly, prompts regime changes) with an endogenous theory of democratic stability (which explains the causes leading to the consolidation of democracy) (Przeworski and Limongi 1997). Once we recognize the role played by varying levels of information, however, we do not need to set aside a theoretical model based on long-run explanatory variables. Both the distribution and types of assets continue to determine the type of stable political regime in a given country. Yet, at the same time, certain political events, by prompting citizens to update their beliefs on the probability of survival of the existing political arrangement, play a considerable role in triggering shifts in the institutional order. Thus events such as the defeat of the Kaiser in 1918, the defeat of its military in the Falkland's war and the collapse of the rupiah in 1997 signaled the political weakness of the ruling elite of, respectively, Germany, Argentina, and Indonesia in such a way that made democracy inevitable for each country.

The introduction of uncertainty and variable information flows may also explain why political transitions and revolutions seem to follow a wave-like pattern across the world (Huntington 1991).[12] In the aftermath of certain key events at the international level, such a shift in the internal politics or collapse of a world power, the domestic social sectors of different nations reestimate their chances of achieving their goals given how other elites have performed abroad. This reassessment precipitates swift political changes in their respective political arenas. Examples range from the Greece of Thucydides, where internal crises in Athens and Sparta automatically sparked considerable social unrest in other city-states, to the Paris Revolutions of 1830 and 1840, which, by questioning the strength of the Holy Alliance, ushered in a string of Liberal revolts across the European continent, to the collapse of several Belle Epoque regimes at the

[11] For this standpoint, see O'Donnell and Schmitter (1986) and recent work by Linz (1993) and Linz and Valenzuela (1994).

[12] For a critique of the existence of democratization waves, see Przeworski et al. (2000).

29

end of World War I, which incited the general strikes and revolutionary movements that spread from Sweden to Spain and from Central America to Argentina and Chile in 1918–19.

Timing of the Game

The choice of the political regime can be thought of as resulting from the following game, with the moves and payoffs as summarized in Figure 1.1.

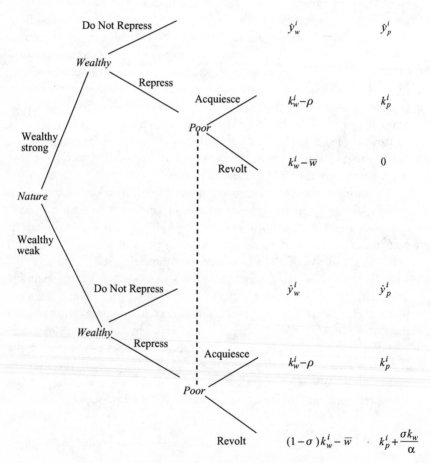

Payoff of the wealthy   *Payoff of the poor*

Figure 1.1 Choice of Political Regime in a Two-Class Model.

Nature determines the exact number of poor and wealthy as well as their respective capital, that is, α, k_p and k_w.

The sequence of the game to decide the political regime unfolds as follows. The wealthy choose whether to repress the poor and maintain an authoritarian regime (or restore it if the inherited regime was a democracy) or to give up their control of the state and accept a democracy. After the wealthy move, the poor respond.

If the rich decide to repress no one, a system of universal suffrage is established in a peaceful manner. Democratic elections take place, a tax is levied on all and the total revenue the tax generates is distributed equally among all citizens. Each wealthy person ends up with her income minus the net transfer and the welfare loss caused by the tax, or formally $\widehat{y}_w^i$. Each poor individual obtains a positive transfer and his final income is $\widehat{y}_p^i$.

If the wealthy choose to maintain (or reimpose) an authoritarian regime, the poor may either revolt or not. If the poor acquiesce to the action of the rich, an authoritarian regime remains in place. Each rich person keeps her income minus the fraction devoted to sustain the nondemocratic regime, so that her income is $k_w^i - \rho$. Each poor individual retains his income k_p^i.

If the poor engage in a successful revolution, they expropriate all of the wealthy's expropriable assets. Conversely, if the revolution fails, the poor's wealth is destroyed. Again, the poor are uncertain about the cost of the repression to the rich. Accordingly, they estimate that the cost of repression is high with probability q, while it is low with probability $(1 - q)$.

Equilibrium of the Game

Consider now how changes in the underlying economic conditions, inequality and specificity, as well as in the costs of repression and in the information available to each side, lead to different political strategies as well as different institutional outcomes.[13] The proofs of the propositions are in Appendix 1.1.

---

[13] Again, the model considers the choice of the political regime at one point in time or, in other words, in the time span of one generation. Nonetheless, the model can easily be made "historical" by extending it to a game played by several generations, each one living at period t and playing a one-shot game in each one of T time periods, $t = 1, \ldots, T$. In that game, agents would take the economic and political variables in the economy at each time (most importantly, wealth inequality, specificity of assets and previous political system) as given and settle on the political system of that generation.

Low Levels of Inequality or Asset Specificity When either the level of inequality or country specificity of wealth is sufficiently low, democracy takes place regardless of the cost of repression.[14]

To show this, recall that, to decide what strategy to follow, the rich compare their income after paying the cost of repression with their after-tax income in a democratic system. For sufficiently low levels of inequality or asset specificity, the tax rate in a democratic setting will be low enough to make the introduction of democracy cheaper than the maintenance of an authoritarian regime (even when the repression cost is low):

$$\widehat{y}_w^i > k_w^i - \rho_l^i$$

Here the dominant strategy of the wealthy is to offer democracy, regardless of the cost of repression (low or high). The main cost of democracy is the redistribution that it brings; thus, if taxes are low, either because inequality is low or because the constraint imposed by the risk that the wealthy will carry their wealth away keeps them low, then the cost of democracy to the wealthy is small. As a consequence, they prefer to choose democracy, and no conflict emerges.

Medium Levels of Inequality and Asset Specificity The likelihood of having a democracy declines in those cases in which either wealth inequality or the level of asset specificity is low but not sufficiently low for democracy to be preferred to repression in all cases. This circumstance takes place whenever the after-tax income of the wealthy under a democracy is higher than the income net of high repression costs but still lower than the income net of low repression costs:

$$k_w^i - \rho_l^i > \widehat{y}_w^i > k_w^i - \rho_b^i$$

When the repression cost is low, the wealthy prefer to repress rather than to allow democratic elections. When the repression cost is high, the wealthy prefer simply to accept a democratic constitution.[15] The decision to maintain an authoritarian regime goes uncontested by the poor for a simple reason. The poor do not revolt because they know that for the rich to repress under these circumstances (medium inequality and medium asset

---

[14] See the proof of proposition 1 in Appendix 1.1.
[15] See the proof of proposition 2 in Appendix 1.1.

specificity), the repression costs must be low and that, therefore, a revolution would fail. Thus, a revolution will not happen and a stable right-wing authoritarian regime will remain in place. (Notice also that the wealthy do not want to try to repress when they have a high repression cost, thus exploiting the poor's beliefs, since in this case they actually prefer the democracy outcome *even if repression would succeed*.)

It is worth stressing that, in this type of society, with medium inequality or medium asset specificity, political stability (either under democracy or authoritarianism) constitutes the normal practice. Again, the fact that repression is taking place must mean that the elite is extremely confident in their ability to overcome a revolution. As a consequence, the action is credible and no revolution takes place. This type of reasoning may explain why certain East Asian economies with relatively widespread equality endured authoritarian regimes for long periods of time in the postwar period. The lack of organizational resources among the opposition (and the support granted by the United States to the governing elites) made repression cheap and authoritarianism an uncontested outcome. Nonetheless, as soon as the resources of the opposition increased rapidly in the 1980s and the end of the Cold War reduced American interest in the stability of the authoritarian regimes (hence depriving the latter of resources), democratization was swift and bloodless (as predicted by the model).

High Levels of Inequality and Asset Specificity   As the levels of inequality and asset specificity go up, the cost of taxation under a democracy becomes higher than the cost of repression that the wealthy have to bear to maintain an authoritarian regime:

$$\widehat{y}_w^i < k_w^i - \rho_b^i$$

With the wealthy betting on a strategy of authoritarian repression, the question we need to explore is how the poor will behave. As already indicated, the poor can either acquiesce to the repression or, depending on how effective the wealthy may be in repressing, engage in a revolution. Remember that the poor have only imperfect knowledge about the repressive capabilities of the rich. Accordingly, and in addition to the gains that they will obtain from a revolutionary victory, the decision of the poor to launch a revolution will depend on the probability, q, that they assign to the existence of a high repression cost (and which, as has been noted, leads to a successful revolution).

33

The poor will not rebel if the expected gain of revolting is smaller than the value of accepting an authoritarian regime:

$$q\left(k_p + \sigma k_w\right) < k_p \tag{4}$$

In short, there is a set of cases in which inequality and specificity are high enough that repression is always preferred to democracy by the wealthy but low enough that the poor do not have much to gain by a revolution. In those circumstances, an authoritarian regime is imposed by the former and accepted by the latter.[16]

Revolutions and Wars   As both inequality of wealth and asset specificity become very high, political confrontation between the classes becomes unavoidable. On the one hand, the rich continue to prefer authoritarianism to democracy:

$$\widehat{y}_w^i < k_w^i - \rho_b^i$$

On the other hand, the poor now have an incentive to revolt since the expected gains of a revolution are higher than the gains from acquiescing to the status quo:

$$q\left(k_p + \sigma k_w\right) > k_p$$

Consider next what the strategies of each party will be and the political outcomes in those circumstances. If the costs of repression are low, the rich will always repress, knowing that an authoritarian regime will eventually prevail.

If the costs of repression are high, the wealthy have no dominant strategy to follow. On the one hand, they will not always choose a repressive strategy. If they did, the poor would systematically try their luck and revolt. As a consequence, the wealthy's strategy would not be optimal when repression was indeed expensive. On the other hand, the rich will not always avoid repression either. That strategy would make the poor believe that those that repress have a low cost of repression, and this in turn would give the wealthy an incentive to repress (and exploit the beliefs of the poor) even in cases in which the cost of repression was high. Since the wealthy cannot follow a pure dominant strategy, they will simply repress with a certain probability (or, in game-theoretic terms, follow mixed strategies) just enough to make the poor indifferent between revolution and acquiescence.

---

[16] See the proof of proposition 3 in Appendix 1.1.

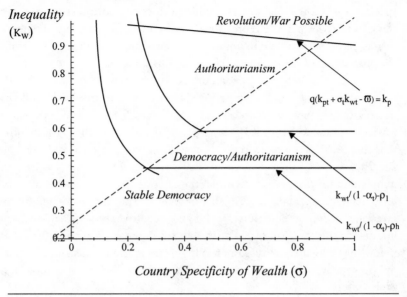

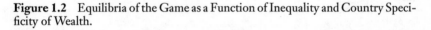

Parameters of Simulation:
$\alpha = 0.2$; $q = 0.1$; $\rho_l = 0.4$; $\rho_h = 0.7$.

Figure 1.2 Equilibria of the Game as a Function of Inequality and Country Specificity of Wealth.

Within this high inequality/high specificity equilibrium, as the levels of inequality and specificity increase, and thus the assets the poor may grab also increase, the probability of having a revolution will increase too.[17] A cursory look at where revolutions and guerrilla movements have historically occurred confirm the formal results: Czarist Russia, mid-twentieth-century China, Viet Nam, Cambodia, Cuba and Central American countries and many sub-Saharan African nations are eminently agricultural economies with sharp inequalities in the distribution of land (Moore 1966, Wolf 1969). The empirical analysis of Chapter 2 shows that this informal observation holds in a systematic way.[18]

Figure 1.2, which is built upon a simulation of the equilibria of the model for a particular set of parameters, summarizes graphically the powerful role of two economic parameters – the distribution of wealth and the country

[17] See the proof of proposition 4 in Appendix 1.1.

[18] Recent research by Collier and Hoeffler (2001) on the causes of violence and civil wars shows them to be highly correlated to the importance of fixed resources in the economy.

specificity of capital – as well as the importance of political resources, captured by the parameter of repression costs, in the choice of political regimes.

Figure 1.2 shows the four equilibria of the game for an example in which the proportion of the population in the wealthy class is 20 percent, with the class controlling between 20 percent and 100 percent of the wealth in the economy ($0.2 \leq k_w \leq 1$). The poor estimate ex ante the likelihood that the wealthy are unable to suppress a revolution (independently of the actual strategies of the wealthy) at 10 percent ($q = 0.1$). Finally, the graph assumes that the per capita cost of repression without war is between 40 percent and 70 percent of the resources available (i.e., $\rho_l = 0.4$ and $\rho_h = 0.7$). To understand the figure, note first that the discontinuous increasing diagonal line characterizes whether inequality or country-specific wealth determines taxation (i.e., it plots equation (3)). When inequality is higher than what that line determines, the risk of capital mobility bounds the upper limit on taxes. Below that line, inequality is not too high, and optimal redistribution from the perspective of the median voter can be implemented without risk of capital flight.

Again, as in the earlier discussion, a stable democracy prevails at sufficiently low levels of *either* inequality or specificity of wealth, even if the poor are demobilized and the costs of repression are low – this is the area delimited by the axis to the left and the first curve to the right. As the cost of taxation increases (due to increases in wealth inequality and asset specificity), authoritarianism starts to pay. Still, in that intermediate area, between the two curves, the political solution depends on the size of repression costs. If the latter are low, the wealthy shift to or maintain what will be an uncontested authoritarian regime. If the repression costs are high, as a result of, say, the progressive institutionalization of working-class opposition in trade unions or left-wing parties, the wealthy will concede democracy. Finally, for high levels of inequality and asset specificity, authoritarianism becomes the dominant strategy of the rich. At extremely high values of both parameters, there is an actual risk of civil war, as the repressive stance of the wealthy becomes less credible (they do not really have a choice but to repress) and the poor see substantive gains from the expropriation of the wealth of the country.

A Discussion of Inequality, Asset Specificity and Repression Costs

The formal results obtained in the previous two sections merit a more detailed discussion, both for their theoretical implications and their historical relevance. After considering first the role of income inequality, I next assess the consequences of capital mobility. Finally, I discuss some historical evidence on the impact of political organization and repression costs.

Income Inequality

A more unequal distribution of wealth increases the redistributive demands of the population and the ultimate level of taxes in a democratic system. As the potential level of transfers becomes larger, the authoritarian inclinations of the wealthy increase and the probabilities of democratization and democratic survival decline steadily. Conversely, as the poor grow richer and their income becomes closer to that of the upper class, economic tensions decline, and the rich are increasingly inclined to accept a democratic regime – elections have only a marginal impact on the wealthy's consumption level.

As observed by Aristotle for the Greek world, "where some possess very many things and others nothing, either [rule of] the people in its extreme form must come into being, or unmixed oligarchy, or (. . .) tyranny" leading to a state or city that "is not of free persons but of slaves and masters, the ones consumed by envy, the others by contempt" (*Politics*, IV, 11). For a period closer to our times, the model formally states why highly unequal societies (with high levels of asset specificity, that is, where all or most capital is land) cannot be governed democratically. Big landowners oppose democracy of necessity, as shown by the histories of Prussia, Russia and the Southern states of the United States and attested by Moore's work (Moore 1966) as well as by the political turbulence of Central America (Paige 1997).[19] In an agrarian economy, for democratic institutions to prevail there has to be a radical equality of conditions – such as in the rare case of the Alpine cantons of Switzerland in the Middle and Modern Ages.

As income inequality declines, democracies are easier to establish. Consider the first democratization wave at the turn of the twentieth century. Although data on income inequality is scarce before the postwar period, Williamson (1991) reports that inequality peaked in the United Kingdom in the mid-nineteenth century with the top decile of the population having 62.3 percent of all income. The income share of the top decile slightly declined to 57.5 percent in 1891 and then fell quickly in the following

---

[19] Even well-to-do farmers will oppose democracy if they face a substantial class of laborers. For an example, see the analysis in Lewin (1989) of the reaction among Swedish farmers at the turn of the twentieth century to the extension of universal suffrage.

two decades, stabilizing at around 35 percent after 1910. It is not coincidental that Britain's House of Lords accepted the complete hegemony of the House of Commons in 1911 and that universal male suffrage was introduced in 1918.[20] Similarly, the income share of the top decile declined from 50 percent in 1870 to 38 percent in 1903 in Denmark and from 41 percent in 1870 to 28 percent in 1910 in Norway (Kraus 1981). Similar to the changes in Britain, the eventual appointment of a Liberal cabinet by the king in Denmark in 1906 and the extension of universal suffrage in Norway in 1897 coincided with the previous easing of substantial inequalities. Finally, we can consider the evolution of inequality in twentieth-century Spain. Spain is a crucial example since it includes both a democratic breakdown, in 1936, and a very successful transition to democracy, in the late 1970s. Spain's level of interregional inequality (measured through standard deviation of regional per capita income) stayed at around 0.37 until 1955. It then declined precipitously, due to rapid economic growth and the massive migratory flows to the cities in the 1960s, to 0.24 in 1975 (just before the transition to democracy) (Pérez et al. 1996). In short, the variation in inequality seems to go a long way in explaining both Spain's civil war of 1936–39 and its fully working democracy established in the 1970s.

Asset Specificity

Changes in the level of specificity, and hence the mobility, of capital also alter the incentives and strategies of various actors engaged in the choice of political institutions.[21] At low levels of mobility, which occur in cases of landholding (in plantations or mines), capitalists have a direct and strong

---

[20] Although after 1886 about two thirds of the nation's men were enfranchised in Britain, the electoral law was heavily biased against working-class voters. Using census and electoral-district data, Boix (2000) estimates that before World War I whereas 99 percent of the British middle-class men had the right to vote, about 40 percent of the British working-class men did not have that right. Registration practices (which punished mobility, which tended to be much higher among workers) and an added vote for propertied voters in rural counties further biased the system against low-income sectors.

[21] The relationship between factor mobility and state behavior can be traced back to Montesquieu (1995), 20, chap. 23. This insight has been revisited by Hirschman (1981, chap. 11), who indicates how the threat of exit curbs arbitrary behavior among public officials. This has recently received some formal treatment, but only in a public choice model consisting of a ruler ruling over a representative agent, and hence with no room for heterogeneity of interests, in Rogowski (1998). In economics, the formal analysis of the importance of the role of competition among local authorities in determining taxation and the provision of services dates back to Tiebout (1956).

interest in tutoring the state. Since capital is minimally sensitive to taxes, voters have a high incentive to impose heavy taxes. As a result, capital will invest considerable effort in blocking democracy, especially since the costs to capital of not doing so are high. As capital mobility increases, voters agree on a lower tax rate than the tax they approved under conditions of high asset specificity. The cost for capital of capturing the state becomes larger than the fraction paid by it in taxes, and any resistance from capital to democracy disappears.[22]

As asset specificity declines, the constraining effect of inequality on democracy lessens.[23] This is exemplified by the way in which the process of the industrial revolution affected the choice of the political regime in Britain and, more generally, among all North Atlantic economies. The agrarian nature of the British economy made the introduction of popular government too threatening to the propertied classes. The first stage of industrialization, which arguably increased the degree of income inequality in Britain (Williamson 1985), coincided with a reactionary phase in British politics at the turn of the nineteenth century (Moore 1966: 442–44) and, most likely, with the suspension of long-held representative practices in local government.[24]

As just noted, inequality peaked by the middle of the nineteenth century and remained substantial in the decades that followed – precisely as successive electoral reforms opened the political arena to about two thirds of all British adult men by 1884. A gradual compression in the wage structure in the pre–World War I period undoubtedly eased the costs of transition and made the introduction of universal suffrage possible in 1918. Still, if the level of inequality were the only variable that mattered in determining the likelihood of democracy, we should have predicted that democracy would

---

[22] As remarked by Hirschman (1981) in his discussion of the Kayapó and other stateless societies, whenever all assets are fully tax-elastic, the state completely disappears. This insight probably requires the additional assumption that there is no demand for public goods. Lack of demand for public goods, basically for an army in those societies, would result from either the employment of precarious military technology (with war consisting of individualized, one-on-one combat) or the existence of large unoccupied areas (which make moving away from conflict cheaper than engaging in war). I discuss these questions again in Chapter 6.

[23] The reverse can be equally true. Lower levels of inequality make capital mobility less relevant to the choice of regime. This is precisely the circumstance in democracies of free farmers in some Swiss cantons and in the Northeastern states in the United States.

[24] I am indebted to Steve Pincus for pointing out this last fact to me. That reactionary phase was also related to the revolutionary explosions in France in that period.

come about in Britain later than it did or that Britain would as prone to conflict and even regime reversals as Germany (where the Prussian Junkers effectively blocked the sovereignty of the Reichstag) and, to some extent, France were. The structural changes fostered by industrialization and the types of capital probably mattered as much as any changes in the distribution of wealth. In 1910–13, for example, the ratio of net foreign investment abroad to total domestic savings was 53 percent in Britain, 13 percent in France and 7 percent in Germany (O'Rourke and Williamson 1999: 209). Despite substantial inequality, the emergence of an economy abundant in relatively nonspecific assets made the extension of the franchise a much less painful option to the owners of industrial capital.

It is in that sense that Moore's dictum, that no democracy is possible without a bourgeoisie, makes sense (Moore 1966: 418). The model takes the finding, which underpins most of Moore's book and gives it its title, that landlords have historically blocked any form of representative government and reconciles it with the idea, which emerges from Moore's empirical exploration of English history and perhaps the French case, that a strong bourgeoisie bolstered the chances of democracy. As a result, it dispels the standard accusation that Moore was inconsistent or even obscure by alternatively stressing the political role of landlords and of the industrial bourgeoisie to explain the emergence of democracy in the twentieth century.[25] What appears confusing in Moore, precisely because he does not completely specify the actors' preferences and political strategies, becomes clearer in light of the theory of this chapter. In a weakly industrialized economy, the political solution in place hinges simply on the distribution of rural property. The absence of landlordism constitutes a necessary precondition for the triumph of democracy. In the presence of powerful landowning elites, the urban classes remain politically subordinate in an authoritarian political order built by the elites. By contrast, in a strongly industrialized economy, the presence of inequalities, which would be especially damaging in a rural world, may, but do not necessarily, hinder representative government.

---

[25] Naturally, when using a strict Marxist interpretation of history, there is no logical inconsistency in making those two claims at the same time: the ascendancy of the urban bourgeoisie implied the decline of the feudal aristocracy. Still, both the historical picture drawn by Moore (1966) and the way in which the theoretical model has been developed here suggest a more sophisticated structure of economic relationships and therefore of political solutions. Moreover, employing a Marxist interpretation of political and economic events should be rejected since it would make it impossible to explain why an ascending urban bourgeoisie ended up favoring the introduction of democratic practices.

Whenever the manufacturing and commercial interests dominate and are sufficiently protected from the threat of expropriation or excessive taxation, democracy is eventually established.

Asset Specificity, Economic Development and Globalization   The British example fits into a broader pattern. The process of economic development is, to a considerable extent, the story of a shift from highly immobile fixed assets to progressively more mobile capital, that is, from societies that rely on the exploitation of mines and agricultural land to economies based on manufacturing industries and human capital–intensive businesses. It is not strange that democracy has been found to be well correlated with the level of development in the last decades (Lipset 1959; Barro 1997; Przeworski and Limongi 1997). Development, measured in per capita income, generally proxies for the expansion of economic agents holding more tax-elastic (i.e., less taxable) types of capital – a phenomenon that in turn eases the intensity of the fiscal conflict between laborers and owners of capital.[26]

The growth of financial capital intensifies the nonspecificity of assets as well and therefore advances the cause of democracy. The explosion of financial integration at the turn of the twentieth century (Eichengreen 1996a) coincided with the first wave of democratizations. The latest surge of democratic transitions at the end of the twentieth century has similarly come hand in hand with the intensification of capital mobility across the globe.[27] Notice also that the model explains why rising capital mobility, democratization and some growing dissatisfaction with democracy are taking place simultaneously. Capital mobility enhances the likelihood of a democratic outcome yet at the same time lowers taxes to what many voters may consider unsatisfactory levels.

Asset Specificity and Precontemporary Regimes   The causal primacy of asset specificity over mere levels of per capita income in explaining the

---

[26] Again, taking this idea somewhat further, Appendix 1.2 to the chapter suggests two alternative explanations linking development and democracy.

[27] Capital mobility and economic openness can also be induced by asset holders to insure themselves against high taxation. For example, after studying the democratization processes of El Salvador and South Africa, Wood notes that to protect themselves against the expropriatory measures of the majority "economic elites may seek to integrate domestic markets into the global economy during the negotiation period [leading to democracy] . . . despite well-founded beliefs that not all firms in all sectors would be likely to weather increased competition" (2000: 206–7).

type of political regime has additional theoretical and empirical advantages. It solves two important paradoxes of current democratization theory. First, it accounts for the presence of representative institutions in pre-twentieth-century societies (which often had per capita income levels that, in statistical studies based on the sample of post–World War II nations, predict authoritarianism). Second, it explains why, despite their wealth most oil economies remain authoritarian. Moreover, asset specificity also gives us a clearer insight into the conditions that relate the size of the country, the presence of imperial structures and the likelihood of democracy.

The role of asset specificity has a direct application to pre-contemporary historical periods. The contrast between the semidemocratic institutions of commercial Athens and the harsh tyrannical regime in Sparta in the fifth century B.C. may be rooted in the very different types of capital assets of each society. Similarly, in the face of growing and generalized pressures from absolutist kings to collect revenue, proto-parliamentarian regimes endured in the sixteenth and seventeeth centuries precisely in those European areas that had high concentrations of commercial capitalists – along the Flanders–North Italy axis and in certain coastal areas of the Western Mediterranean basin (Tilly 1990). Thus, for example, in 1632, when the count-duke of Olivares, then prime minister to the Spanish king, attempted to impose the absolutist institutions of Castile on Catalonia, he was appalled to discover that the Catalans were "hard and terrible, because their form of government departs little, if at all, from that of a republic."[28] Finally, high levels of mobility may well have been the reason for the predominance of democratic arrangements in nineteenth-century frontier societies in the United States: the abundance of available capital made it cheaper for pioneers to move to new lands than to fight over already colonized areas.

Wealthy Dictatorships The role of asset specificity and its impact on taxation also solves an important paradox in the current empirical work on the relationship between development and democracy. Although the probability of a democratic regime has been found to increase with per capita income, the literature has also detected a set of extremely wealthy yet authoritarian regimes – mainly oil-exporting countries. For the period

[28] Quoted in Elliott (1986: 443).

42

1950–90, 80 percent of all countries with a per capita income over $8,000 and exporting no oil were democracies. The proportion is roughly reversed among high per capita income countries whose export revenues from oil amounted to 50 percent or more of total trade revenues.[29]

Przeworski and Limongi (1997) have attempted to remedy this anomaly in the modernization theory of democracy by developing the following exogenous theory of democratization. Although the level of per capita income positively affects the prospects of democratic consolidation, it cannot be employed, they claim, to predict the probability that a transition to democracy will occur. As a result, given a positive and randomly distributed probability that every authoritarian regime will collapse every year, the most developed countries will become stable democracies over time. But this is not incompatible with the persistence of a set of wealthy nations that, in the absence of a regime breakdown, have remained authoritarian.

A simpler theoretical solution is to acknowledge that wealthy dictatorships are the direct consequence of a strong concentration of fixed natural resources. As stressed earlier, a high per capita income is related to democracy only to the extent that the former originates in relatively mobile, or, more generally, hard-to-tax, kinds of capital, such as money or most types of human capital. For this very reason, the model predicts that high-income countries that base their prosperity on fixed natural resources, such as oil, should remain authoritarian in spite of their wealth. To avoid expropriation of their fixed assets, the owners will systematically crush any democratic movement. This explanation is also more robust from an empirical point of view for the following reason. According to the data presented in Przeworski and Limongi (1997) and Przeworski et al. (2000), the rate at which democracies break down declines with income – in line with modernization theory. But, as a matter of fact, the probability of democratic transitions is not randomly distributed (the result one should expect for the exogenous theory of democratization to hold). Instead, the probability of democratic transitions is positively correlated with income level in the sample of low- and middle-income nations and negatively correlated for high-income nations. This specific pattern of authoritarian breakdown requires a certain causal theory – the closest seems to be the changing structure of types of capital.[30]

---

[29] For a recent analysis of the relationship between oil and democracy, see Ross (2001).

[30] For a detailed critique of the premises and empirical analysis of Pzreworski and Limongi (1997) and Przeworski et al. (2000), see Boix and Stokes (2002).

Size of Countries, Politically Fragmented Continents and the Emergence of Democracy The mobility of capital, and therefore the likelihood of a democratic regime, is mostly conditional on the type of asset, that is, on how liquid the asset is and how easily it can be redeployed abroad. Still, asset mobility is also affected by the size of the territory controlled by the tax setter. The larger the geographical area controlled by the state, the higher the costs of moving abroad. Crossing the border from downtown Luxembourg into Germany takes a fraction of the time needed to move away from central Siberia into a different country. Accordingly, in large countries, the owners of capital may have a much higher incentive to control the policy-making process. In short, size is negatively correlated with democracy.[31]

The reduction that capital mobility operates on both taxes and the resistance to democratic institutions may explain in part why democracy emerged in Western Europe rather than in China and why proto-parliamentarian institutions collapsed in several European states in the sixteenth and seventeenth centuries. In imperial China, a vast and unified territory drove the tax-elasticity of capital close to zero. In the very fragmented Europe of the fourteenth and fifteenth centuries, limited forms of democracy appeared in those cities and small territories with abundant commercial, and therefore cheaply movable, capital. But, then, as Europe consolidated into ever larger political units after the 1500s, representative institutions became rarer.

Political Mobilization and Repression Costs

As already discussed, changes in the level of income inequality and asset specificity go a long way in explaining shifts in the constitutional structure across nations and time. Nonetheless, the theoretical model would be incomplete if we did not pay attention to the organizational and technical resources available to each agent to fight the opposite group. In a sense, this is self-evident: as stressed repeatedly in setting up the model, rich and poor assess both the income benefits associated with each political regime *and* the costs of achieving their preferred solution. However, what I wish to emphasize and explore here is that, holding the level of inequality and capital mobility constant, political transitions from or

---

[31] For evidence on the positive relationship between smallness and democracy, see Diamond (1999: 117–21) and Hiscox and Lake (2001). For the seminal analysis on the relationship between size and democracy, see Dahl and Tufte (1973).

to democracy are also spurred by a shift in the balance of power among classes – whereas, up until the previous subsection, I had underlined how changes in the distribution and nature of assets affected the type of political regime.

A change in the distribution of political resources among classes (in favor of, say, the poor) shifts the institutional status quo in two divergent directions depending on the underlying economic and social conditions. At medium or even low levels of inequality and asset specificity, the mobilization of the worse-off sectors increases the likelihood of a peaceful transition from authoritarianism to democracy. As has been discussed, for moderate inequality and asset specificity, an authoritarian regime is advantageous to the wealthy only if their repression costs are low. Thus, once the poor accumulate political resources and overcome their collective action problems, organizing in unions and political parties, and are able to sustain mass demonstrations and general strikes, the old elites reestimate their chances of success and eventually accept liberalizing the political arena and holding elections. Formally, the change in repression costs shifts the inequality expression $k_w^i - \rho_l^i > \widehat{y}_w^i$ to $\widehat{y}_w^i > k_w^i - \rho_h^i$.[32]

By contrast, at high levels of inequality and asset specificity, the gradual mobilization of the poor triggers a change as well in the political arena, albeit in a completely different direction. As the worse-off overcome their collective-action problems and establish political mechanisms of action, that is, as they acknowledge that their chances of revolutionary victory increase, their incentives for engaging in violent forms of protest go up. But, given the highly skewed distribution of assets among the population, the wealthy still favor the use of repression. As a result, the previous situation of stable authoritarianism is now replaced by an increase in clashes between the two classes (and a positive probability of a communist regime).

The mobilization of the lower classes across all Europe at the turn of the twentieth century serves as a good illustration of the divergent consequences of a shift in the repression costs of the old elites. In Western Europe, with declining levels of economic inequality and abundant industrial and financial capital, the mobilization of the working class finally pushed the old regime elites to liberalize the electoral regime after the First World War. While only 11 percent of the population was unionized in

---

[32] The converse can also happen. A weakening of the lower classes can facilitate an authoritarian coup.

Britain in 1892, about 45 percent had joined trade unions by 1920 (Scase 1977). Similarly, in Belgium, union membership exploded from less than 6 percent of the nonagricultural labor force to over 40 percent from 1910 to 1920 (Strikwerda 1997). In Germany, unionized workers were 12 percent of the labor force in 1910 and about 48 percent twenty years later. In the Netherlands, the percentage went up from 9 percent in 1910 to 30 percent in 1930 (Rothstein 1989; Strikwerda 1997). In Sweden and Norway, about one third of all industrial workers were unionized on the eve of World War I (Luebbert 1991: 170). In correspondence with its growing strength, the labor movement launched powerful general strikes, basically directed at forcing constitutional changes, in countries such as Belgium in the early 1890s and in Sweden in the 1910s. Still, the agitation of the labor movement did not lead to civil confrontation. Rather, democratic transitions fell in line in a peaceful manner across Europe in the 1910s and constitutional democracies remained consolidated in most Atlantic economies despite the crisis of the 1930s.

The successful democratic transitions in Northern Europe make for a powerful contrast with the political development of the highly unequal and profoundly rural countries of Southern and Eastern Europe. Much like the Atlantic economies, the European periphery witnessed a substantial mobilization of the urban and rural working classes in the first third of the twentieth century. In Italy, trade unions expanded their following by ten in the 1910s and the Socialist party gathered a third of the votes in 1919. In Spain, unions organized significant portions of the industrial workforce and of agricultural laborers. In both countries, the end of World War I was followed by a cascade of industrial strikes and political violence. In Hungary, Bela Kun established, for a brief time, a revolutionary regime after the collapse of the Austro-Hungarian monarchy. In all these cases, the response from the elites to the red scare differed completely from the strategies of their counterparts in North Atlantic Europe. In Italy, Mussolini took power in 1922. In Spain, Primo de Rivera imposed a military dictatorship from 1923 until 1930. The Spanish Republic that followed crumbled quickly. In response to a Socialist-led uprising in Asturias in 1934 and to the electoral victory of the Popular Front in 1936, a military coup spawned a three-year-long cruel civil war. In Portugal, an unstable and hardly democratic republican regime collapsed after a few years in the late 1910s. By the 1930s, all of the Eastern European countries except Czechoslovakia were under authoritarian control. In one instance, the spiral of mobilization and repression led to a revolution and to the type of left-wing dictatorship the model predicts for highly unequal countries: Russia.

The Role of the Middle Class and the Formation of Cross-class Coalitions

The Middle Class

Although history offers evidence of societies sharply divided between the rich, or propertied, and the poor, or propertyless, the social scale is generally composed by a gradation of economic sectors or classes. To reflect a more complex social world, I now model a game in which, in addition to rich and poor, there is a middle class of individuals. I denote each individual in the middle class as m, with income y_m. The ordering of the income of each class is $y_w > y_m > y_p$.

With three classes, the following political regimes are feasible: an authoritarian regime controlled by the wealthy; a limited democracy, in which both the rich and the middle class vote; a full democracy, where all classes are enfranchised; and two revolutionary regimes – one in which the middle class and the poor expropriate from the wealthy and impose a democratic system (in which the middle class pays a net transfer) and a communist one in which the poor expropriate from both rich and middle-class individuals. Given their position in the income scale, middle-class individuals prefer a restrictive democracy (in which only the wealthy and the middle class vote) to either a regime controlled by the wealthy or a universal suffrage system. Whether they prefer a universal suffrage democracy to an authoritarian system (with only the wealthy voting in the latter) will depend on whether their income is above average income (in which case they would incur a negative transfer under full democracy) or below average income (in which case full democracy is to their advantage). Whether the middle class will support the expropriation of assets from the rich will depend on their assessment of the benefits of acquiring new assets relative to the transfers to be paid to the poor.

To explore how having a third agent affects the analysis, assume that the political regime is decided through the set of moves described in Figure 1.3. The underlying logic of the game is identical to the one examined earlier; the only difference is that cross-class alliances emerge as a possible outcome. With three actors in society, the rich must first decide whether they

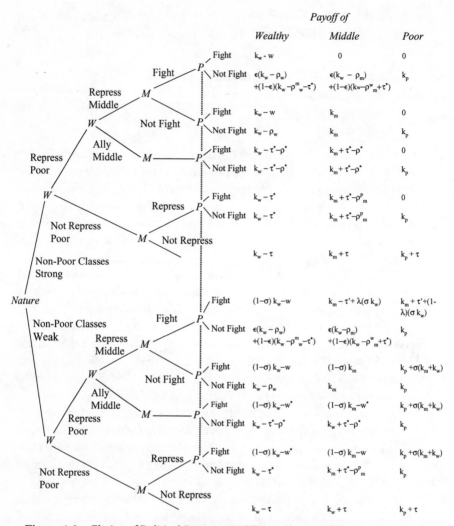

Figure 1.3 Choice of Political Regime in a Three-Class Model.

will repress (all or any of) the other agents. Should they decide to repress no one, M (the middle class) may either repress P (the poor) or not. If neither the wealthy nor the middle class represses, a system of universal suffrage is peacefully established. If the middle class represses, there is some probability that the poor may revolt and impose a left-wing dictatorship.

If the rich decide on a repressive strategy, they must in turn consider whether to repress both the middle class and the poor (to sustain a fully authoritarian regime in which only the wealthy decide) or to ally themselves with the middle class against the poor (therefore introducing a limited democracy). After the rich move, the middle class responds. If the wealthy decide to repress M, M may either fight against or acquiesce to the authoritarian regime. If the wealthy decide to co-opt M, the middle class simply joins them – since, as has been pointed out, a restrictive democracy is strictly preferred by M to either an authoritarian regime or universal suffrage.

The last move is made by the poor. In those circumstances in which at least one class decides to repress the poor, P must decide whether to rebel or to acquiesce. Depending on the previous moves of the wealthy and the middle class, the pattern of alliances will be different for P alone against the other two classes, allied with the middle class against the rich, fighting just the rich (with the middle class taking a passive position), or fighting just the middle class (with the rich abstaining).

In those circumstances in which two (contiguous) classes may find it to their advantage to oppose the third class, the former two share the cost of repression: this can be denoted as ρ^* (with $\rho^* < \rho$ always for each separate class). Under those particular conditions (as will be shown) in which one class may abstain in the determination of the regime and leave the other two fighting each other, we can denote the cost to the wealthy of fighting M as ρ_w^m; the cost to the middle class of fighting the rich alone as ρ_m^w; and the cost to the middle class of fighting P alone as ρ_m^p.

Let τ be the net transfer under universal suffrage and τ^* the net transfer under a restrictive democracy.

As in the previous game, the poor (but neither the rich nor the middle class) know about the repression costs of the other classes only in a probabilistic manner. For the middle class, instead, there is complete information about the cost of repression of the wealthy. As a result, the decision of the middle class to fight or not (if repressed) is determined by a parameter ϵ (with $0 \leq \epsilon \leq 1$); victory takes place with a probability ϵ and defeat with a probability $1 - \epsilon$.

The reactions of the rich and the middle class vary according to which strategy the poor are anticipated to pick among the following alternatives: either they never rebel (the expected gains of a revolutionary coup do not exceed the current income); they rebel if the middle class does (only the expected gains of that joint revolutionary attempt exceed their current income); or they have an incentive to rebel alone (the expected gains of revolution beat the current income y_p). Here I consider mainly the first choice, in which the poor have no incentive to rebel – a discussion of the strategies of each agent is enough to describe how the evolution of assets and the relative position of each class affect the political outcome.

From Authoritarianism to Limited Democracy: The Role of the Middle Class If the poor are anticipated to acquiesce to the regime in place, the upper class has now to consider the following set of political strategies: maintaining an authoritarian regime, co-opting the middle class into limited democracy or accepting universal suffrage. Whether the wealthy will continue to impose an authoritarian regime depends on the political resources of the middle class. But, as in the two-classes model, the outcome hinges on the distribution of assets among the classes – and on the tax consequences of that distribution.

To understand how different distributions of assets lead to different political outcomes, consider first a situation in which wealth differences are important both between the wealthy and the middle class and between the middle class and the lower class. This distribution is depicted in Figure 1.4.A. In this case, the differences between the two classes, P and M, are sufficiently high to lead to $\tau^* - \tau > \rho_m^p$ or, in other words, to give the middle class an incentive to repress the poor (if the rich decided, for some reason, not to repress the lower class) and impose a limited democracy regime (since the gains for the middle class from a limited regime are larger

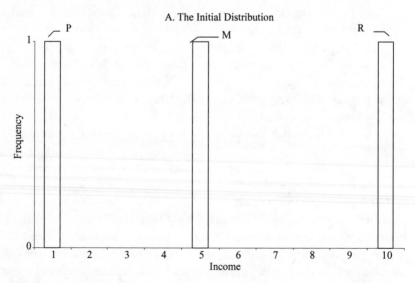

Figure 1.4 Changing Income Distributions.

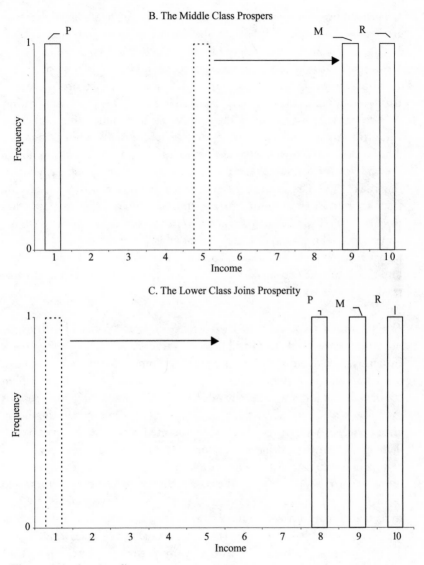

Figure 1.4 (*continued*)

than the costs to them to repress the poor). This result in turn leads the wealthy to compare their payoffs under limited democracy (the outcome from letting the middle class repress the poor) and under authoritarianism (the outcome from repressing both the poor and the middle classes). Given a sufficiently large distance between the rich and the middle class, the probability of paying transfers to the middle class would be higher than repressing the latter, or $\epsilon\tau^* > \rho_w^m$, and the rich would lean toward authoritarianism. In short, in a society in which the upper class is well ahead in assets relative to the other classes, authoritarianism should prevail.

Notice, however, that as the middle class becomes richer and more similar to the upper class (a scenario depicted in Figure 1.4.B), τ^* will decline. As a result, the cost borne by the rich of war to subdue the middle class will grow larger than the transfers to be paid under a limited democracy. The wealthy will be well advised to switch to a strategy of co-optation of the middle class (or, under certain circumstances, even to a strategy of letting the middle class alone repress the poor). In other words, the transition from an authoritarian regime to a system of limited democracy will take place as a middle class emerges as a separate sector, equal in wealth to the upper class. This process has a close resemblance to the political development of Europe in the nineteenth century: as the bourgeoisie made its way into the economic and social scene, a system of limited democracy became predominant across that continent.

From Limited Democracy to Universal Suffrage Notice also from the previous discussion that the middle class is not a "natural" ally of the poor. In purely redistributive terms, a system of limited democracy is in most cases a dominant strategy for the middle class. Even if the rich are willing to concede the full franchise, the middle class will always step in to repress the lower classes whenever the cost of repression is lower than the difference between the transfer obtained in a limited regime and in a universal democracy (remember that $\tau^* > \tau$ for the middle class always).

It is only when $\tau^* - \tau < \rho_m^p$ (and the rich have decided not to pursue a repressive strategy) that the middle class will not repress the poor. For this to be the case, the differences between M and P should have declined enough to reduce the gap between τ^* and τ to a minimum. The comparative costs of repression dissuade the middle class from imposing a restricted suffrage.[33] This process of income equalization, in which the poor catch up with M and cease to be a threat, is described in Figure 1.4.C.

To sum up, the transition from an authoritarian regime (in the hands of the upper class) to universal democracy hinges on the distribution of resources. With just a minority in possession of most resources, a democratic

---

[33] Naturally, as the poor become closer to the middle class in income per capita, it is also to the advantage of the well-to-do to abstain from any repressive strategy, since $\rho^* > \tau^* - \tau$.

outcome is implausible. As the distribution of economic assets changes, the regime gradually opens up to new voters. Universal suffrage is feasible only after a considerable amount of equalization has already taken place.

Multiple Actors   A model with more actors would lead to similar conclusions. Naturally, the more fragmented the social space, the slower the transition from authoritarianism to full democracy. The upper segments would be able to co-opt the middle segments one at a time, and the political clout of the poorest would be greatly reduced. Thus, one can predict that the more fragmented the working class is, the higher the degree of equality that must be achieved for full democracy to be introduced.[34] A derivation of this result is that democracy will take place in ethnically divided societies only at levels of equality higher than exist in homogeneous societies.

Cross-sectoral Alliances

So far I have employed what is essentially a class-based or factor-based model of politics to explain regime transitions. In the basic model, a class of wealthy individuals, characterized by one type of capital (either oil, land, human capital or financial assets) with the same level of asset specificity, is confronted by a set of poor individuals, essentially unskilled laborers. In the previous subsection, I introduced some gradation in the returns to assets held by individuals, thereby developing a more complex social structure with at least three classes. But even in that discussion the framework still reflects a class-based economy, where group membership and the corresponding political interests are defined by income level. In this subsection, I explore what happens if we relax the assumption that the assets of the class of wealthy individuals or capitalists are homogeneous, that is, that they have the same level of mobility.

Once we accept the possibility of having different types of capital (as a result of different levels of specificity), even within the same income class, two main results emerge. First, we can easily model an economy with several economic sectors coexisting within any single territory. In other words, instead of having only classes, that is, income-defined social groups, as economic and political players, we can describe a society with a multiplicity

---

[34] This is similar to saying in a two-actor model that the lower the repression costs of the rich, the lower τ must be for a democracy to succeed.

of sectors, defined by the specificity of their assets, within (or across) factors. In this sense, this extension accommodates, without doing any violence to the initial model, the most recent literature applying sectoral models of politics to trade (Frieden 1991; Alt and Gilligan 1994; Hiscox 2001) and to the formation of the welfare state (Baldwin 1990; Mares 2001).

Second, allowing for sectoral variation among capitalists may considerably change the predictions of the political game, in which the lower, middle and rich classes struck deals purely as a function of their income, described earlier. More specifically, whenever the level of asset specificity or capital mobility is not positively correlated with income, the political interests and strategies of each class of capitalists need not correspond with the predictions of the preceding subsection. Instead of a coalitional structure in which the middle class plays a pivotal role and allies itself with either the upper or the lower class, the middle class may now face the joint opposition of the remaining classes. A class–cleavage structure may give way to sector-based cleavages so that the predictions about the agents behind democratization and authoritarian repression may be altered.

To clarify this insight, Figure 1.5.A depicts the location of three different economic sectors in terms of their income (along the vertical axis) and the specificity of their assets (along the horizontal axis): L, that is, a working class that bases its income on labor; K_B representing a urban class or bourgeoisie; and K_T as a class of landowners. Labor, which receives the lowest returns, is very nonspecific. In turn, rural and urban capitalists have the same return and vary very slightly in the specificity of their assets. In addition, Figure 1.5.A, which actually parallels Figure 1.2, shows, using a set of concave lines, the tax burden associated with different levels of income and asset specificity under a democratic regime (where the median voter belongs to L). For either low income or low specificity, taxes should be low. As both parameters rise, the tax burden increases. The position of each sector on democracy then varies with the expected tax burden. In Figure 1.5.A, where the returns from land and urban capital, as well as their asset specificity, are identical, the political cleavage will take place along income lines: L will oppose K_B and K_T.

Consider, by contrast, a case in which commercial capital is much more sensitive than land to taxes because it can either easily flee the country or underreport its returns. In this example, commercial capitalists will expect a much lower tax rate than K_T under a democracy. This simple difference will unsettle the predictions of class-based models. Defying the strict linearity based on income described earlier, labor and the bourgeoisie may now

A. Class-Based Alliance: Capital versus Labor

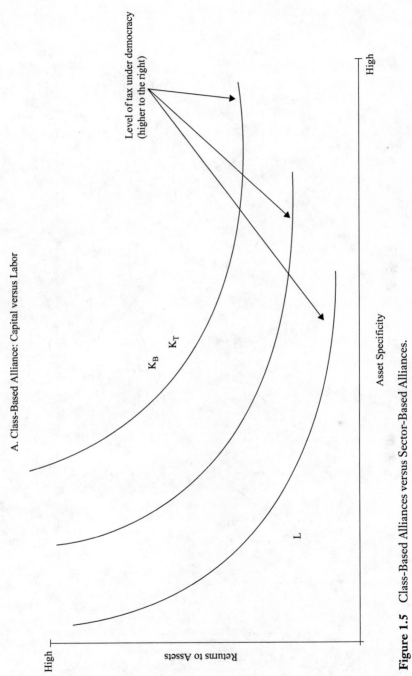

Level of tax under democracy
(higher to the right)

K_B K_T

L

Returns to Assets

High

High

Asset Specificity

Figure 1.5   Class-Based Alliances versus Sector-Based Alliances.

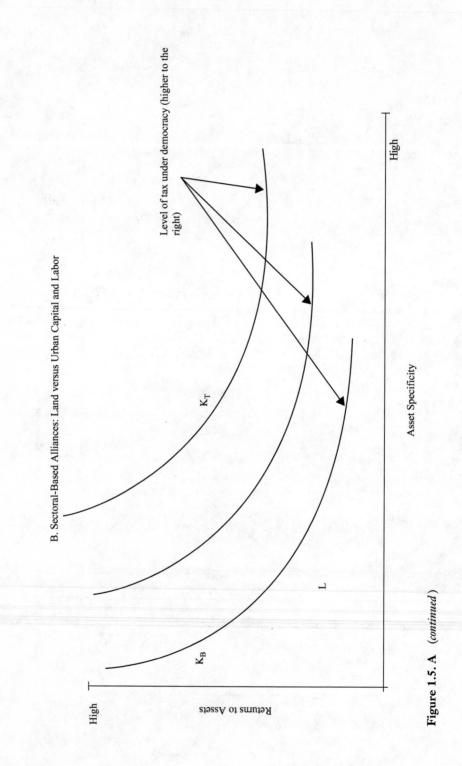

B. Sectoral-Based Alliances: Land versus Urban Capital and Labor

Level of tax under democracy (higher to the right)

High

Asset Specificity

Returns to Assets

High

K_T

K_B

L

Figure 1.5. A (*continued*)

decide to strike a coalition against the landowning class. This possibility is represented in Figure 1.5.B. In this instance, a wealthy industrial bourgeoisie draws a much higher return than the class of well-to-do farmers. Still, since it holds much more mobile assets, it expects more moderate taxes than rural capital in a democratic setting and has no qualms about seeking an alliance with urban labor (in favor of democratic institutions) against the farming class.

Urban–rural cleavages were pervasive in several European countries, such as Denmark and Sweden, in the nineteenth century (precisely before the emergence of the socialist movement representing the industrial working class made income distribution across factors central again) (Lipset and Rokkan 1967). Similarly, the exclusion of the countryside from political decisions by the urban commercial class (with the tacit support of the lower classes in the cities) was a central feature of several Swiss cantons until at least the mid-nineteenth century. The political confrontation between town and countryside characterized other nations as well, such as post-bellum United States (Rogowski 1989), and can be seen in the party system of pre-1918 Britain.

The formation of an urban-rural cleavage has generally been accounted for as a result of disputes over trade policy (Gourevitch 1986; Rogowski 1989). Commercial debates were undoubtedly at the center of politics in the late nineteenth century. But notice that, all in all, tariffs were simply another form of taxation – in fact, they were the key type of taxation until state bureaucracies were sufficiently developed to establish income taxation. The type of wealth distribution and specificity in each country must have mattered to account for the type of cleavage structure that arose. To sum up, although calculations over trade gains and losses matter in explaining political alignments, both sectoral and class-based cleavages can be accounted for in a very straightforward manner through a simple model of taxation.

Conclusions

This chapter has developed a comprehensive theory to account for the occurrence of democracies, authoritarian regimes and left-wing dictatorships as a result of the distribution and nature of economic assets and of the political balance of power among different social groups. Stable democracies take place whenever inequality is low or wealth is either mobile or difficult to tax. Excessive differences among the rich and the poor push the former to restrict the franchise to avoid the redistributive consequences of a fully democratic system, unless capital mobility restrains the ability of the poor to expropriate this wealth.

In examining the underlying causes of variation in types of political regimes, the model also details the processes through which political transitions take place and why systematic violence occurs. To do so, it introduces a component that, although by now central in international relations to account for wars, has eluded the study of domestic politics: the (varying) amount of information that all actors have about the relative capabilities vis-à-vis their opponents. Rational actors will engage in revolutionary action and civil wars only if they are uncertain about the outcome of their choices. With full knowledge of the ultimate consequences of the game, no agent has any incentive to pay the extra costs of war, and, as a result, transitions from or to a democratic system will occur in a peaceful manner (propelled by shifts in the structure of the economy and the resources of the parties). By contrast, given some uncertainty about the power of the wealthy and provided that inequality and asset specificity are high, political agents become more prone to engage in political conflicts and some countries experience systematic civil unrest.

Both for analytical convenience and to build a relatively parsimonious theory of political transitions, the chapter begins by making a rather simplified set of assumptions about the number and nature of political actors. In the initial model, only two classes (or, in the language of economic theory, only two representative agents) struggle over the type of political constitution. The model is then extended in ways that strengthen its theoretical and empirical leverage. Employing a three-class model, with upper, middle and lower social groups, it examines the political strategies of different classes in a way that sheds light on the gradual process of democratization that took place in the advanced world in the nineteenth century and the first third of the twentieth century. Similarly, the introduction of variability in the specificity of assets leads to the generation of simple yet powerful cross-sectoral models of politics.

This model of political transition seems to have considerable empirical purchase on the history of political development. It matches and gives internal consistency to Moore's insight about the antidemocratic nature of landlords; at the same time, it accounts for Moore's intuition about the bourgeoisie's benign role in the process of extending universal suffrage. It explains why economic development, by equalizing conditions and reducing the weight of immobile assets, fosters democracy. Similarly, and without

Conclusions

resorting to any new or ad hoc variables, it explains why the ruling elites of most wealthy oil producers resist the liberalization of their government's institutions. Naturally, these insights need further systematic empirical corroboration. This task is undertaken in the next two chapters employing both detailed econometric and historical evidence.

APPENDIX 1.1

Proving the Results of the Initial Game

Proof of Proposition 1. Low Levels of Inequality or Asset Specificity

Whenever either inequality is sufficiently low or specificity σ_t is sufficiently low, taxation is low (3) and democracy is preferred to successful repression even when repression is not costly. That is, the wealthy prefer to accept a democracy whenever $\hat{y}_w^i > k_w^i - \rho_l$. In this case, it is the dominant strategy for the wealthy to offer democracy, regardless of whether the cost of repression is high or low. Democracy arrives then in any Nash equilibrium of the game. □

Proof of Proposition 2. Medium Levels of Inequality and Asset Specificity

Consider the situation in which $k_w^i - \rho_l > \hat{y}_w^i > k_w^i - \rho_b$. Clearly, in this case, when repression cost is low, the wealthy prefer to repress rather than to concede democracy. Conversely, they prefer no repression when the cost is high. To show that this is a (Bayesian perfect) equilibrium, it suffices to show that the poor never revolt given the beliefs determined by this strategy and that the wealthy prefer this (separating) equilibrium to trying to imitate one another. First, given the separating beliefs, the poor never revolt: the only time the poor would like to do so is when they are being repressed. But in this case the cost of repression is sufficiently low so that repression would ultimately succeed, with extremely bad results for the poor. Second, the wealthy do not want to try to repress when they have a high repression cost, since in this case they actually prefer the democracy outcome even if repression would succeed. Third, the wealthy who are lucky enough to enjoy low-cost repression technology clearly do not want to allow for democracy. □

Proof of Proposition 3. High Levels of Inequality and Asset Specificity

We are now in situations in which $\hat{y}_w^i < k_w^i - \rho_b$, that is, the wealthy would prefer repression (if successful) to democracy. We need to show that the "pooling" equilibrium described by the proposition is indeed a Bayesian perfect equilibrium. First, for repression to succeed and authoritarianism to emerge as the form of government, it is necessary that, given the probability of success of a revolution, the poor prefer not to revolt. Since under both "types" of repression costs the wealthy choose the same authoritarian regime, the beliefs of the poor are given by the initial probability of a high repression cost, q. Then the expected gain of revolting is smaller than the value of accepting an imposed authoritarian regime if, even when the poor win the civil war, they obtain less than they currently have:

$$q \left(\frac{k_p}{\alpha} + \frac{\sigma k_w}{\alpha} \right) < \frac{k_p}{\alpha} \tag{5}$$

If (5) holds, then the poor never prefer to revolt. But it is clear that, for all exogenous q, there exists some σ small enough and some k_w small enough such that the condition noted holds and the pooling equilibrium proposed is indeed an equilibrium. Thus, if this condition holds, and $\widehat{y}_w^i < k_w^i - \rho_b$, the wealthy are better off repressing regardless of the actual repression cost; given that the wealthy repress, nonupdated beliefs $\beta = q$ are optimal; and given these beliefs, the poor do indeed prefer not to revolt. Parameters that fulfill these two conditions can easily be found as long as q is not too high (an example is derived in Figure 1.2). When these two conditions hold, the pooling candidate equilibrium described in proposition 3 is a Bayesian perfect equilibrium. □

Proof of Proposition 4. The Conditions Leading to Political Violence

First, assume (5) does not hold, so that the poor prefer to revolt, and also assume inequality and specificity are high enough so that the democracy payoff is not preferred by the wealthy regardless of the cost of repression $\widehat{y}_w < k_w^i - \rho_b$. Clearly, since (5) does not hold, the equilibrium described in proposition 3 is not an equilibrium now, since if the wealthy were to always choose repression the poor would always try their luck and revolt, with the consequence that the strategy of the wealthy would not be optimal when repression is expensive. The other pure strategy equilibrium, in which the wealthy do not repress if their cost of repression is high, is also not an equilibrium, as given the beliefs it would engender (the poor would believe that anyone who represses has a low cost of repression) the wealthy would be better off deviating when repression is actually costly. The equilibrium must then have the wealthy following a mixed strategy when they have a high cost of repression.

Constructing such an equilibrium is straightforward. First, for mixing to take place, beliefs about the probability of victory by the poor in a revolution β must be such that the poor are indifferent between initiating a revolution and provoking a civil war,

$$\beta \left(\frac{k_p}{\alpha} + \frac{\sigma k_w}{\alpha} \right) = \frac{k_p}{\alpha}$$

This implies beliefs given by:

$$\beta = \frac{k_p}{k_p + \sigma k_w} \tag{6}$$

The beliefs of the poor are determined by the actual strategy of the wealthy by Bayes rule. Calling the probability that the wealthy choose to repress when the cost of repression is high p_A, we have $\beta = p_A q / (p_A q + (1 - q))$. Imposing that these beliefs be correct determines p_A as a function of β. Substituting in β from (6) we have the probability of repression when its cost is high given by:

$$p_A = \frac{1-q}{q} \frac{1}{\sigma} \frac{1-k_w}{k_w} \tag{7}$$

Finally, the probability that the poor revolt in that period (p_R) is then determined by the indifference condition of the wealthy who face a high repression cost. For them to be indifferent, we must have:

$$(1 - p_R)[k_w^i - \rho_b] = \widehat{y}_w^i \tag{8}$$

And this equation defines implicitly the probability of a civil war as a function of the structural parameters of the economy. □

Alternative Explanations for the Development–Democracy Correlation

Consider two alternative models to explain why, independently of how development may change the distribution and specificity of assets, the likelihood of democratization (or, at least, of democratic consolidation) increases with per capita income.

1. Tax-Elasticity of Income

Assume that higher incomes are more sensitive to tax rates than lower incomes – in other words, that the leisure-work substitution effect becomes steeper with incomes $(\partial^2 y_i/\partial \tau < 0)$. If, as a result of economic development (and a higher average per capita income), the income of well-to-do agents increases in absolute terms, the fall in total revenues (as a result of their shifting to leisure) should become sharper for the same tax level. Thus constrained by the response of the well-off, the median voter will impose lower taxes. Repression will become more expensive in relative terms, and democracy will be more likely.[*]

To shed light on this argument, consider two economies with the same distributive pattern, that is, with the same ratio of high versus low incomes, but with a different average per capita income (and, naturally, a different median per capita income). The rich in the society with a higher average per capita income are more sensitive to any tax rate than the rich in the poorer society. As a result, the tax rate at which the median voter maximizes his disposable income is lower in the former economy than in the latter one. Since redistributive pressures are lower in the richer society, democracy is cheaper to establish.

2. Declining Marginal Utility of Income

In the initial model, the welfare of each individual is a linear function of income. Consider, instead, the possibility that the marginal utility of additional income declines with income, with a structure $U(y_i) = (y_i)^\alpha$ for $0 < \alpha < 1$. That is, for low incomes, below or barely above the threshold of subsistence, each additional unit

---

[*] I am indebted to Alícia Adserà for first bringing this argument to my attention.

of income increases individual utility almost proportionally. As income increases, utility increases at a slower pace. At very high income levels, the marginal utility of additional income approaches zero. Hence, the disutility that a transfer imposes on the upper class declines as their per capita income increases. Thus, as growth occurs and per capita income of the upper classes rises, the benefits of a repression strategy decline, and democracy becomes more likely.

2

Empirical Evidence

Two broad structural conditions, the distribution of income among individuals and the mobility of assets, determine both the type of political regime and the extent of political violence in any country in the long run. At low levels of inequality, the extent of distributional demands from less well-off individuals subsides to make democracy and its tax burden bearable to the richest sectors. Similarly, as asset specificity declines, the threat of expropriation tapers off and democracy becomes acceptable to capital owners. By contrast, in highly unequal countries whose wealth is mainly immobile, class conflict becomes intense: the owners of capital generally resort to an authoritarian strategy to defend their wealth while the poor tend to rebel to level the distribution of assets across society. I now turn to assess the empirical validity of the theoretical model by examining through econometric analysis data spanning 1850 to 1990 on both the type of political regime and the degree of political conflict. Chapter 3 strengthens the results by looking at qualitative evidence extracted from the evolution of Switzerland's cantons and the states of the United States in the last three centuries.

This chapter is organized as follows. In the first section, I discuss the definition and measurement of democracy (and authoritarianism) and describe the distribution of political regimes and political transitions across the world in the last two centuries. In the second and third sections, I employ statistical tools to determine the impact of inequality and asset specificity on the likelihood of a transition to a democratic system from an authoritarian regime (or, conversely, from democracy to dictatorship) using two cross-temporal cross-national panels. The first data set, from 1950 to 1990, contains direct data on income inequality, taken from Deininger and Squire (1996), as well as proxies for asset specificity, such as the proportion of wealth generated by oil, agriculture and types of human capital. The second panel contains observations from the mid-nineteenth century to the late twentieth century and taps inequality indirectly, through the distribution of rural property and the level of literacy. The fourth section of this chapter examines the impact of inequality and asset specificity on the occurrence of civil conflicts, again employing those two data sets. I postpone the summary of the evidence gathered in this chapter to the last section of Chapter 3.

Political Regimes and Political Transitions since 1800

Figure 2.1 displays both the absolute number of democracies and the proportion of democratic regimes among sovereign nations across the world every year from 1800 to 1994.

A country is defined as a democracy if it meets three conditions: (1) the legislature is elected in free multiparty elections; (2) the executive is directly or indirectly elected in popular elections and is responsible either directly to voters or to a legislature elected according to the first condition; (3) a majority of the population (more precisely, at least 50 percent of adult men) has the right to vote. The first two conditions follow Przeworski's definition and coding of democracy (Przeworski et al. 2000).[1] The third condition has been added to track the substantial variation in the extension of the franchise across countries before World War II – after 1950 all nations with free competitive elections (as well as most without) had universal suffrage (at least for men).

To clarify these requirements, consider the following set of examples. The Russian empire can be easily classified as autocratic since it did not meet any of the conditions. By contrast, with its competitive elections, responsible executive and universal male suffrage between 1848 and 1851 and after 1870, France belongs to the democratic camp. Many other nineteenth-century countries fell in between in how many conditions they fulfilled. Although the United Kingdom was governed by an executive accountable to a parliament elected through free and competitive elections since, at least, the first electoral reform of 1832, its enfranchised electorate remained small until the end of the nineteenth century – encompassing only one seventh of all adult men till the late 1860s and about one third afterwards. The electoral reform of 1885 extended the franchise to more than half of the adult men in Britain, turning the United Kingdom into a democracy according

---

[1] For a full discussion of the rules that apply to the first two conditions, see Przeworski et al. (2000), chap. 1.

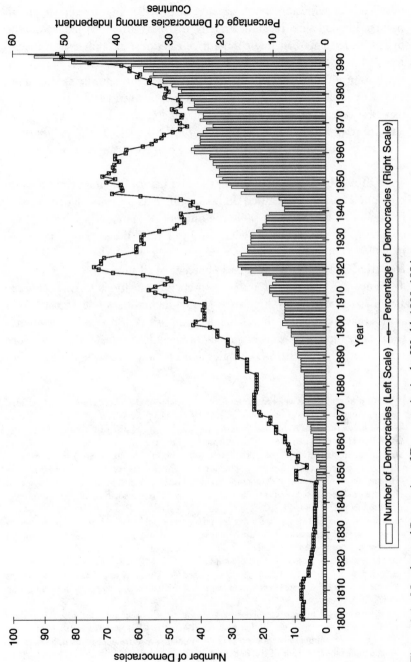

Figure 2.1 Number and Proportion of Democracies in the World, 1800–1994.

to this book's definition. The German case provides an interesting counterpoint to Britain. Since its unification in 1870 and until the Weimar Republic in 1919, Germany had free competitive elections and universal male suffrage (thus meeting conditions 1 and 3), but the executive, controlled by the Kaiser, did not have to rely on a parliamentary majority. Accordingly, Germany is classified as an authoritarian regime until 1918.[2] Appendix 2.1 lists all sovereign countries between 1800 and 1994 and their democratic or authoritarian nature.[3] For the period from 1950 to 1990, the classification is taken from Przeworski et al. (2000).[4] The rest of the data set has been developed by Boix and Rosato (2001).

As shown by Figure 2.1, during the first half of the nineteenth century only one country, the United States, qualified as a democracy. Following the revolutionary wave of 1848, the number of democracies grew from 3 countries that year (France, Switzerland and the United States), that is, less than 6 percent of all independent states, to 18 nations, that is, a third of all countries, in 1914, and to 28, or 44 percent of all states, in 1921.

Figure 2.2 displays the annual number of transitions to democracy in already sovereign states. Figure 2.3 shows the number of democratic transitions that coincided with independence. Until World War I, most democratic transitions occurred in already independent states – the exceptions were several former British colonies and Norway. After 1918, democracy

---

[2] Condition 1 excludes as well those cases in which, in a bicameral system, there is an unelected chamber with veto power over the popularly elected chamber. Although the British House of Lords has the right to block legislation approved in the House of Commons, it has not exercised such power in the last two centuries. In the constitutional crisis of 1909–10, in which the British upper house initially rejected the cabinet's budget, the House of Lords eventually conceded the supremacy of the lower chamber – this concession is used to classify Britain (and similar cases) as democratic backward through time under the assumption that, had the crisis erupted earlier, the elected house would have also affirmed its position over the unelected chamber.

[3] In some exceptional cases, the index includes transitional years of two types: sovereign countries under occupation (e.g., the Netherlands, 1940–44) or situations of intense internal conflict or constitutional crisis that are difficult to code.

[4] There is only one exception in the coding. Whereas in Przeworski, Argentina is coded as a democracy from 1950 to 1954, in this book Argentina is coded as an authoritarian regime to make the regime consistent with the nondemocratic practices in place in the 1940s.

Przeworski's data base correlates very strongly with other indexes. The Coppedge-Reinicke scale for 1978, the Bollen scale for 1965, the Gurr scale for 1950–86 and the Gastil index of political liberties for 1972–90 predict respectively 92 percent, 85 percent, 91 percent and 93 percent of the outcomes of Przeworski's scale (Przeworski et al. 2000: 56–57).

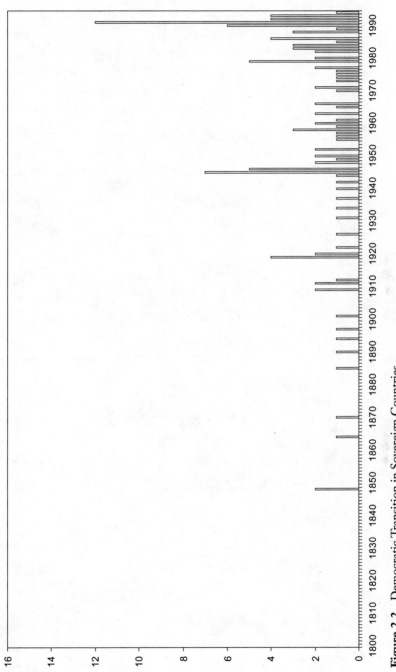

Figure 2.2 Democratic Transition in Sovereign Countries.

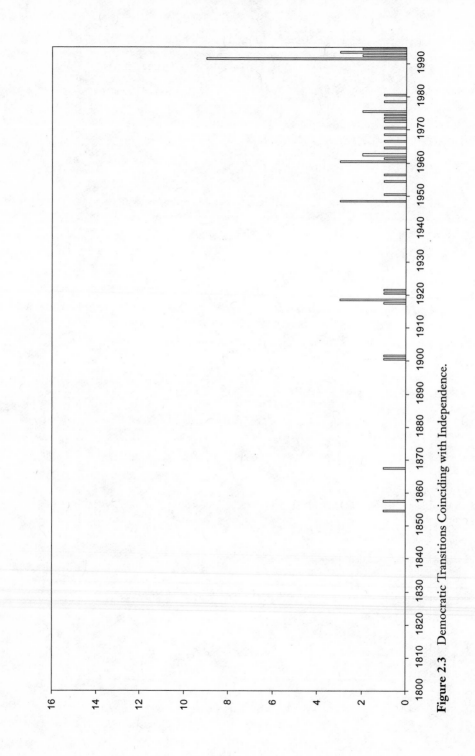

Figure 2.3 Democratic Transitions Coinciding with Independence.

expanded through both the demise of previously authoritarian regimes, such as Germany and Austria, and the birth of new countries in Eastern Europe resulting from the collapse of the Russian and the Austro-Hungarian empires.

After peaking in the early 1920s, the number of democracies experienced an absolute decline to 13 countries in 1940. This represented around 20 percent of the universe of cases. A second and rather fast wave of democratization took place right after World War II. By 1950 there were 34 democracies, that is, more than in the peak year of 1921. Nonetheless, due to an increase in the number of independent states, the proportion of democracies remained, at around 40 percent, similar to the one registered three decades before.

The number of democratic regimes stayed the same, with a slight decline due to the authoritarian backlash experienced in several Latin American countries, until the mid-1970s. By contrast, the number underwent a dramatic fall in relative terms in that same period to about 26 percent of all states by 1969. As is apparent from observing Figures 2.4 and 2.5, which indicate, respectively, the annual number of democratic breakdowns and the annual number of authoritarian regimes introduced with independence, the decline in the proportion of democracies in the period after World War II occurred for rather different reasons than those for the democratization reversal in the interwar period. In the interwar period, the fall was due to both the regime breakdowns in Italy, Germany, Spain and most Eastern European countries in the 1920s and early 1930s and the military occupations at the beginning of World War II. In the postwar period, the decline in the proportion of democracies resulted from the organization of most newly born countries into one-party or military dictatorships.

Figure 2.1 captures as well the third, rather rapid democratization wave that started in the mid-1970s in Southern Europe, extended to Latin America in the following decade and culminated with the fall of the Soviet Union in the early 1990s. By the mid-1990s, the number of democracies had risen to 95, or 51 percent of the universe of countries.

Empirical Analysis of the Post–World War II Period

Empirical Strategy

The model developed in Chapter 1 predicts that the probability of transition in country i between different political systems (j and k) is a function of

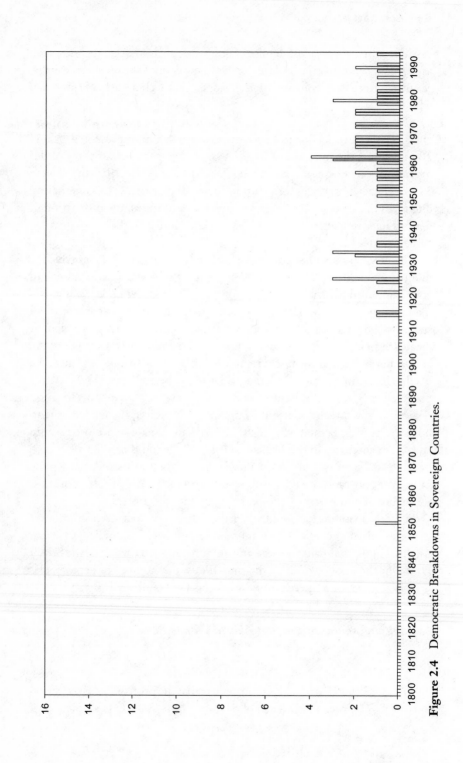

Figure 2.4 Democratic Breakdowns in Sovereign Countries.

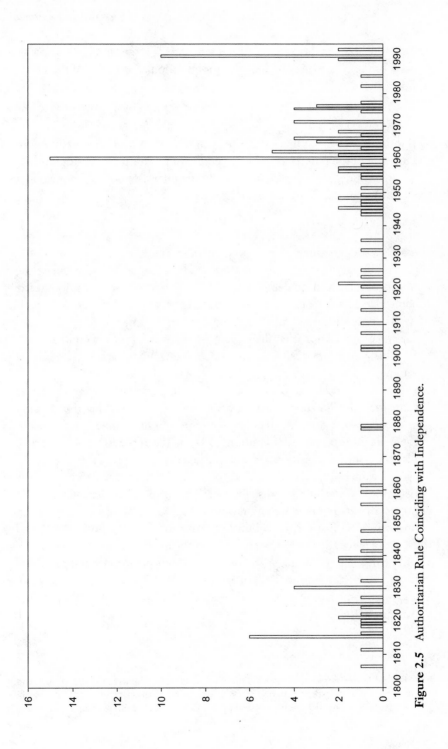

Figure 2.5 Authoritarian Rule Coinciding with Independence.

the level of inequality, the country specificity of assets and the repression costs of the rich (which include the mobilization capabilities of the poor). Formally:

$$P^i_{jk}(t) = F_{jk}(k_w, \sigma_t, \alpha_t, \rho_{lj}, \rho_{bj}) \tag{1}$$

But the model also implies that the evolution of inequality is partly a consequence of the political system, given that different political systems lead to different degrees of redistribution (high under a democracy, none under authoritarianism). This can be written as follows:

$$k_{wt} = f(k_{wt-1}, S_{t-1}) \tag{2}$$

where f is a function.[5]

As is apparent, these two equations make it impossible to estimate the impact of inequality on democracy in a cross-country sample without using some instrument. For example, evidence that countries with more inequality are those with less democracy would fail to identify the direction of the effect, since we know that democracy has a lessening effect on inequality. In other words, inequality is in part an endogenous variable to political regime.

The best strategy to overcome this problem consists in examining and estimating the dynamic structure of the political game. Even if inequality is an endogenous variable to political regime, it is determined previously to the political game we are examining. Players (both the rich and the poor) play the political transition game conditional on the level of inequality (and asset specificity) they encounter at the start of the period, which we know determines the extent of redistribution they can expect under each possible political system. Thus, we should estimate a model, already described in proposition (1), of the probability of transition from authoritarianism to democracy (or the other way around).

Let the state of country i be $S_{it} = 1$ if it is a democracy and $S_{it} = 0$ if it is an authoritarian regime. Let $x_{it} = (\sigma^i_t, k^i_{wt}, \alpha^i_t, \rho^i_{lD}, \rho^i_{bD}, \rho^i_{lA}, \rho^i_{bA})$. Then we can write the empirical counterpart of the model (1), following Amemiya (1985) as:

$$P(S_{it} = 1|S_{it-1}) = \Phi(\beta' x_{it} + \gamma' x_{it} S_{i,t-1}) \tag{3}$$

---

[5] This is less clear for asset specificity. Still, if we assume that democracies foster growth and that growth leads to the generation of less specific assets, then asset specificity is also partly endogenous to political institutions. See a discussion in Chapter 6.

Where Φ is a normal cumulative distribution function. In what follows, I estimate this model by maximum likelihood, where the likelihood function is:

$$\ell = \prod_i \prod_t \Phi_{it}^{y_{it}}[1 - \Phi_{it}]^{1-y_{it}} \tag{4}$$

where F is given by (3).[6]

In testing the model empirically, it is important to note that, even though the outcomes of the game are deterministic in one case as the actors play pure strategies (the probability of transition to democracy is 1 in proposition [1] in Chapter 1), the empirical counterparts of these outcomes are not deterministic even when the actors do play these strategies. An important reason is that a lot of randomness exists outside of the decisions of the actors.[7] As a result, to estimate the model, I assume that the probability of transition between states is governed, conditional on the observables, by a normal distribution. For the standard reasons in time-series models, the estimators of the impact of inequality (and the other exogenous or predetermined variables) on the probability of a political transition, conditional on the starting state, are consistent and unbiased.

Data

As pointed out in the introduction to the chapter, I first test the model employing a data set that runs from 1950 to 1990 and that contains direct observations of income inequality as well as several measures of asset specificity. Although most of the data points come from the period after 1960, there are observations for about twelve to twenty countries for the 1950s. The number of countries for which data is available peaks at over fifty in the last decade of the sample.

Dependent Variable: Democracy Democracy is a dichotomous variable that, following the coding requirements described in the section on political transitions and political regimes since 1800, takes the value of 1 whenever each country is a democracy in a given year and 0 otherwise.

---

[6] See Amemiya (1985: chap. 11) for the estimation and the asymptotic properties of this dynamic probit model. For a previous application of the model to democratic transitions, see Przeworski et al. (2000).

[7] In theoretical rigor, the strategy played is democracy; the outcome may be a lottery that places some weight $1 - \varepsilon$ on democracy and a weight ε on an authoritarian outcome. None of the analysis is affected by this interpretation.

Independent Variables (1) *Inequality:* Data on inequality are taken from Deininger and Squire (1996), who have gathered a data set of cross-national cross-time observations including Gini coefficients and the proportion of income in the hand of each quintile. This data set consists of 692 "high-quality" (that is, comparable) observations – 587 of them with Gini coefficients. For the estimation, I have employed an adjusted Gini coefficient to control for cross-national variation in the methods used to measure income distribution.[8] The year-country adjusted Gini coefficient employed in the sample is a five-year average of adjusted Gini coefficients. This procedure minimizes the volatility in the inequality measures and maximizes the number of observations (approximately doubling them).[9]

(2) *Country specificity of wealth:* The country specificity of wealth, and hence the average loss of value of the assets of a country as they are moved to another country and therefore their nonexpropriability, is determined by several factors:

(a) *Average share of the agricultural sector* over GDP, which increases the level of asset specificity given that the wealth attached to the land is almost entirely immobile. The measure is constructed by the World Bank and available for the period 1970–90.

(b) Similarly, the *ratio of fuel exports over total exports* reflects highly immobile, and thus country-specific, wealth. The measure comes from World Bank tables, and it is available for 1970–90.

---

[8] This variation is a function of the choice of the recipient unit (individual or household), the use of gross versus net income and the use of expenditure or income. Following the suggestions of Deininger and Squire (1996), the adjusted Gini is equal to the Gini coefficient plus 6.6 points in observations based on expenditure (versus income) and 3 points in observations using net rather than gross income. The results reported do not vary if we use unadjusted Gini coefficients.

[9] A second dataset on inequality has been put together by the United Nations University's World Institute for Development Economics Research (UNU-WIDER 2000). Although this data set contains 5,067 data points, there are only 1,532 "high quality" observations encompassing all the population. Once we exclude from the latter the data points from Deininger and Squire (1996) and drop observations that report, using different income definitions or reference units, the same country and year, we are left with 281 observations for the period 1950–90. In 202 out of these 281 data points, we already have Deininger and Squire observations – both data sets are highly correlated with a coefficient of 0.902. Accordingly, the UNU-WIDER data set adds only 79 country-year Ginis – about 150 new observations once we calculate the five-year average. Given the very little additional information we would obtain from employing this new data set, I have decided to use the Deininger and Squire data set on income inequality in my estimations. Results do not change and in fact become more robust if we include the WIDER data on Ginis in the model to be presented. They are available from the author on request.

(c) *Average years of schooling*, which approximate the mobility generated by human capital. The level of asset specificity and the possibility of expropriation decline on average with an increase in the importance of human capital. The measure is taken from Barro and Lee (1993).

(d) *Level of economic concentration:* In countries where economic activity is highly concentrated in a few sectors, all assets in the economy become more fully specialized to a small number of uses. As a result, the likelihood that those assets will be employed in other uses is smaller. In other words, holding the size of the economy constant, the higher the concentration of all the activities in an economy in a particular industry, the higher the loss of productivity the assets in this economy will experience when redeployed, that is, the higher the general level of asset specificity. I measure this variable through a Hirsch-Herfindhal index of concentration based on 239 three-digit standard international trade classification categories of exports as estimated by UNCTAD. It varies from 0.06 (a highly diversified economy) to 1 (whenever only one product is exported).

Notice that, as discussed in the introductory chapter, previous scholars have alternatively employed some of these variables to test different theories of democratization. Modernization theorists have claimed that rising education levels generate a more articulate, politically better organized and more tolerant public that in turn facilitates the introduction of democracy (Lipset 1959; Deutsch 1961). Similarly, scholars have related the shift to an industrial economy to the formation of an autonomous workforce with the capacity to think for themselves on the job and to develop bargaining tools to deal on equal terms with the elites (Dahl 1971, chap. 4). Finally, Middle East scholars have suggested that oil-derived resources both reduce the demand for political accountability from voters and endow governments with money to finance patronage structures and to repress opposition groups (Ross 2001). By contrast, the strength of this book's approach lies first in the fact that a single model, with precise microfoundations, rather than a diverse set of (substantially structural) theories, can reconcile a wide variety of empirical findings. Moreover, the model I present can encompass historical circumstances, also apparent both in the analysis of the 1850–1980 sample and in the case studies (pursued in Chapter 3), that can hardly be accommodated by cultural arguments based on toleration and attitude change. Finally, I consider a set of control variables that tap these cultural or ideational arguments.

Control Variables   I include as well the following control variables:

(a) The level of development, measured through the value of real per capita income (in constant dollars, Chain Index, expressed in international prices, base 1985), taken from the Penn World Tables. The level of development has been consistently found to affect the type of political regime, particularly after World War II (Lipset 1959; Przeworski et al. 2000).[10] Although, according to this book level of development should enter the analysis only indirectly, through its relation with inequality and country specificity of wealth, I have decided to include it as a control variable and, to some extent, as a proxy for omitted measures of specificity.[11]

(b) Percentage of the population of each country that belong to the three most widely spread religions (Catholicism, Islam and Protestantism) using the data reported in La Porta et al. (1998). These three measures of religious beliefs and practices tap the cultural and ethical norms that may influence the legitimacy that democratic practices may have in the population (Huntington 1991: 77–85).

(c) Level of religious fractionalization, measured as a Hirsch-Herfindhal index of fractionalization based on the data on religious membership in LaPorta et al. (1998).

(d) Level of ethnic fractionalization, measured through an index built by LaPorta et al. (1998) by averaging five different sources in Easterly and Levine (1997).

(e) Lagged growth rate, which the literature has found to affect the stability of political regimes, particularly authoritarian systems (Przeworski et al. 2000).

Results

Table 2.1 explores the impact of inequality and development on political regime using the dynamic specification described in equation (3). For each estimation, I obtain two sets of parameters. The first parameter (the beta coefficient) estimates the probability of transition from authoritarianism to

---

[10] For a detailed discussion of the theoretical and empirical relationship between democracy and per capita income, before and after 1950, see Boix and Stokes (2002).

[11] Concerning inequality, as nations develop, both the mean and dispersion of inequality declines. For economies with a per capita income lower than $5,000 (constant prices of 1985), the average Gini index is 42.5 with a standard deviation of 10.4. For economies with a per capita income above $10,000, the mean Gini index is 34.2 with a standard deviation of 3.6.

Empirical Analysis of Post War Period

Table 2.1. *Regime Transitions, 1950–90*

Dependent Variable: (1) Probability of Transition to Democracy: Beta coefficient;
(2) Probability of Stable Democracy: Sum of Alpha and Beta coefficients

Independent Variables	Model 1A (All countries)		Model 1B (Excl. Soviet countries)		Model 2A (All countries)	
	Beta	Alpha	Beta	Alpha	Beta	Alpha
Constant	−3.350***	−17.533*	−1.393	−19.487**	−3.471**	−1.112
	(1.040)	(9.004)	(1.200)	(9.024)	(1.594)	(4.570)
Gini index[a]	−0.019^	0.040	−0.052***	0.073^	−0.013	−0.018
	(0.013)	(0.055)	(0.017)	(0.057)	(0.018)	(0.045)
Per capita income (in thousand $)[b]	0.082^^	1.953**	0.083^	1.951***		
	(0.074)	(0.816)	(0.073)	(0.815)		
Average years[c] of schooling					0.030	0.301
					(0.100)	(0.221)
Percent of Catholics[e]	0.002	0.047**	0.009*	0.040*	0.003	0.017
	(0.004)	(0.021)	(0.005)	(0.021)	(0.005)	(0.012)
Percent of Protestants[e]	0.055**	0.377	0.071***	0.360	0.055**	0.155
	(0.022)	(0.350)	(0.025)	(0.351)	(0.023)	(0.180)
Percent of Muslims[e]	0.002	1.407***	0.007	1.402***	0.003	0.470**
	(0.005)	(0.542)	(0.006)	(0.542)	(0.006)	(0.196)
Religious fractionalization[f]	2.220**	10.937*	1.231	11.296**	2.189**	3.400
	(1.046)	(5.751)	(1.070)	(5.755)	(1.111)	(3.260)
Ethnic fractionalization[g]	0.380	−4.341**	0.062	−4.023*	0.461	−4.115***
	(0.594)	(2.183)	(0.582)	(2.181)	(0.622)	(1.604)
Growth rate	−0.022	0.092*	−0.018	0.088*	−0.136	0.048
	(0.022)	(0.052)	(0.022)	(0.052)	(0.252)	(0.045)
Log-likelihood	−76.50		−70.25		−79.68	
Prob > Chi-square	0.0000		0.0000		0.0000	
Pseudo R^2	0.8887		0.8913		0.8654	
Number of observations	1042		1002		919	

Independent Variables	Model 2B (Excl. Soviet countries)		Model 3A (All countries)		Model 3B (Excl. Soviet countries)	
	Beta	Alpha	Beta	Alpha	Beta	Alpha
Constant	−2.720*	−1.864	−2.526**	−16.628*	−0.797	−18.357*
	(1.630)	(4.600)	(1.238)	(9.911)	(1.449)	(9.939)
Gini index[a]	−0.036*	0.005	−0.035**	−0.223^	−0.077***	−0.181^
	(0.019)	(0.046)	(0.017)	(0.180)	(0.025)	(0.181)

(continued)

Table 2.1 (*continued*)

Independent Variables	Model 2B (Excl. Soviet countries)		Model 3A (All countries)		Model 3B (Excl. Soviet countries)	
	Beta	Alpha	Beta	Alpha	Beta	Alpha
Average years[c] of schooling	0.138 (0.110)	0.193 (0.225)				
Share of Agricultural Sector[d]			0.000 (0.014)	−0.351** (0.141)	−0.007 (0.014)	−0.344** (0.141)
Percent of Catholics[e]	0.010* (0.006)	0.010 (0.012)	0.007 (0.005)	0.066* (0.039)	0.015** (0.007)	0.058 (0.039)
Percent of Protestants[e]	0.071*** (0.025)	0.138 (0.180)	0.026 (0.034)	1.025 (0.808)	0.058 (0.042)	0.992 (0.808)
Percent of Muslims[e]	0.011 (0.007)	0.461** (0.196)	0.002 (0.005)	1.530** (0.716)	0.008 (0.006)	1.524** (0.716)
Religious fractionalization[f]	1.432 (1.150)	4.151 (3.270)	2.251* (1.337)	35.820** (16.918)	2.010 (1.364)	36.062** (16.920)
Ethnic fractionalization[g]	0.231 (0.621)	−3.885* (1.603)	0.518 (0.678)	−2.740 (4.984)	0.505 (0.661)	−2.728 (4.981)
Growth Rate	−0.010 (0.026)	0.045 (0.046)	−0.014 (0.025)	−0.015 (0.090)	−0.002 (0.026)	−0.028 (0.090)
Log-likelihood	−73.87		−53.441		−48.620	
Prob > Chi-square	0.0000		0.0000		0.0000	
Pseudo R^2	0.8676		0.8923		0.8958	
Number of observations	888		733		701	

Independent Variables	Model 4A (All countries)		Model 4B (Excl. Soviet countries)		Model 5 (All countries – no Soviet-dominated cases)	
	Beta	Alpha	Beta	Alpha	Beta	Alpha
Constant	−2.256 (1.502)	2.985 (3.273)	−1.257 (1.591)	1.986 (3.315)	−2.422 (1.842)	6.127 (4.875)
Gini index[a]	−0.032^^^ (0.020)	−0.041^^^ (0.045)	−0.057** (0.023)	−0.017^^ (0.046)	−0.013 (0.024)	−0.062 (0.055)
Fuel as percentage of exports[b]	−0.065^^^ (0.043)	0.206* (0.105)	−0.051 (0.039)	0.191* (0.103)		
Exports concentration index[i]					−3.047* (1.795)	−0.432 (2.849)
Percent of Catholics[e]	0.008 (0.006)	0.003 (0.011)	0.014** (0.006)	−0.003 (0.011)	0.005 (0.006)	0.021 (0.015)

Empirical Analysis of Post War Period

Independent Variables	Model 4A (All countries)		Model 4B (Excl. Soviet countries)		Model 5 (All countries – no Soviet-dominated cases)	
	Beta	Alpha	Beta	Alpha	Beta	Alpha
Percent of Protestants[e]	0.019 (0.040)	0.342 (0.263)	0.056 (0.046)	0.306 (0.264)	0.035 (0.055)	0.122 (0.183)
Percent of Muslims[e]	0.003 (0.006)	0.329** (0.172)	0.007 (0.006)	0.325* (0.172)	0.003 (0.007)	0.344* (0.171)
Religious fractionalization[f]	2.032 (1.519)	1.434 (3.482)	1.631 (1.476)	1.835 (3.464)	1.968 (1.485)	−0.344 (4.356)
Ethnic fractionalization[g]	0.528 (0.659)	−4.228** (1.928)	0.431 (0.636)	−4.131** (1.920)	0.456 (0.724)	−4.918** (2.128)
Growth rate	0.004 (0.028)	0.062 (0.053)	0.006 (0.028)	0.059 (0.054)	−0.004 (0.036)	0.049 (0.057)
Log-likelihood	−61.639		−58.255		−55.879	
Prob > Chi-square	0.0000		0.0000		0.0000	
Pseudo R^2	0.8841		0.8838		0.8946	
Number of observations	797		766		818	

[a] Five-year moving average of adjusted Gini coefficients. Data taken from Deininger and Squire (1996).

[b] Real per capita income (in constant dollars, Chain Index, expressed in international prices, base 1985), taken from the Penn World Tables.

[c] Average years of schooling, as reported in Barro and Lee (1993).

[d] Average share of the agricultural sector over GDP, taken from the World Bank.

[e] *Source:* LaPorta et al. (1998).

[f] Level of religious fractionalization, measured as a Hirsch-Herfindhal index of fractionalization based on the data on religious membership in LaPorta et al. (1998).

[g] Level of ethnic fractionalization, measured through an index built by LaPorta et al. (1998) by averaging five different sources in Easterly and Levine (1997).

[h] Ratio of fuel exports over total exports, taken from World Bank tables, only available for 1970–90.

[i] Level of economic concentration, measured through a Hirsch-Herfindhal index of concentration based on 239 three-digit standard international trade classification categories of exports as estimated by UNCTAD.

Estimation: Dynamic probit model.

Standard errors in parenthesis.

*** $p < 0.01$; ** $p < 0.05$; * $p < 0.01$.

^^^ $p < 0.01$ in joint test of interactive terms and its components; ^^ $p < 0.05$ in joint test of interactive terms and its components; ^ $p < 0.01$ in joint test of interactive terms and its components.

democracy. The sum of the two coefficients (beta and alpha) indicates the probability that an already democratic system will not break down.

Model 1A regresses per capita income and the Gini index on regime transitions using all the available observations from sovereign states. Model 1B repeats the estimation excluding all the countries under Soviet control – this is a factor that, although exogenous to the model, must be taken care of since it directly hindered the development of democracy in Eastern Europe. While maintaining the measure of income inequality, subsequent regressions (in Models 2 to 5) consider the impact of different measures of asset specificity: the level of education, the size of the primary sector, the share of oil exports and the extent of economic concentration.[12] Again, for each model, I estimate the regression for all the countries as well as for a restricted universe that excludes the Soviet countries.

Models 1A and 1B show that per capita income, which I take here as a first approximation of asset specificity (and which is generally employed in the literature on the empirical causes of democratization), positively affects the likelihood of a democratic transition (the beta coefficient) and, in particular, the stability of a democratic regime (the sum of the alpha and beta coefficients). In turn, a decline in income inequality is associated with an increase in the probability of a democratic transition (beta coefficient) – this is especially true when we exclude the Soviet-dominated cases (Model 1B). Growing income inequality is associated with a higher probability of democratic stability (since the sum of the beta and alpha coefficients is positive). Still, this result, which is an exception in all the tests, holds only for very low levels of per capita income. At medium and high levels of per capita income, income inequality has no independent impact on the likelihood of democratic breakdowns. This can be seen in Table 2.2, which simulates the annual probability of experiencing both a democratic transition and a democratic breakdown for different levels of per capita income and economic inequality.[13] Table 2.2.A shows that for a high Gini index (the maximum in the sample is 0.66 in Zimbabwe in 1950), the yearly probability of a democratic transition is close to 0. By contrast, for a highly equal society, that probability rises to over 0.10 even for very low levels of development. In turn, Table 2.2.B shows that, in the period from 1950 to 1990, the probability of a democratic breakdown was 0 in countries with a per capita income equal to or higher than $5,000. More inequality seems to increase the probability of a coup in medium-income countries, but the

---

[12] The introduction of the log value of the adjusted Gini coefficient (a possibility if we think that the positive marginal impact of equality on democracy decreases after a certain threshold of equality has been surpassed) does not affect the results – and in fact strengthens some of them.

[13] The results, based on the estimates in Model 1B in Table 2.1, are obtained by changing the variables of interest while holding the other variables at their median values.

Table 2.2. *Predicted Probability of Regime Transition by Per Capita Income and Income Inequality, 1950–90*

A. Predicted Probability of Transition from Authoritarianism to Democracy by Per Capita Income and Income Inequality, 1950–90

Gini Index	Per Capita Income (1985 $)					
	1,000	3,000	5,000	7,000	9,000	11,000
70	0.000	0.000	0.000	0.001	0.001	0.002
60	0.001	0.001	0.002	0.003	0.006	0.009
50	0.004	0.006	0.010	0.015	0.022	0.033
40	0.016	0.023	0.034	0.049	0.069	0.094
30	0.052	0.072	0.097	0.129	0.168	0.213
20	0.134	0.174	0.220	0.272	0.330	0.393

B. Predicted Probability of Democratic Breakdown by Per Capita Income and Income Inequality, 1950–90

Gini Index	Per Capita Income (1985 $)					
	1,000	3,000	5,000	7,000	9,000	11,000
70	1.000	0.693	0.000	0.000	0.000	0.000
60	1.000	0.761	0.000	0.000	0.000	0.000
50	1.000	0.820	0.001	0.000	0.000	0.000
40	1.000	0.868	0.002	0.000	0.000	0.000
30	1.000	0.907	0.003	0.000	0.000	0.000
20	1.000	0.937	0.006	0.000	0.000	0.000

Simulation based on Table 2.1, Model 1B.
All other variables are set at their median value.

effect, swamped by the role of per capita income, is not very reliable from a statistical point of view.

Before I describe the remaining models, consider the results for the control variables. The religious composition of the population seems to have no systematic effect on the type of regime. A higher degree of religious fragmentation increases the success rate of democratic regimes, mainly in semideveloped economies. A simulation of the regression estimates shows that for medium levels of income, between $2,000 and $5,000 approximately, and moderate inequality, religious fragmentation reduces the chances of a democratic breakdown to 0 if it attains very high levels. By contrast, for both low and high levels of per capita income and the Gini index, religious fragmentation plays a marginal role: the probability of a regime transition is driven basically by level of development and inequality. Finally, in line with previous literature on the causes of democratization, ethnic fractionalization strongly increases the likelihood of democratic breakdowns, particularly, again, among middle-income countries. For countries with per capita incomes between $3,500 and $5,500, and medium levels of inequality, the probability of a democratic breakdown goes from 0 in a homogeneous country to close to 1 in a completely fragmented polity. In either very poor or very rich countries, development completely neutralizes the effect of ethnic fragmentation.

Model 2 in Table 2.1 examines the effect of inequality and average years of education. Both variables perform in the way expected. Income inequality either blocks the introduction of democracy or jeopardizes a preexisting democratic regime. Higher levels of human capital, in turn, contribute to the process of democratization. Because they are strongly correlated, their coefficients are not statistically significant in Model 2A. A joint test of the inequality and human capital variables shows, however, that they are significant at the 10 percent level (and at the 1 percent level in Model 2B). In Model 2B, the beta coefficient of inequality is significant on its own. Table 2.3, which simulates the annual probability of experiencing both a democratic transition and a democratic breakdown for different degrees of economic inequality and human capital, shows that it is the combination of both factors that bolsters democratization. As shown in Table 2.3.A, with a high Gini index, the yearly probability of a democratic transition is close to 0. By contrast, for a relatively equal society, the annual probability of a democratic transition climbs to a range that extends from 0.03 (in a country with just one year of schooling) to 0.25 for a nation with high levels of human capital. In turn, as shown in Table 2.3.B, the probability of a democratic breakdown approximates 90 percent in highly unequal societies (especially with high levels of asset specificity) and then declines very sharply as equality and human capital become more widespread.

Model 3 in Table 2.1 examines the impact of income inequality and the share of agriculture as a proportion of GDP. Income inequality both delays democratization and is more conducive to authoritarian coups. In turn, while agricultural societies seem to have no impact on democratic transition, they lead to a high frequency of democratic breakdowns. Again, Table 2.4 simulates the annual probability of regime transitions for these two factors. Notice in Table 2.4.B how the likelihood of an authoritarian coup results from the interaction of both variables. It is only when income

Table 2.3. *Predicted Probability of Regime Transition by Education Levels and Income Inequality, 1950–90*

A. Predicted Probability of Transition from Authoritarianism to Democracy by Education Levels and Income Inequality, 1950–90

Gini Index	Average Years of Education				
	1	3	5	7	9
70	0.000	0.000	0.001	0.003	0.006
60	0.001	0.001	0.003	0.008	0.016
50	0.002	0.004	0.010	0.020	0.037
40	0.006	0.012	0.024	0.045	0.078
30	0.015	0.030	0.054	0.091	0.146
20	0.036	0.064	0.107	0.167	0.245

B. Predicted Probability of Democratic Breakdown by Education Levels and Income Inequality, 1950–90

Gini Index	Average Years of Education				
	1	3	5	7	9
70	0.948	0.832	0.618	0.359	0.153
60	0.905	0.742	0.495	0.250	0.090
50	0.840	0.631	0.371	0.161	0.049
40	0.752	0.507	0.260	0.096	0.025
30	0.643	0.383	0.169	0.053	0.011
20	0.520	0.270	0.101	0.026	0.005

Simulation based on Table 2.1, Model 2B.
All other variables are set at their median value.

inequality takes middle values and land becomes marginal in the economy that democracies become stable.

Model 4 in Table 2.1 runs income inequality and the size of the oil sector on regime transitions. The presence of an oil economy acts as a heavy constraint on the possibility of democratization. As depicted in the simulation in Table 2.5.A, for economies in which fuel exports represent more than one third of all exports, the probability of democratic transitions is 0, regardless of the distribution of income. The simulation in Table 2.5.B suggests that no democratic breakdowns take place in oil economies. The result must be qualified by the observation that, consistent with the model, there is an extremely low probability of transition from authoritarian to democratic regimes in oil economies, as just described. As a result, only three oil

Table 2.4. *Predicted Probability of Regime Transition by Size of Agricultural Sector and Income Inequality, 1950–90*

A. Predicted Probability of Transition from Authoritarianism to Democracy by Size of Agricultural Sector and Income Inequality, 1950–90

Gini Index	Share of Agricultural Sector over GDP			
	0	20	40	60
70	0.000	0.000	0.000	0.000
60	0.000	0.000	0.000	0.000
50	0.005	0.003	0.002	0.001
40	0.033	0.024	0.018	0.013
30	0.143	0.115	0.091	0.071
20	0.383	0.333	0.287	0.243

B. Predicted Probability of Democratic Breakdown by Size of Agricultural Sector and Income Inequality, 1950–90

Gini Index	Share of Agricultural Sector over GDP			
	0	20	40	60
70	1.000	1.000	1.000	1.000
60	0.917	1.000	1.000	1.000
50	0.116	1.000	1.000	1.000
40	0.000	0.999	1.000	1.000
30	0.000	0.747	1.000	1.000
20	0.000	0.028	1.000	1.000

Simulation based on Table 2.1, Model 3.
All other variables are set at their median value.

countries in the sample (Norway, Trinidad and Tobago, Venezuela) were democracies; none of them had experienced a transition to authoritarianism (at least before 1990). With such a low number of cases, any conclusions about the impact of oil on an authoritarian backlash can be only tentative.

Finally, Model 5 in Table 2.1 examines the joint effect of inequality and economic concentration on regime transitions (in this case there are no Soviet-dominated countries in the universe under observation). Economic inequality acts as a deterrent to democracy – but its coefficients are not statistically significant. In turn, the diversification of productive activities both pushes the yearly probability of a democratic transition upward – by between 8 and 20 percent depending on the level of income inequality – and

Table 2.5. *Predicted Probability of Regime Transition by Size of Oil Sector and Income Inequality, 1950–90*

A. Predicted Probability of Transition from Authoritarianism to Democracy by Size of Oil Sector and Income Inequality, 1950–90

Gini Index	Fuel as Percentage of Exports					
	0	20	40	60	80	100
70	0.000	0.000	0.000	0.000	0.000	0.000
60	0.002	0.000	0.000	0.000	0.000	0.000
50	0.009	0.000	0.000	0.000	0.000	0.000
40	0.037	0.003	0.000	0.000	0.000	0.000
30	0.111	0.013	0.001	0.000	0.000	0.000
20	0.256	0.048	0.004	0.000	0.000	0.000

B. Predicted Probability of Democratic Breakdown by Size of Oil Sector and Income Inequality, 1950–90

Gini Index	Fuel as Percentage of Exports					
	0	20	40	60	80	100
70	0.834	0.033	0.000	0.000	0.000	0.000
60	0.593	0.005	0.000	0.000	0.000	0.000
50	0.309	0.000	0.000	0.000	0.000	0.000
40	0.108	0.000	0.000	0.000	0.000	0.000
30	0.024	0.000	0.000	0.000	0.000	0.000
20	0.003	0.000	0.000	0.000	0.000	0.000

Simulation based on Table 2.1, Model 4B.
All other variables are set at their median value.

lowers the probability of a democratic breakdown. As concentration declines, the probability of an authoritarian coup falls and practically disappears in an economy in which inequality is medium or low (I do not show here the simulations from which these results are taken).

Table 2.1 has estimated the yearly probabilities of regime transitions as a way to overcome the potential endogeneity of the independent variables, particularly inequality, to the type of political regime. The results, which in themselves satisfactorily approximate the model being tested, can also be employed to calculate what the long-term political dynamics of any given country will be, that is, what type of regime will be in place in any given country over an extended period, say one hundred years, given certain structural parameters. To exemplify this, let us take the estimated probabilities of political transition every year reported in Model 1 and use them to build the regime path of several countries differing in levels of economic development and inequality: country A has a per capita income of $2,000 and a high level of income inequality (a Gini index of 0.65); country B has a per capita income of $2,000 yet little inequality (a Gini index of 0.35); country C has a per capita income of $6,000 and high inequality; finally, country D is both developed and relatively equal. Assuming that these countries all start as authoritarian, their political dynamics are sharply different. The level of inequality shapes the chances of making a democratic transition. Whereas in the two relatively equal countries (B and D) a democratic regime emerges after 15 to 20 years of dictatorship, in the unequal countries the authoritarian regime remains in place for more than 90 years (up to 120 years in country A). Once democratic regimes are established, their stability levels differ, driven by the level of development. In the two developed countries, democracy lasts forever. In the two under-developed countries, democracy collapses relatively quickly, generally after 1 or 2 years. Then, again, in the unequal country, the authoritarian regime lasts for another century, while in the equal nation a new transition happens after less than 20 years of dictatorship.

Empirical Analysis since the Mid-Nineteenth Century

In this section I expand the inquiry to a broader data set that spans the years 1850 to 1980. There are at least two reasons that make this analysis strongly advisable. First, it increases the set of observations considerably – almost by a factor of 3 – thus making our tests more robust.

More importantly, it allows us to explore the democratization dynamics of those countries that were independent before World War II. As is apparent from Figures 2.1 to 2.3, half of all democratic transitions between 1800 and 1990 took place before 1950. Moreover, the rate of success in democratizing before World War II had a very strong effect on the probability of being democratic after it. Among countries that existed before 1939, almost 90 percent of those that were democratic in the 1950s had already been democratic thirty years before. Similarly, over four fifths of the dictatorships of the postwar period were authoritarian in the 1920s. In short, we need to begin with the nineteenth century for our study of how and why regimes changed. Modeling and testing a theory of political development without looking at the political transitions of the second half of the nineteenth century and the first half of the twentieth century would be tantamount to advancing a theory of economic growth and development that ignored the foundations and nature of the industrial revolution.

Data

The logic of the measures I use for this period is similar to the previous analysis. Here I discuss only differences in the data. Since data on income inequality for any country before World War II is quite scarce, I rely on two indicators that predict the extent of economic inequality rather well: the distribution of agricultural property and the quality of human capital. In addition, the index of human capital as well as an index of occupational diversification proxy for the level of asset specificity (once I control for per capita income, which can be affected by other factors such as extractive resources in each country).

The distribution of agricultural property is measured through the area of family farms as a percentage of the total area of holdings. This measure, gathered and reported by Vanhanen (1997), is based on defining as family farms those "farms that provide employment for not more than four people, including family members, [...] that are cultivated by the holder family itself and [...] that are owned by the cultivator family or held in ownerlike possession" (Vanhanen 1997: 48).

The definition, which aims at distinguishing "family farms" from large farms cultivated mainly by hired workers, is not dependent on the actual size of the farm – the size of the farm varies with the type of product and the agricultural technology being used.[14] The percentage of family farms captures the degree of concentration and therefore inequality in the ownership of land. The data set, reported in averages for each decade, ranges from 1850 to 1979. It varies from countries with 0 percent of family farms to countries where 94 percent of the agricultural land is owned through family farms: the mean of the sample is 30 percent with a standard deviation of 23 percent. An extensive literature has related the unequal distribution of land to an unbalanced distribution of income. For the period after 1950, for which I have both the Deininger and Squire data and Vanhanen's measure of the proportion of family farms, it is possible to show that they are indeed well correlated. Excluding the cases of socialist economies, the correlation

---

[14] A detailed discussion and description of the data can be found in Vanhanen (1997: 49–51) and the sources quoted therein.

coefficient among the Gini index and the percentage of family farms is −0.66. For countries with a per capita income below $2,000 the correlation coefficient is −0.75.

To measure the quality of human capital, I rely on Vanhanen's "index of knowledge distribution," which consists in the arithmetic mean of the percentage of literates in the adult population and the "level of students." The level of students is the number of students per 100,000 inhabitants, normalized so that 1,000 students per 100,000 inhabitants corresponds to a level of 100 percent. The Vanhanen index of education, which also extends from 1850 to 1979, varies from 0.5 to 99 percent with a mean of 29.2 and a standard deviation of 22.7. The coefficient of correlation of this index of education and the Gini index reported by Deininger and Squire for the period 1950–90 is −0.59.

The index of occupational diversification, also developed by Vanhanen, is the average of the percentage of nonagricultural population and the percentage of urban population. The urban population is defined as population living in cities of 20,000 or more inhabitants.

To measure per capita income, I have merged the previous data from the Penn World Tables with the per capita income data reported by Maddison (1995) after adjusting the Maddison data to make it comparable with the Penn World Tables data set.

Results

The combination of the previous data gives us a panel of over 6,500 country-year observations without per capita income and of over 3,300 observations when per capita income is included.[15] The results of the estimations (again using a dynamic probit model) are reported in Table 2.6.

Model 1 excludes per capita income. Model 2 includes it. In both cases, I report the estimations for all countries (column A in each model) and for all countries excluding those under Soviet control (column B). The coefficients of the independent variables are in line with the theoretical expectations – except for the beta coefficient of family farms. Higher levels of economic equality (in the countryside in the form of more family farms and in general

---

[15] To obtain a yearly series of observations on family farms, education and occupational structure, I have taken each data point provided by Vanhanen (1997) for each decade and then interpolated the missing observations (using a linear structure).

Table 2.6. *Estimating the Probability of Political Transition, 1850–1980*

Dependent Variable: (1) Probability of Transition to Democracy: Beta coefficient; (2) Probability of Stable Democracy: Sum of Alpha and Beta coefficients

Independent Variable	Model 1A (All countries) Beta	Model 1A (All countries) Alpha	Model 1B (Excl. Soviet countries) Beta	Model 1B (Excl. Soviet countries) Alpha	Model 2A (All countries) Beta	Model 2A (All countries) Alpha	Model 2B (Excl. Soviet countries) Beta	Model 2B (Excl. Soviet countries) Alpha
Constant	-2.9790*** (0.1557)	3.4590*** (0.2809)	-3.0602*** (0.1679)	3.5402*** (0.2879)	-2.447*** (0.2375)	3.0080*** (0.3586)	-2.4324*** (0.2415)	2.993*** (0.3612)
Percentage of family farms[a]	-0.0028^^^ (0.0038)	0.0190*** (0.0062)	-0.0016^^^ (0.0045)	0.0178*** (0.0067)	-0.0060^^^ (0.0051)	0.0195*** (0.0074)	-0.0083^^^ (0.0056)	0.0217*** (0.0078)
Index of education[b]	0.0088* (0.0053)	-0.0018^^^ (0.0098)	0.0159*** (0.0060)	-0.0088^^^ (0.0102)	0.0066^^^ (0.0065)	0.0010^^^ (0.0114)	0.0132* (0.0075)	-0.0057^^^ (0.0120)
Index of occupational diversification[c]	0.0174*** (0.0060)	-0.0010^^^ (0.0099)	0.0144*** (0.0063)	0.0020^^^ (0.0101)	0.0110^^^ (0.0096)	-0.0024^^^ (0.0145)	0.0075^^^ (0.0101)	0.0011^^^ (0.0150)
Per capita income (in thousands)[d]					-0.0085^^^ (0.0968)	0.1267^^^ (0.1484)	-0.0193^^^ (0.1026)	0.1375^^^ (0.152)
Log-likelihood	-392.39		-385.14		-281.66		-278.84	
Prob > Chi-square	0.0000		0.0000		0.0000		0.0000	
Pseudo R^2	0.8987		0.8988		0.8759		0.8744	
Number of observations	6537		6332		3275		3203	

Democratic institutions: Own code (Boix and Rosato 2001) for 1850–1949 and Przeworski (2000) for the 1950–90.

[a] Area of family farms as a percentage of the total area of holdings. *Source:* Vanhanen (1997).

[b] Arithmetic mean of the percentage of literates in the adult population and the "level of students." The level of students is the number of students per 100,000 inhabitants normalized so that 1,000 students per 100,000 inhabitants corresponds to a level of 100 percent. *Source:* Vanhanen (1997).

[c] Arithmetic mean of percentage of nonagricultural population and percentage of urban population. Urban population is defined as population living in cities of 20,000 or more inhabitants. *Source:* Vanhanen (1997).

[d] Per capita income: Log of per capita GDP in $ in 1985 constant prices. *Source:* World Penn Tables and Maddison (1995).

Estimation: Dynamic probit model.

Standard errors in parenthesis.

*** $p < 0.01$; ** $p < 0.05$; * $p < 0.01$

^^^ $p < 0.01$ in joint test of interactive terms and its components; ^^ $p < 0.05$ in joint test of interactive terms and its components; ^ $p < 0.01$ in joint test of interactive terms and its components.

through higher literacy levels) and more nonspecific assets (through more human capital and a more diversified economic structure) increase both the chances of a democratic transition and the stability of democratic regimes.[16]

Notice that the results in Model 1 hold even after I introduce per capita income as a control in Model 2. Per capita income is weakly significant from a statistical and a substantial point of view. This appears to confirm the fact that per capita income, as employed in the modernization literature in postwar samples, is simply a proxy for other more fundamental factors.

To clarify the results in Table 2.6, Table 2.7 simulates, based on Model 1B, the annual probability of democratic transition and democratic breakdown as a function of economic structure, that is, the average of urbanization and industrialization, and the percentage of family farms. On the one hand, the probability of having a democratic transition is driven by the type of economic structure (Table 2.7.A). As the economy becomes more diversified, the chances of a transition increase considerably – from less than 1 percent if less than one fourth of the economy is urbanized and industrialized, to over 6 percent if more than three fourths are modern. The role of the distribution of rural property in affecting regime transitions is negative but extremely marginal.

On the other hand, both factors are equally important in determining the robustness of democracies (Table 2.7.B). The probability of a democratic breakdown in any given year reaches 25 percent in highly unequal and underdeveloped countries. Yet as either rural equality or industrialization increase, the authoritarian threat disappears. In a highly rural economy, the probability of a democratic breakdown falls to 1 percent as one moves from a country controlled by landowners (Russia before the Stolypin reforms and the Soviet Revolution, Spain for most of the twentieth century, as well as most Latin American nations) to one with a highly fragmented property system (like that prevailing in Norway, where, at the turn of the twentieth century, family farms represented almost four fifths of all land). Similarly, even when the distribution of property remains highly unequal, the chances of an authoritarian backlash disappear as most of the economy ceases to be based on fixed assets.

---

[16] Results about the impact of rural equality do not change when we regress a composite variable of "Family farms*Occupational diversification" to adjust for the size of the countryside – in fact, the impact of rural inequality increases. Results ave available from the author.

Table 2.7. *Predicted Probability of Regime Transition by Urban and Industrial Structure and Distribution of Property, 1850–1980*

A. Predicted Probability of Transition from Authoritarianism to Democracy by Urban and Industrial Structure and Distribution of Property, 1850–1980

Average of Urban Population and Manufacturing Sector	Percentage of Family Farms				
	0	25	50	75	100
0	0.004	0.003	0.003	0.003	0.002
25	0.011	0.010	0.009	0.008	0.007
50	0.026	0.024	0.022	0.020	0.018
75	0.057	0.052	0.048	0.044	0.041
100	0.111	0.103	0.096	0.090	0.083

B. Predicted Probability of Democratic Breakdown by Urban and Industrial Structure and Distribution of Property, 1850–1980

Average of Urban Population and Manufacturing Sector	Percentage of Family Farms				
	0	25	50	75	100
0	0.255	0.144	0.071	0.031	0.011
25	0.143	0.070	0.030	0.011	0.004
50	0.070	0.030	0.011	0.004	0.001
75	0.030	0.011	0.003	0.001	0.000
100	0.011	0.003	0.001	0.000	0.000

Simulation based on Table 2.6, Model 1B.
Index of knowledge distribution set at 25 percent.

Revolutions and Civil Wars

Besides specifying the conditions under which authoritarianism or democracy will prevail, the model also predicts that, at high levels of income inequality and asset specificity, and given some uncertainty about the technology of repression in the hands of the wealthy, revolutions and some forms of armed conflict should erupt with some positive probability. In this section I test this proposition on the two samples. The data on civil wars is taken from the Correlates of War Project developed by Singer and Small (1993). This data set includes data from 1816 through 1992. A civil war is defined as a conflict in which military action took place, the national government at the time was involved, both sides in the war effected resistance, and at least 1,000 battle deaths resulted. Although some revolutions may therefore not be included in the sample, the data set fits my interest in violent and sustained activities leading to a potential change in the control of the state.

Table 2.8 displays the results of a probit model on the likelihood of a war starting (Models 1 and 2) for the period 1950 to 1990. To test the theory, in Model 1 I regress the beginning or occurrence of civil wars on the Gini index, agriculture as a percentage of GDP and the interaction of those terms. As control variables I add the index of economic concentration, the percentage of fuel exports, the index of ethnic fractionalization, its square (since political scientists have recently claimed that ethnic fragmentation and violence are related in a curvilinear fashion [Bates 1999]), religious fractionalization, political regime and continental dummies for Africa and Latin America, which seem particularly prone to violent episodes. Model 2 adds a control for per capita income, generally used by the literature but one that is well correlated to measures such as agriculture and, in part, to inequality.

As predicted in the model, income inequality and the size of fixed assets do not lead to more civil war starts – in fact, their signs are negative. It is the interaction of inequality and high levels of country-specific wealth that make civil wars more likely. Either at low levels of inequality or in very industrialized societies, the likelihood of war is quite small or insignificant. For high Gini indexes and a heavily agrarian economy, the likelihood of a civil war quickly rises to over 0.3. A higher index of export concentration increases the probability of a civil war – probably because the prize of victory, and therefore the incentive to engage in war, goes up with the easiness with which resources can be expropriated. The size of fuel exports does not seem to be relevant.[17] Ethnic fragmentation leads to a higher probability of a civil war in a curvilinear function. The highest levels of violence take place in societies where approximately two balanced ethnic groups contend for power – with all the other variables at the median values. The probability of a civil war is about 20 percent higher in societies where there are two ethnic groups of the same size than in countries that are either completely fractionalized or fully homogeneous. Still, these parameters are not statistically significant. Neither religious fragmentation nor political regime are statistically significant either. Finally, I do not find regional effects on the likelihood of domestic conflict.[18]

---

[17] For recent empirical work on the relationship between civil war and the importance of fixed resources in the economy, see Collier and Hoeffler (2001).

[18] Africa drops out from the first two models because of a multicollinearity problem. The interactive term of education and inequality behaves in the same direction predicted by the model.

Table 2.8. *The Causes of Civil Wars, 1950–90*

Independent Variables	Onset of Civil War		Annual Probability of Civil War			
	Model 1	Model 2	Model 3	Model 4	Model 5	Model 6
Constant	2.812	9.296	−2.219	−1.637	0.912	0.105
	(4.728)	(12.492)	(1.909)	(3.428)	(4.550)	(7.645)
Civil war in previous year				3.271***		3.244***
				(0.408)		(0.408)
Gini index	−0.253*	−0.267*	−0.065	−0.080	−0.065	−0.079
	(0.144)	(0.154)	(0.047)	(0.085)	(0.049)	(0.087)
Share of agriculture over GDP	−0.329*	−0.340*	−0.114*	−0.134	−0.119	−0.134
	(0.185)	(0.195)	(0.066)	(0.113)	(0.073)	(0.121)
Gini index * Share of agriculture over GDP/100	0.914*	0.901*	0.329**	0.390	0.313*	0.374
	(0.515)	(0.517)	(0.166)	(0.296)	(0.172)	(0.300)
Index of economic concentration	4.598**	4.051*	2.492**	1.811	2.301**	1.640
	(2.192)	(2.381)	(0.999)	(1.624)	(1.042)	(1.762)
Fuel as percentage of exports	−0.022	−0.025	−0.017**	−0.009	−0.017*	−0.009
	(0.025)	(0.026)	(0.009)	(0.014)	(0.009)	(0.014)
Ethnic fractionalization	5.007	4.817	3.529**	1.914	3.483*	1.865
	(4.440)	(4.964)	(1.777)	(2.984)	(1.798)	(3.045)
(Ethnic fractionalization)^2	−3.881	−4.129	−1.932**	−0.805	−2.276	−0.984
	(5.298)	(5.754)	(2.212)	(3.802)	(2.267)	(3.851)
Religious fractionalization	2.587	1.760	2.094	1.684	1.849	1.548
	(1.978)	(2.748)	(0.861)	(1.441)	(0.969)	(1.609)
Democratic regime	−0.623	−0.733	−0.440*	−0.424	−0.441*	−0.428
	(0.492)	(0.537)	(0.250)	(0.377)	(0.250)	(0.374)
Africa			−1.321***	−1.779**	−1.378***	−1.802***
			(0.516)	(0.881)	(0.521)	(0.886)
Latin America	0.159	0.520	0.045	0.097	0.068	0.125
	(1.129)	(1.448)	(0.437)	(0.747)	(0.445)	(0.766)
Per capita income (log value)		−0.599			−0.327	−0.187
		(1.013)			(0.395)	(0.659)
Log-likelihood	−21.482	−20.892	−85.836	−33.263	−84.583	−33.0437
Prob > Chi-square	0.0082	0.0094	0.0000	0.0000	0.0000	0.0000
Pseudo R^2	0.3562	0.3735	0.3145	0.7346	0.3240	0.7359
Number of observations	577	575	663	663	661	661

Estimation: Probit model.
Standard errors in parenthesis.
***$p < 0.01$; **$p < 0.05$; *$p < 0.01$.
^^^$p < 0.01$ in joint test of interactive terms and its components; ^^$p < 0.05$ in joint test of interactive terms and its components; ^$p < 0.01$ in joint test of interactive terms and its components.

Table 2.9. *The Causes of Civil Wars, 1850–1980*

Independent Variables	Onset of Civil Wars			Annual Probability of Civil War		
	Model 1	Model 2	Model 3	Model 4	Model 5	Model 6
Constant	-2.169*** (0.141)	-1.480 (1.202)	-1.720*** (0.097)	-2.214*** (0.131)	1.199 (0.760)	-1.364 (1.080)
Civil war in previous year				2.668*** (0.101)		2.749*** (0.163)
Percentage of family farms[a]	0.006 (0.006)	-0.001 (0.010)	0.014*** (0.004)	0.010** (0.005)	0.003 (0.007)	0.000^ (0.009)
Index of occupational diversification[b]	-0.002 (0.006)	-0.008 (0.011)	-0.005 (0.004)	-0.002 (0.005)	0.000 (0.008)	-0.005^ (0.010)
Percentage of family farms*	-0.043** (0.021)	-0.022 (0.029)	-0.068*** (0.015)	-0.051*** (0.019)	-0.036* (0.021)	-0.026^ (0.027)
Index of occupational diversification/100						
Democracy in previous year	0.189 (0.145)	0.287 (0.177)	0.393*** (0.096)	0.229* (0.127)	0.361*** (0.120)	0.236 (0.157)
Per capita income (log value)		-0.074 (0.188)			-0.413*** (0.119)	-0.096 (0.165)
Log-likelihood	-366.15	-138.18	-889.43	-497.08	-354.60	-190.81
Prob > Chi-square	0.0001	0.0038	0.0000	0.0000	0.0000	0.0000
Pseudo R^2	0.0326	0.0592	0.0572	0.4731	0.1094	0.5208
Number of observations	6574	3286	6574	6574	3286	3286

[a] Area of family farms as a percentage of the total area of holdings. *Source:* Vanhanen (1997).

[b] Arithmetic mean of percentage of nonagricultural population and percentage of urban population. Urban population is defined as population living in cities of 20,000 or more inhabitants. *Source:* Vanhanen (1997).

Estimation: Probit model.

Standard errors in parenthesis.

*** $p < 0.01$; ** $p < 0.05$; * $p < 0.05$. ^^^ $p < 0.01$ in joint test of interactive terms and its components; ^^ $p < 0.05$ in joint test of interactive terms and its components; ^ $p < 0.01$ in joint test of interactive terms and its components.

Models 3 to 6 in Table 2.8 explore the annual probability of civil war. The latter two (Models 5 and 6) introduce a control for per capita income. Models 4 and 6 include a control for the occurrence of war in the previous year. Regardless of the introduction of per capita income, the interactive term "Gini index*Share of agriculture" fits the theoretical expectations and is statistically significant if there is no control for lagged war. If this control is introduced, the variable ceases to be significant – still, the coefficient remains very stable. The same result takes place for economic concentration, fuel exports, ethnic fractionalization (and its square value) and democratic regime: they stop being statistically significant once the lagged value of war is introduced.

Table 2.9 explores the same relationship for the sample of 1850 to 1980. Neither the level of literacy nor the type of economic structure alone makes any impact on the likelihood of a civil war. Instead, the interaction of a non-industrial economy and an increasing skew in the distribution of property leads to the start of civil wars (Model 1). Once we introduce a control for per capita income, in Model 2, the interactive term loses its statistical significance – however, in a joint test with per capita income, it is significant at the 1 percent level.

Again, Models 3 to 6 in Table 2.9 explore the impact of inequality and asset specificity, alone and jointly, on the annual probability of war for the whole period from 1850 to 1980. Even controlling for per capita income and a lagged value of civil war, the interactive term conforms to our theoretical expectations: unequal agrarian societies have a higher likelihood of experiencing civil strife. Thus, whereas in a highly unequal and agrarian country the annual probability of war is almost 7 percent (if there was no war the previous year), in either equal societies or industrial economies the probability of civil war drops to 0.

List of Political Regimes, 1800–1994

List columns indicate, respectively, country code,[*] country, regime and years.

America

2	United States	Democratic	1800–1994
20	Canada	Democratic	1867–1994
40	Cuba	Authoritarian	1902–1908
		Democratic	1909–1915
		Authoritarian	1916–1939
		Democratic	1940–1952
		Authoritarian	1953–1994
41	Haiti	Authoritarian	1820–1994
42	Dominican Rep.	Authoritarian	1844–1929
		Transitional Period	1930–1931
		Authoritarian	1932–1965
		Democratic	1966–1994
51	Jamaica	Democratic	1962–1994
52	Trinidad	Democratic	1962–1994
70	Mexico	Authoritarian	1822–1994
90	Guatemala	Authoritarian	1839–1944
		Democratic	1945–1953
		Authoritarian	1954–1957
		Democratic	1958–1962
		Authoritarian	1963–1965
		Democratic	1966–1981
		Authoritarian	1982–1985
		Democratic	1986–1994

[*] Country codes follow the numeration established by Jaggers and Gurr (1996) in the "Policy" data set.

Political Regimes, 1800–1994

91	Honduras	Authoritarian	1839–1956
		Democratic	1957–1962
		Authoritarian	1963–1970
		Democratic	1971
		Authoritarian	1972–1981
		Democratic	1982–1994
92	El Salvador	Authoritarian	1841–1983
		Democratic	1984–1994
93	Nicaragua	Authoritarian	1838–1983
		Democratic	1984–1994
94	Costa Rica	Authoritarian	1938–1947
		Democratic	1948–1994
95	Panama	Authoritarian	1903–1949
		Democratic	1950
		Authoritarian	1951
		Democratic	1952–1967
		Authoritarian	1968–1990
		Democratic	1991–1994
99	Great Colombia	Authoritarian	1821–1830
100	Colombia	Authoritarian	1832–1936
		Democratic	1937–1947
		Authoritarian	1948–1957
		Democratic	1958–1994
101	Venezuela	Authoritarian	1830–1958
		Democratic	1959–1994
110	Guyana	Authoritarian	1966–1994
130	Ecuador	Authoritarian	1830–1947
		Democratic	1948–1962
		Authoritarian	1963–1978
		Democratic	1979–1994
135	Peru	Authoritarian	1821–1955
		Democratic	1956–1961
		Authoritarian	1962
		Democratic	1963–1965
		Authoritarian	1966-1979
		Democratic	1980–1989
		Authoritarian	1990–1994
140	Brazil	Authoritarian	1824–1945
		Democratic	1946–1963
		Authoritarian	1964–1978
		Democratic	1979–1994
145	Bolivia	Authoritarian	1825–1978
		Democratic	1979
		Authoritarian	1980–1981
		Democratic	1982–1994
150	Paraguay	Authoritarian	1811–1994

155	Chile	Authoritarian	1818–1908
		Democratic	1909–1924
		Authoritarian	1925–1933
		Democratic	1934–1972
		Authoritarian	1973–1989
		Democratic	1990–1994
160	Argentina	Authoritarian	1825–1911
		Democratic	1912–1930
		Authoritarian	1931–1957
		Democratic	1958–1961
		Authoritarian	1962
		Democratic	1963–1965
		Authoritarian	1966–1972
		Democratic	1973–1975
		Authoritarian	1976–1982
		Democratic	1983–1994
165	Uruguay	Authoritarian	1830–1918
		Democratic	1919–1933
		Authoritarian	1934–1941
		Democratic	1942–1972
		Authoritarian	1973–1984
		Democratic	1985–1994
10051	Bahamas	Democratic	1973–1994
10052	Barbados	Democratic	1966–1994
10053	Belize	Democratic	1981–1994
10056	Dominica	Democratic	1978–1994
10059	Grenada	Democratic	1974–1978
		Authoritarian	1979–1983
		Democratic	1984–1994
10068	St. Kitts & Nevis	Democratic	1984–1994
10069	St. Lucia	Democratic	1980–1994
10070	St. Vincent	Democratic	1981–1994
10082	Suriname	Democratic	1975–1979
		Authoritarian	1980–1987
		Democratic	1988–1989
		Authoritarian	1990
		Democratic	1991–1994
10208	Antigua	Authoritarian	1982–1994

Europe

200	United Kingdom	Authoritarian	1800–1884
		Democratic	1885–1994
205	Ireland	Authoritarian	1921
		Democratic	1922–1994

100

210	Netherlands	Authoritarian	1815–1896
		Democratic	1897–1939
		Occupation	1940–1944
		Democratic	1945–1994
211	Belgium	Authoritarian	1830–1893
		Democratic	1894–1939
		Occupation	1940–1944
		Democratic	1945–1994
212	Luxembourg	Authoritarian	1867–1889
		Democratic	1890-1939
		Occupation	1940–1944
		Democratic	1945–1994
220	France	Authoritarian	1800–1847
		Democratic	1848–1851
		Authoritarian	1852–1869
		Democratic	1870–1939
		Authoritarian	1940–1943
		Transitional Period	1944–1945
		Democratic	1946–1994
225	Switzerland	Democratic	1848–1994
230	Spain	Authoritarian	1800–1930
		Democratic	1931–1936
		Authoritarian	1937–1976
		Democratic	1977–1994
235	Portugal	Authoritarian	1800
		Occupation	1801
		Authoritarian	1802–1806
		Occupation	1807–1819
		Transitional Period	1820–1822
		Authoritarian	1823–1909
		Transitional Period	1910
		Democratic	1911–1925
		Authoritarian	1926–1975
		Democratic	1976–1994
245	Bavaria	Authoritarian	1800–1871
255	Germany	Authoritarian	1800–1806
		Occupation	1807–1812
		Authoritarian	1813–1917
		Transitional Period	1918
		Democratic	1919–1932
		Authoritarian	1933–1945
		Democratic	1990–1994
260	West Germany	Transitional Period	1945–1948
		Democratic	1949–1990
265	East Germany	Authoritarian	1945–1990

267	Baden	Authoritarian	1819–1871
269	Saxony	Authoritarian	1806–1812
		Occupation	1813
		Authoritarian	1814–1847
		Transitional Period	1848
		Authoritarian	1849–1871
271	Wuttenberg	Authoritarian	1800–1871
290	Poland	Democratic	1918–1925
		Authoritarian	1926–1938
		Occupation	1939–1944
		Transitional Period	1945–1947
		Authoritarian	1948–1988
		Democratic	1989–1994
305	Austria	Authoritarian	1800–1917
		Transitional Period	1918–1919
		Democratic	1920–1932
		Authoritarian	1933–1937
		Occupation	1938–1944
		Transitional Period	1945
		Democratic	1946–1994
310	Hungary	Authoritarian	1867–1917
		Transitional Period	1918
		Authoritarian	1919–1943
		Occupation	1944
		Transitional Period	1945–1947
		Authoritarian	1948–1989
		Democratic	1990–1994
315	Czechoslovakia	Democratic	1918–1938
		Occupation	1939–1944
		Democratic	1945–1946
		Transitional Period	1947
		Authoritarian	1948–1989
		Democratic	1990–1992
315	Czech Rep.	Democratic	1993–1994
317	Slovak Rep.	Democratic	1993–1994
324	Saboya	Authoritarian	1815–1860
325	Italy	Authoritarian	1861–1918
		Democratic	1919–1921
		Authoritarian	1922–1945
		Democratic	1946–1994
327	Papal Estates	Authoritarian	1815–1848
		Transitional Period	1849
		Authoritarian	1850–1870
329	Sicily	Authoritarian	1816–1860
332	Modena	Authoritarian	1815–1860
335	Parma	Authoritarian	1815–1860

337	Tuscany	Authoritarian	1815–1860
339	Albania	Authoritarian	1914
		Transitional Period	1915–1924
		Authoritarian	1925–1938
		Occupation	1939–1944
		Transitional Period	1945
		Authoritarian	1946–1991
		Democratic	1992–1994
342	Serbia	Authoritarian	1878–1920
343	Macedonia	Democratic	1991–1994
344	Croatia	Authoritarian	1991–1994
345	Yugoslavia	Democratic	1921–1928
		Authoritarian	1929–1940
		Occupation	1941–1943
		Transitional Period	1944–1945
		Authoritarian	1946–1991
346	Bosnia	Transitional Period	1992–1994
347	Yugoslavia-Serbia	Authoritarian	1992–1994
349	Slovenia	Democratic	1991–1994
350	Greece	Authoritarian	1827–1861
		Transitional Period	1862–1863
		Democratic	1864–1914
		Authoritarian	1915–1925
		Democratic	1926–1935
		Authoritarian	1936–1940
		Occupation	1941–1943
		Democratic	1944–1966
		Authoritarian	1967–1973
		Democratic	1974–1994
352	Cyprus	Authoritarian	1960–1962
		Transitional Period	1963–1964
		Authoritarian	1965–1973
		Transitional Period	1974
		Authoritarian	1975–1976
		Democratic	1977–1994
355	Bulgaria	Authoritarian	1879–1912
		Transitional Period	1913–1914
		Authoritarian	1915–1941
		Occupation	1942–1943
		Transitional Period	1944–1946
		Authoritarian	1947–1989
		Democratic	1990–1994
360	Romania	Authoritarian	1859–1915
		Occupation	1916
		Authoritarian	1917–1939
		Transitional Period	1940

		Authoritarian	1941–1943
		Transitional Period	1944–1947
		Authoritarian	1948–1990
		Democratic	1991–1994
364	Soviet Union	Authoritarian	1922–1991
365	Russia	Authoritarian	1800–1811
		Occupation	1812
		Authoritarian	1813–1922
		Authoritarian	1992
		Democratic	1993–1994
366	Estonia	Transitional Period	1917–1918
		Democratic	1919–1933
		Authoritarian	1934–1940
		Transitional Period	1988–1990
		Democratic	1991–1994
367	Latvia	Democratic	1920–1933
		Authoritarian	1934–1940
		Transitional Period	1989–1990
		Authoritarian	1991–1992
		Democratic	1993–1994
368	Lithuania	Transitional Period	1918–1919
		Democratic	1920–1925
		Authoritarian	1926–1940
		Transitional Period	1990
		Authoritarian	1991
		Democratic	1992–1994
369	Ukraine	Democratic	1991–1994
370	Belarus	Democratic	1991–1993
		Authoritarian	1994
371	Armenia	Democratic	1991–1994
372	Georgia	Authoritarian	1991
		Democratic	1992–1994
373	Azerbaijan	Authoritarian	1991–1994
375	Finland	Democratic	1917–1994
380	Sweden	Authoritarian	1800–1910
		Democratic	1911–1994
385	Norway	Democratic	1900–1939
		Occupation	1940–1944
		Democratic	1945–1994
390	Denmark	Authoritarian	1800–1900
		Democratic	1901–1939
		Occupation	1940–1944
		Democratic	1945–1994
395	Iceland	Democratic	1918–1994
2132	Malta	Democratic	1964–1994
2202	Andorra	Democratic	1994

Political Regimes, 1800–1994

2235	Liechtenstein	Democratic	1991–1994
2239	Monaco	Democratic	1994
2301	San Marino	Democratic	1993–1994

Africa

404	Guinea-Bissau	Authoritarian	1974–1993
		Democratic	1994
411	Equatorial Guinea	Authoritarian	1968–1994
420	Gambia	Authoritarian	1965–1994
432	Mali	Authoritarian	1960–1994
433	Senegal	Authoritarian	1960–1994
434	Benin	Authoritarian	1960–1990
		Democratic	1991–1994
435	Mauritania	Authoritarian	1960–1994
436	Niger	Authoritarian	1960–1994
437	Cote D'Ivoire	Authoritarian	1960–1994
438	Guinea	Authoritarian	1958–1994
439	Burkina Faso	Authoritarian	1960–1994
450	Liberia	Authoritarian	1847–1994
451	Sierra Leone	Democratic	1961–1966
		Authoritarian	1967–1994
452	Ghana	Authoritarian	1957–1969
		Democratic	1970–1971
		Authoritarian	1972–1978
		Democratic	1979–1980
		Authoritarian	1981–1994
461	Togo	Authoritarian	1960–1994
471	Cameroon	Authoritarian	1960–1994
475	Nigeria	Democratic	1960–1965
		Authoritarian	1966–1978
		Democratic	1979–1982
		Authoritarian	1983–1994
481	Gabon	Authoritarian	1960–1994
482	Central African Rep.	Authoritarian	1960–1992
		Democratic	1993–1994
483	Chad	Authoritarian	1960–1994
484	Rep. of Congo	Democratic	1960–1962
		Authoritarian	1963–1994
490	Dem. Rep. of Congo	Authoritarian	1960–1994
500	Uganda	Authoritarian	1962–1979
		Democratic	1980–1984
		Authoritarian	1985–1994
501	Kenya	Authoritarian	1963–1994
510	Tanzania	Authoritarian	1961–1994
516	Burundi	Authoritarian	1962–1994

517	Rwanda	Authoritarian	1962–1994
520	Somalia	Democratic	1960–1968
		Authoritarian	1969–1994
522	Djibouti	Authoritarian	1977–1994
529	Ethiopia	Authoritarian	1855–1935
		Occupation	1936–1941
		Authoritarian	1942–1993
531	Eritrea	Authoritarian	1993–1994
540	Angola	Authoritarian	1975–1994
541	Mozambique	Authoritarian	1975–1994
551	Zambia	Authoritarian	1964–1994
552	Zimbabwe	Authoritarian	1965–1994
553	Malawi	Authoritarian	1964–1994
560	South Africa	Authoritarian	1910–1994
564	Orange Free State	Democratic	1854–1902
565	Namibia	Authoritarian	1990–1994
570	Lesotho	Authoritarian	1966–1994
571	Botswana	Authoritarian	1966–1994
572	Swaziland	Authoritarian	1968–1994
580	Madagascar	Authoritarian	1960–1992
		Democratic	1993–1994
581	Comoros	Authoritarian	1975–1994
590	Mauritius	Democratic	1968–1994
600	Morocco	Authoritarian	1800–1911
		Occupation	1912
		Authoritarian	1956–1994
615	Algeria	Authoritarian	1962–1994
616	Tunisia	Authoritarian	1956–1994
620	Libya	Authoritarian	1951–1994
625	Sudan	Democratic	1956–1957
		Authoritarian	1958–1964
		Democratic	1965–1968
		Authoritarian	1969–1985
		Democratic	1986–1988
		Authoritarian	1989–1994
4008	Cape Verde Is.	Authoritarian	1975–1994
4038	Seychelles	Authoritarian	1976–1994
4252	Sao Tome	Authoritarian	1976–1990
		Democratic	1991–1994

Asia

630	Iran	Authoritarian	1800–1905
		Transitional Period	1906–1924
		Authoritarian	1925–1994
640	Turkey	Authoritarian	1800–1918

Political Regimes, 1800–1994

		Occupation	1919–1921
		Transitional Period	1922
		Authoritarian	1923–1960
		Democratic	1961–1979
		Authoritarian	1980–1982
		Democratic	1983–1994
645	Iraq	Authoritarian	1932–1994
651	Egypt	Authoritarian	1922–1934
		Transitional Period	1935
		Authoritarian	1936–1994
652	Syria	Authoritarian	1944–1994
660	Lebanon	Authoritarian	1943–1970
		Democratic	1971–1975
		Transitional Period	1976–1989
		Authoritarian	1990–1994
663	Jordan	Authoritarian	1946–1994
666	Israel	Democratic	1948–1994
670	Saudi Arabia	Authoritarian	1926–1994
678	Yemen – Arab Rep.	Authoritarian	1918–1945
		Transitional Period	1946–1947
		Authoritarian	1948–1989
679	Yemen	Authoritarian	1990–1994
680	Yemen, People's Dem. Rep.	Authoritarian	1968–1990
690	Kuwait	Authoritarian	1961–1994
692	Bahrain	Authoritarian	1971–1994
694	Qatar	Authoritarian	1971–1994
696	United Arab Emirates	Authoritarian	1971–1994
698	Oman	Authoritarian	1800–1994
700	Afghanistan	Authoritarian	1800–1994
701	Turkmenistan	Authoritarian	1991–1994
702	Tajikistan	Authoritarian	1991–1994
703	Kyrgyzstan Rep.	Democratic	1991–1994
704	Uzbekistan	Authoritarian	1991–1994
705	Kazakhstan	Authoritarian	1991–1994
710	China	Authoritarian	1800–1859
		Transitional Period	1860–1861
		Authoritarian	1862–1910
		Transitional Period	1911
		Authoritarian	1912
		Transitional Period	1913
		Authoritarian	1914–1938
		Occupation	1939–1945
		Authoritarian	1946–1994
712	Mongolia	Authoritarian	1924–1989
		Democratic	1990–1994
713	Taiwan	Authoritarian	1949–1994

730	Korea	Authoritarian	1800–1910
731	North Korea	Authoritarian	1948–1994
732	South Korea	Authoritarian	1948–1959
		Democratic	1960
		Authoritarian	1961–1987
		Democratic	1988–1994
740	Japan	Authoritarian	1800–1857
		Transitional Period	1858–1867
		Authoritarian	1868–1944
		Transitional Period	1945–1949
		Authoritarian	1950–1951
		Democratic	1952–1994
750	India	Democratic	1950–1994
760	Bhutan	Authoritarian	1907–1994
769	Pakistan	Authoritarian	1947–1949
		Democratic	1950–1955
		Authoritarian	1956–1971
		Democratic	1972–1976
		Authoritarian	1977–1987
		Democratic	1988–1994
771	Bangladesh	Authoritarian	1971–1985
		Democratic	1986–1994
775	Myanmar	Democratic	1948–1957
		Authoritarian	1958–1959
		Democratic	1960–1961
		Authoritarian	1962–1994
780	Sri Lanka	Democratic	1948–1976
		Authoritarian	1977–1990
		Democratic	1991–1994
790	Nepal	Authoritarian	1800–1990
		Democratic	1991–1994
800	Thailand	Authoritarian	1800–1931
		Transitional Period	1932–1934
		Authoritarian	1935–1940
		Occupation	1941
		Authoritarian	1942–1974
		Democratic	1975
		Authoritarian	1976–1982
		Democratic	1983–1990
		Authoritarian	1991
		Democratic	1992–1994
811	Cambodia	Authoritarian	1949–1952
		Transitional Period	1953–1954
		Authoritarian	1955–1969
		Transitional Period	1970–1971
		Authoritarian	1972–1974

Political Regimes, 1800–1994

		Transitional Period	1975
		Authoritarian	1976–1994
812	Laos	Democratic	1954–1958
		Authoritarian	1959–1994
816	North Vietnam	Authoritarian	1954–1975
817	South Vietnam	Authoritarian	1955–1975
818	Vietnam	Authoritarian	1976–1994
820	Malaysia	Authoritarian	1957–1994
830	Singapore	Authoritarian	1965–1994
840	Philippines	Authoritarian	1935–1940
		Occupation	1941–1944
		Authoritarian	1945
		Democratic	1946–1964
		Authoritarian	1965–1985
		Democratic	1986–1994
850	Indonesia	Authoritarian	1945–1954
		Democratic	1955–1956
		Authoritarian	1957–1994
7213	Brunei	Authoritarian	1985–1994
7241	Maldives	Authoritarian	1966–1994

Australasia

900	Australia	Democratic	1901–1994
910	Papua N. Guinea	Democratic	1975–1994
920	New Zealand	Democratic	1857–1994
950	Fiji	Democratic	1970–1986
		Authoritarian	1987–1994
9149	Solomon Is.	Democratic	1978–1994
9151	Vanuatu	Democratic	1980–1994
9152	W. Samoa	Authoritarian	1962–1994
9220	Federated States of Micronesia	Democratic	1992–1994
9242	Marshall Is.	Democratic	1992–1994

3

Historical Evidence

This chapter moves away from the large econometric tests undertaken in Chapter 2. Instead, it examines the democratization process within two countries: the cantons of Switzerland from the late Middle Ages until the mid-nineteenth century and the states of the United States from colonial times until the mid-twentieth century. These two cases are examined mainly to determine the interests and strategies of different political actors and economic sectors in the choice of political regimes and therefore to overcome the limitations of purely statistical work.

The choice of these two countries seems advisable for at least three reasons. First, making good one of the criteria emphasized in standard scientific research (Cook and Campbell 1979), they add external validity to the statistical results. Whereas the statistics show the model to be accurate at the national level, the comparative analysis of Swiss cantons and American states shows that the model matches the evolution of subnational territories too. Second, both Switzerland and the United States, which were based on confederal or loose federal arrangements for relatively long periods of history, showed the kind of wide variation in democratic practices and structural conditions needed to trace the social conditions that underlie different franchise regimes. Finally, both countries remained, for very different reasons, substantially aloof from world politics and the impact of international wars. Its nearly insular geography sheltered the United States from the waves of European revolutions. The status of neutrality, guaranteed by all the great European powers, ensured Switzerland the minimal autonomy it needed to develop its own political institutions. Because it is true that the revolutionary episodes that agitated Europe from 1789 to 1848 directly affected Swiss politics, the different evolution of

Germany in the same period is instructive here. In the eighteenth century, numerous small German towns had political arrangements (and economic structures) similar to those in several Swiss cities (Walker 1998). Likewise, in the nineteenth century, particularly in 1848, they also attempted to democratize. But whereas the Swiss cantons were successful in democratizing between 1830 and 1848, the western and southwestern German cities saw their democratic impulses eventually thwarted by Austria and Prussia.

The first section traces the differences between the democratic Alpine cantons, the oligarchical bourgeois cantons such as Basel and Zurich, the aristocratic governments of Berne and Fribourg and the social upheavals of Geneva from the fourteenth to the eighteenth centuries to their respective levels of economic equality and specialization. It then examines Switzerland's industrialization, which took off at the end of the eighteenth century, and differing rates of cross-cantonal democratization from the Congress of Vienna in 1815 until the unifying reform of the Swiss constitution in 1874. The second section describes the evolution of American states. Before the Civil War, the practice of universal male suffrage on the frontier, as well as the progressive democratization of several Northeast states after independence, contrasted with the exclusion of the black population in the plantation economy of the South and the maintenance or reintroduction of restrictive electoral laws in states like Rhode Island and Massachusetts as they experienced early industrialization and the emergence of an incipient class cleavage. After the 1880s, once the Northern coalition that led the Civil War and the Reconstruction effort had crumbled, electoral restrictions reappeared following the theoretical insights of the model. In the relatively equal (and sparsely populated) areas of the Midwest and the Plains, democracy remained in place. In the highly unequal agrarian economies of the South, the poll tax, strict registration procedures and literacy and property requirements were introduced to exclude the black population and parts of the poor white electorate. In the North, the inflow of poor migrant workers heightened inequality and fostered important middle-class movements intent on imposing restrictive electoral rules at the turn of the twentieth century. But the type of assets in the Northern industrial and financial centers may explain why, on the Northeastern seaboard, despite wage differentials that were closer to those in the South than in the Midwest, suffrage restrictions remained much milder.

111

Democracy in the Swiss Cantons

Until the adoption of the federal constitution of 1848, Switzerland was a confederation of cantons with each one enjoying de facto complete sovereignty over its corresponding political and franchise arrangements. From the creation of a permanent alliance among several Alpine communities at the end of the thirteenth century, which gradually expanded to incorporate several urban cantons, until the first third of the nineteenth century, cantonal constitutions fell into three distinctive categories: democracies, landowning aristocracies and urban oligarchies.

The Alpine cantons (Appenzell, Glaris, Schwytz, Unterwald, Uri and Zug) were organized as *participatory democracies*. Political sovereignty remained in the hands of the *landsgemeinde*, a popular assembly formed by all adult men. Although some families seem to have played a substantial role in the direction of public affairs (Rappard 1914; Bonjour 1952; Capitani 1986), the popular assemblies met regularly and, throughout the eighteenth century, successfully warded off repeated attempts at oligarchical control. That type of political regime matches the theoretical predictions well. Economic and social relations were relatively equal in the Alpine cantons: there were no cities; all of the farming communities were composed of free men, engaged in the exploitation of dairy and forest products; and many of the economic activities in those communities required continuous cooperative arrangements among all individuals, thereby strengthening the latter's interdependence and equality (Berger 1983).[1]

By contrast, in the remaining cantons, each of which generally had a town surrounded by a rural hinterland, the countryside was excluded from (or at most played a marginal role in) the process of government. Wealth was concentrated in the cantonal capital. The inhabitants of the bourgs milked the peasantry through extensive feudal rights and restrictions on competition (in Zurich, for example, farmers had to buy and sell textiles using urban intermediaries since from at least the mid-seventeenth century). The countryside contained the poorest, and, to the urban oligarchy, most threatening, segments of the population: only half of the rural population had enough land to feed a family, and, in the eighteenth century, between one fourth and one fifth systematically depended on public assistance (Capitani 1986: 442–43). In line with the theoretical predictions of

---

[1] Democratic practices were also relatively extended in the Grisons and Valais. Although they did not have *landsgemeinden*, they employed referenda mechanisms.

the book, all significant revolts took place among the peasantry (in cantons governed by the city): in northern Switzerland in the late sixteenth century and in central Switzerland in 1653; then again in Zurich, Fribourg, Valais and Vaud in the 1780s and 1790s (Van Muyden 1899). As pointed out by Rappard (1912), cantonal position on the French invasion of 1798 was correlated with the weight of feudal structures across cantons. In Vaud and in the Plains of Berne, where feudal dues still existed, the peasantry welcomed revolutionary ideas. In the Alpine cantons and in the Oberland of Berne, where feudalism had disappeared, anti-French sentiment ran very high.

Among the nondemocratic cantons, the constitutional arrangements varied as a function of the predominant assets in each city. In Berne, Luzern, Fribourg and Soleure, a small yet powerful aristocratic clique with extensive properties in the rural areas confronted a very weak commercial bourgeoisie. That *landowning aristocracy* exercised a tight control over government. By the mid-eighteenth century, 79 families controlled all of the seats of the Grand Council (cantonal assembly) of Berne – with 14 families having close to half the seats. In Soleure, the Grand Council was in the hands of 34 families at the end of the eighteenth century. In Luzern, the 36 members of the Senate were appointed for life, with the children usually succeeding their parents (Rappard 1912). In contrast, in Zurich, Basel, Saint-Gall and Schaffhausen, a *bourgeois coalition* controlled the cantonal government: the merchant class governed with some participation of the guilds. Generally, cantons were governed by two councils (the Small and the Grand Council) elected, directly or indirectly, by all the bourgeois, that is, the inhabitants of the city, organized in tribes (*Zunft*) operating as both electoral colleges and professional associations. The broader representative basis of those cantons was directly related to their economic structures. At least until the sixteenth century, they had important commercial and financial links to Germany and Italy. Moreover, inequality was probably mild by European standards. In then-prosperous Schaffhausen, the largest fortunes oscillated between 13,000 and 19,000 gulden at the turn of the sixteenth century. In contemporary Augsburg and Nuremberg, fortunes ten to fifteen times those figures were not unusual (Steinberg 1996). In mid-eighteenth-century Zurich, the top decile of all households controlled slightly over one half of all the wealth (Biucchi 1973) – in England, the top decile controlled close to 85 percent (Lindert 1991).

Figures 3.1 and 3.2 summarize in a graphical manner the previous analysis. Figure 3.1 depicts the distribution of different types of cantons in

113

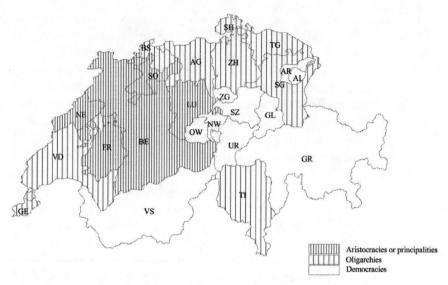

Figure 3.1 Democracy in Switzerland before 1830.

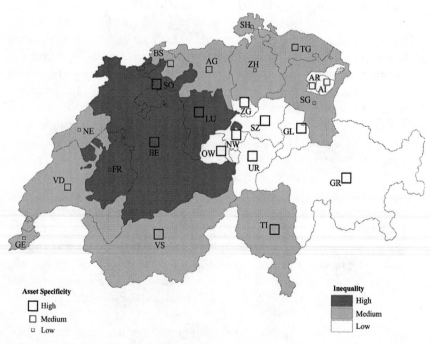

Figure 3.2 Inequality and Type of Assets in Switzerland in the 1830s.

114

Switzerland in the late 1820s, just before the democratization wave that followed the revolution of 1830.[2] Figure 3.2 displays the overall structural traits of each canton's economy: the level of economic equality and the extension of industrial activity (which proxies for the declining role of fixed assets). Although these two dimensions are measured in rather rough ways, mostly based on descriptive accounts and on fragmentary statistical data, they generally fit the theoretical predictions of the book.[3] A substantial level of democratic practice survived in the core of Switzerland, which was characterized by relative rural equality. Medium levels of representation were in place in the industrial northeast. By contrast, aristocratic regimes were dominant in the unequal and fixed-asset cantons of the west.

The principality of Neuchatel and, to some extent, the city of Geneva are the main exceptions to our theoretical expectations – even with few landed interests, democratic practices reigned in those places for only brief periods of time, if at all. Although Neuchatel had an extensive watchmaking industry, mainly organized in family craft shops, its control by Prussia until the mid-nineteenth century hindered the development of any democratic institution.

For most of the Ancien Régime and until 1841, Geneva was governed by the upper segments of the bourgeoisie, who controlled the Small Council as well as the syndics, or executive body, in a polarized political environment. After a popular explosion overthrew this oligarchical regime in 1782, French troops reestablished it immediately. A democratic regime was introduced in 1788–89 and then aborted in 1795. Under the new constitution of 1814, only one sixth of the canton's adult men were enfranchised (Rappard 1942). Two reasons seem to explain the very limited democracy of Geneva. First, in contrast with other urban cantons, Geneva had only a small rural hinterland. Whereas urban classes in Zurich and Basel were allied (along sectoral or cross-class lines) against the peasantry, the class cleavage in Geneva emerged as an exclusively urban phenomenon (Capitani 1986). Second, within the city of Geneva sharp wealth inequalities divided the rich, who lived in the upper part of the city, and "les gens de métier qui occupaient, avec les réfugiés, les rues basses" (Van Muyden 1899: 356).

---

[2] The map is based on the description provided by Franscini (1827) of the governmental institutions in each canton by the late 1820s.

[3] The information used to build Figure 3.2 has been extracted from Franscini (1827, 1855), Rappard (1914), Bergier (1984) and Capitani (1986).

The variation in regime type found across cantons cannot be attributed either to level of income or to religion. To determine cantonal wealth, I have employed three alternative measures: the daily wage paid by each canton to a soldier in 1818, the proportion of rural population in a canton and the 1851 per capita cantonal contribution to the federal government. To measure the effect of religious practices, which are substantially heterogeneous across Swiss cantons, I employ the proportion of Catholics in the late 1820s.[4] The level of democracy and a soldier's pay show a correlation coefficient of −0.82. Rural population and democracy show a correlation coefficient of 0.23. Finally, the correlation between cantonal contributions to the federal government and level of democracy is −0.68. In short, these results remind us that economic development does not explain political regime and that when it does so, in the worldwide sample for the period after World War II, it must be a proxy for other explanatory factors. In turn, the percentage of Catholics and democracy show a correlation coefficient of 0.38. Any Weberian thesis relating democracy and Protestantism must also be rejected for the case of Switzerland.[5]

Besides explaining political differences across cantons, the type and distribution of wealth seem to account well for changes in democratic or authoritarian practices over time. After the sixteenth century, the Swiss economy experienced two important changes. On the one hand, a growing population drove wages down, made pauperism a widespread phenomenon and sharpened economic inequalities (Bergier 1984; Capitani 1986). On the other hand, the decline of Mediterranean trade (Braudel 1984) and permanent wars in the continental theater stifled the burgeoning commercial and financial life in place in late medieval Switzerland. These two phenomena pushed the urban elites to increase their oligarchical practices. Across all cities, the number of families with access to the Grand Council dropped to between one fourth and one third in the sixteenth century (Körner 1986: 366). In the seventeenth century, Secret Councils were created to

---

[4] For these calculations, I have coded the level of democracy in each canton from 0 (the absolutist princedom of Neuchatel) to 10 (several Alpine cantons, where all men were entitled to vote). The measures of soldiers' pay and rural population come from Franscini (1827). The measure on cantonal contributions is taken from Franscini (1855).

[5] In a multivariate regression, the proportion of Catholics is statistically insignificant. The best fit to explain democracy is

$$\text{Democracy} = 21.54 - 10.86^{**} \text{ Percent Rural } - 0.56^{***} \text{ Soldier's Pay}$$

$$R^2 = 0.72; {}^{***}p < 0.01; {}^{**}p < 0.05.$$

take control of the daily management of public affairs. Still, the triumph of authoritarian tendencies varied across cantons. In Fribourg, public positions were formally forbidden to any citizen whose name did not appear in the so-called *livre de la grand bourgeoisie* in 1627. In Soleure and Luzern, very restrictive electoral practices were instituted around 1700. But in the commercial city of Zurich, merchants and guilds blocked the formation of an oligarchy in 1713.

The institutions of the Ancien Régime collapsed with the French invasions of 1798 and the Napoleonic creation of a centralized Helvetian Republic, yet they were put back in place by the Mediation Act signed in 1803 between Napoleon and the Swiss Diet. A new confederal pact in 1815, signed by 22 cantons (the old ones, several new cantons born from the old "baillages" administered until 1798 by the old states, and Geneva), gave full de facto political sovereignty to its parties. The old political systems emerged practically intact to last for another decade and a half. With hindsight, however, it is apparent that most of the oligarchical cantons owed their institutions to the international balance of power that had emerged out of the Congress of Vienna of 1815. In the winter and spring of 1830–31, after the July Revolution of 1830 in Paris toppled the reactionary regime of Louis XVIII, a wave of popular revolts, mostly of rural origin, swept across Switzerland. With the exception of aristocratic Berne, where the army was mobilized temporarily against the countryside, the adoption of liberal constitutions took place peacefully.[6] The economic changes that had taken place in Switzerland in the last half century lay behind that smooth political transition. Since the mid-eighteenth century, the cotton and silk industries had grown rapidly – by some accounts they employed 12 percent of the population and by 1770 represented one third of the national product (Bergier 1984: 170). Most of the textile industry relied on an extensive put-out system that supplemented the income of substantial parts of the peasantry (Steinberg 1996). By 1850 the industrial sector employed 33 percent of the labor force (Andrey 1986: 510). Already, by 1820, Switzerland was the first country in exports per capita in the world – at a rate twice the English level and three times the Belgian one. Similarly dramatic changes took place in the financial sector. At the beginning of the nineteenth century Switzerland was slightly ahead of England in the per capita number of savings deposits

---

[6] In Geneva, a set of gradual reforms extended the franchise to about one third of the adult men in 1832 and one half in 1835 (Rappard 1942). Universal male suffrage was approved in 1841.

(Biucchi 1973). Private bankers in Basel, Geneva and Zurich began to invest heavily abroad as early as the end of the eighteenth century (Landes 1969: 168).[7] Savings and non-private banks mushroomed from just three in 1800 to over one hundred in 1835 (Andrey 1986: 524). The expansion of investment opportunities explains why the suppression of feudal rights (and of franchise restrictions) was met with little resistance among aristocratic families (Bergier 1984: 99).

Still, the extent of radical change in Switzerland should not be exaggerated. Even after the revolutionary period of 1830–31, it took another four decades to introduce male universal suffrage. Cities were still overrepresented in the cantons of Basel, Luzern, Saint-Gall, Schaffhausen, Soleure and Zurich, and franchise requirements remained restrictive for certain social segments until the 1840s. The federal constitution of 1848 theoretically granted the right to vote to all male residents 20 years old or older. But it let the cantons determine subjective conditions, such as income and literacy, that could restrict the franchise (Gruner 1978). As a result, the extension of the franchise continued to vary substantially – mostly in line with the type of political regime in place during the Ancien Régime – from over 95 percent in Alpine cantons such as Schwytz to less than 80 percent in Berne, Luzern and Fribourg and to an exceptionally low 55 percent in Basel city.[8] Only after new electoral laws were passed in the early 1870s did universal male suffrage become established across Switzerland. By that time, the process of industrialization had shaped an economy capable of softening the level of redistributive tensions.

Democracy in America

The decision of the 1787 constitutional convention in Philadelphia to grant states complete autonomy over electoral matters resulted in a wide variety of franchise requirements and electorates in the United States. With the probable exception of the decade immediately following the Civil War, this diversity lasted until the second half of the twentieth century.

In the colonial period, the franchise was conceived as a privilege restricted to the propertied classes, who were considered the only legitimate

---

[7] In 1913, Switzerland had a gross stock of direct foreign investment abroad of about $700 per inhabitant – compared to $440 for Britain, $320 for the Netherlands and $70 for Germany (Bairoch 1990).

[8] My own estimations, based on data from Gruner (1978). The average proportion of registered voters as a percentage of population in 1848–66 and the level of democracy before 1830 (calculated from Franscini [1827]) shows a correlation coefficient of 0.50.

stakeholders in the commonwealth. Following British legal precedents dating from the fifteenth century, most of the colonies limited the right to vote to freeholders. The freehold qualification varied across colonies; in the Northern settlements it was a minimum value of land or of income from land, and to the south of New York it was in the form of acres.[9] Connecticut, Massachusetts and Pennsylvania had alternatives to the real estate qualification in the form of either personal property or the payment of taxes. Finally, in several localities, the franchise was granted to persons in the categories of freeman or town dweller (Williamson 1960). As recognized by contemporary travelers to colonial America and attested to by recent studies, the colonies were fairly equal societies, at least in comparison to Europe. At the time of independence, the top decile of adult white men held slightly over one half of all the wealth (Lindert 1991). As a result, the franchise was widely extended among white men. Around three quarters of adult white men could vote in Connecticut, Georgia, New Hampshire, rural Pennsylvania, Rhode Island and South Carolina. The franchise encompassed 50 to 60 percent of adult men in Maryland, Massachusetts, New York, Philadelphia and Virginia (Williamson 1960; Dinkin 1977).

The American Revolution led to some expansion in the franchise. With the exceptions of Pennsylvania, where the legal threshold was drastically reduced, and Massachusetts, where the eastern counties managed to stiffen the voting requirements, most former colonies moderately eased their legal restrictions. By 1790, roughly 60 to 70 percent of all adult white men had the right to vote (Keyssar 2000: 24). The process of democratization continued in the first half of the nineteenth century. Most of the original states dismantled their property qualifications between 1800 and 1825, and, except for Louisiana, no state admitted to the Union after 1790 introduced them. Even though paying taxes was often substituted for owning property as the requirement, the small size of the required tax (generally a minimal poll tax) as well as the extension of the vote to men who had served in the militia led to something close to universal male suffrage in most states (Williamson 1960, Chap. 14). In New York, for example, after taxpayers and militiamen were allowed to vote in 1821, the state's electorate for the assembly expanded from 78 to 90 percent (Williamson 1960: 195–204).

---

[9] In New York and Virginia the freehold qualification encompassed tenants holding the land through indefinite leases.

The antebellum expansion of the electorate can be traced back to a set of immediate factors: military mobilization, such as for the War of 1812, which led to an exchange of votes for army enrollment; the slavery conflict, which pushed Southern landowners in the 1840s and 1850s to enfranchise poor whites to form a solid coalition against blacks and Northerners; a decline in the relative numbers of freeholders and growth of other "middle-class" occupations, which required that legal conditions be changed to avoid a significant drop in the electorate; and, finally, growing party competition, which spurred some politicians to expand the franchise to mobilize new voters in their favor.

Nevertheless, the gradual enlargement of the electorate in the United States was ultimately made possible by variables that fall in line with our theoretical expectations. Equality of conditions (among the white population) remained stable (and higher than in other countries) at least until 1850. Whereas the top 1 percent of men held 29 percent of gross assets in the United States in 1860, the proportion was 61 percent in the United Kingdom in 1875 (Lindert 1991). Margo and Villaflor (1987) have shown that, between 1820 and 1850, the ratio between the wages of skilled and unskilled workers remained stable at around 1.5 in the Northeast, 2 in the Midwest and 1.9 in the South. In the same period, it shot up from 2 to 2.6 in England (Williamson 1991). Under those conditions, American politicians could rest assured about the marginal redistributive consequences of expanding the franchise.

Three key exceptions to the antebellum expansion of the franchise operate as counterfactuals showing that the level of equality and the considerable mobility generated by abundant frontier land lay behind the ease with which democracy was sustained and even expanded in the United States in the period. First, the resistance to abolishing slavery, and hence to granting citizenship to the poorest section of Southern society, mounted to the point of igniting a generalized war.

Second, the extension of the franchise came to a halt in those Northeastern areas experiencing an industrial revolution and the rapid formation of an urban proletariat. Massachusetts maintained taxpaying conditions that made sure that, on the eve of the Civil War, the proportion of enfranchised men remained similar to that at the time of independence (Williamson 1960: 195). In Rhode Island, where the preindependence freeholding electoral requirement remained in place, the growth of manufacturing caused the proportion of men who lacked the right to vote to double from less than one fourth in the 1770s to about two fifths in 1841.[10] Several reform attempts in the first third of the nineteenth century were rebuffed by a coalition of conservatives and landowners in control of the legislature. Eventually, widespread popular action to extend the franchise led to the emergence of a People's Convention in 1841 that, defying the constitutional authority of the existing legislature, granted the right to vote to all men, reapportioned the electoral districts and appointed a new governor. Shortly after, a military confrontation between the democratic movement and an alliance of landowners and urban businessmen led to the defeat of the former in the spring of 1842. Immediately afterward, new legislation was passed, easing the electoral restrictions although still disenfranchising close to one third of men, mostly workers and recently naturalized immigrants.

Finally, the limits of antebellum American democracy can also be seen in how the surge of unskilled immigrants since the mid-1840s stirred substantial political action to limit the immigrants' access to the ballot box. The Know-Nothing movement attracted about one million members and harvested considerable electoral support in 1854–56 under the banner of lengthy residence periods, literacy tests and systematic registration procedures. Although the movement often failed, it did succeed in getting strict registration procedures imposed in New York City and its county, literacy tests approved in Connecticut and Massachusetts and nonwhites in Oregon and propertyless whites in Georgia disenfranchised.

The Civil War temporarily made franchise conditions much more uniform and liberal across the country. The Reconstruction Act of 1867 imposed military rule in the South, with its end conditional on the Southern states' ratification of the Fourteenth Amendment, and approval of state constitutions guaranteeing blacks the right to vote. The removal of the last federal troops from the South in the mid-1870s, however, opened a period in which blacks were excluded from elections – through violence and fraud at first, and then through new legislation and state constitutional amendments. In a first wave of legislation between 1890 and 1895, the Southern states introduced the poll tax, complex registration procedures

---

[10] The distribution of the right to vote was clearly biased against urban districts. In Providence only one third of the adult men could vote. In rural areas, the franchise covered over 50 percent of adult men. District apportionment was also heavily weighed against cities. Providence held only 4 out of 72 seats in the General Assembly.

and the secret ballot, which de facto disenfranchised illiterate voters. In a second round of legislation, from 1898 to 1903, the literacy test and property requirements tightened the conditions for voting.

Racial motives were clearly behind the redefinition of the franchise. But purely economic or class considerations were also fundamental to the legal changes that swept the South at the turn of the twentieth century. As Kousser (1974) shows in detail, the introduction of exclusionary procedures was generally fought along class lines. The white landowning class, who controlled the black-belt counties, was interested in cheapening agricultural labor and minimizing taxes. Opposing the landowners were both white voters in uphill counties, where the agrarian structure was more equal and blacks remained a minority, and black representatives. To soften the opposition of poor white farmers, black-belt politicians often conceded special clauses (such as having fought in the Civil War oneself or being the son or grandson of someone who could vote before the war) to minimize the effects of the literacy test.

The introduction of restrictions devastated voter turnout among blacks and lower-class whites. By the mid-1900s, the percentage of registered black voters was below 10 percent in Alabama, Georgia, Louisiana, Mississippi and North Carolina and barely over that figure in South Carolina and Virginia (Kousser 1974, Table 2.3, p. 61). Overall turnout declined by at least half, to figures that ranged from 50 percent in North Carolina to about 15 percent in Mississippi. My own estimates, based on the ecological inference techniques developed by King (1997), indicate that turnout had declined to about 47 percent of white men and 9 percent of black men in the South (excluding Texas and Florida) in the presidential elections of 1908.[11]

The fall in voter turnout in the South had significant policy consequences. Spending on education was heavily biased against both blacks and poor whites. In North Carolina, in 1906–10, the expenditure was less than $1.80 per child for black and for poor white children, yet it was $5.36 per child for rich whites (Kousser 1980). Whereas in Mississippi state tax revenue totaled $4.30 per capita, in Ohio it equaled $16.29 – still two times larger than the former once we control for per capita income. Moreover, a wide set of rules, such as draconian vagrancy laws (subjecting anyone without a job to possible arrest) and laws giving landowners complete control

---

[11] The data on racial distributions are taken from the census of 1910. The results match Kousser's (1974) previous estimates, based on regression analysis, indicating declines in white turnout to around 50 percent and in black participation to less than 10 percent.

over their tenants' crops, were passed to cheapen the supply of labor and sustain the traditional Southern economy (Keyssar 2000). The structure of political participation that developed in the South also had repercussions on the construction of social policies at the federal level during the New Deal period. To sustain a cheap, non-unionized workforce, which was essential to the sharecropping system dominant in the South, Southern Democrats succeeded in defining the Old Age Insurance program of 1935 in restrictive terms that excluded nine tenths of black workers. Similarly, the Old Age Assistance program was tied to state financing and had no minimum benefit, and its management was based on considerable local administrative autonomy (Bensel 1984; Alston and Ferrie 1985; Quadagno 1988; Robertson 1989).

As shown in Figure 3.3, which plots the degree of formal restrictions across states in 1910, the exclusionary practices of the South were markedly different from the prevailing electoral rules in the rest of the Union. Replicating what was done for Switzerland, Figure 3.4 depicts the level of wage inequality, measured as the ratio of the salary of officials and managers to the wage of domestic servants in 1919, and the proportion of fixed capital, proxied by the percentage of farm population in 1919.[12] Electoral requirements were rare in the Midwest and the Plains. In many states, franchise conditions were so lax that, until the 1910s and early 1920s, the right to vote was automatically given to noncitizens who declared their intent to naturalize in the future. The lack of barriers to suffrage was undoubtedly related to the equality of their economic conditions. Whereas the ratio of the salary of officials and managers to the wage of domestic servants averaged almost 3.8 in the Southern states, it was just 2.5 in the Plains states.

In the industrial states in the North, wage dispersion was high, at least until the First World War. The ratio of the salary of managers to the wage of domestic servants was similar to that in the South: 3.7 in Illinois and Michigan; 3.8 in New Jersey, New York and Massachusetts; and 4.2 in Rhode Island. Moreover, inequality increased in this period. The ratio of unskilled workers' wages to the returns of all factors per laborer fell by 1.5 percent annually between 1870 and 1913 (O'Rourke and Williamson 1999). That widening income gap, driven by the arrival of about 25 million immigrants, naturally agitated public opinion, particularly the opinion of Northeastern urban elites, in favor of a more restrictive franchise.

---

[12] Both measures are calculated based on data provided by Leven (1925).

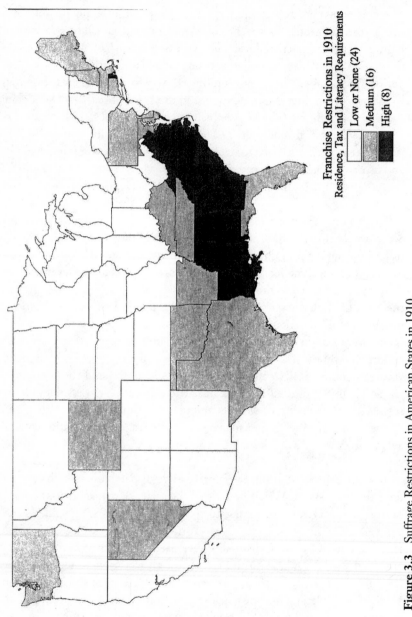

Figure 3.3   Suffrage Restrictions in American States in 1910.

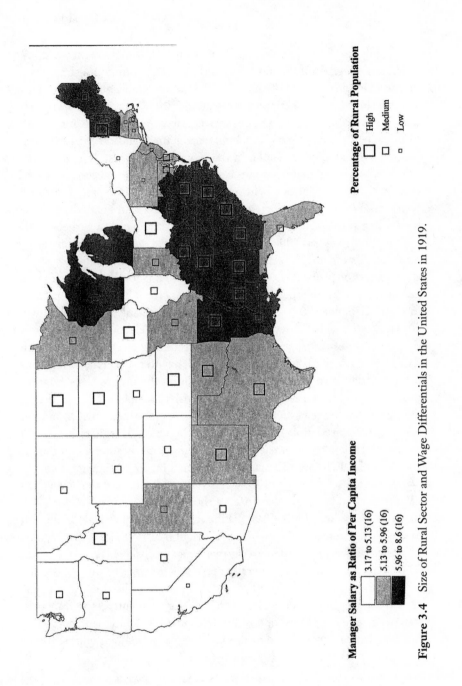

Manager Salary as Ratio of Per Capita Income

☐ 3.17 to 5.13 (16)

☐ 5.13 to 5.96 (16)

■ 5.96 to 8.6 (16)

Percentage of Rural Population

☐ High

☐ Medium

▫ Low

Figure 3.4 Size of Rural Sector and Wage Differentials in the United States in 1919.

Already in their discussion of the Fifteenth Amendment in 1869, Northern congressmen opposed extending the prohibition against voter discrimination by reason of race to include other conditions, such as place of birth, property ownership or level of education – their goal was to retain the states' power to exclude, if necessary, the poor and immigrants from the ballot box. In the postbellum period, the exclusion of paupers was approved in half a dozen states on the Northeastern coast. The introduction of a taxpaying qualification was attempted, with no success, in several constitutional conventions held in the 1880s. More sweeping and direct restrictive requirements, such as passing a literacy test, generally failed – they either were blocked by the Democratic constituencies or garnered only mild support (Keyssar 2000). Still, the progressive movement, animated by professionals and middle-class reformers, succeeded in introducing systematic registration procedures – the proportion of non-Southern counties with personal registration procedures rose from 30 percent in 1900 to 52 percent in 1930 (Kleppner 1987) – as well as diverse mechanisms, such as the use of city managers, to shelter local administrations from elections. The progressive drive against corruption was aimed at reducing electoral fraud. But it also implied a wish to discourage the turnout of voters who cast their ballots based on their own self-interest rather than on the progressives' conception of the public interest, and therefore a wish to temper the consequences of universal suffrage, which one contemporary reformer called, "another name for a licensed mobocracy."[13] The introduction of registration mechanisms had a depressive impact on turnout, particularly among immigrants and the poor. Electoral participation declined by 20 percentage points in non-Southern states between 1900 and 1925, and a third of the decline has been attributed to the introduction of those mechanisms (Kleppner 1982; Piven and Cloward 1988). Class distinctions seem to have been important in vote differentials. In the presidential election of 1908, for example, only 17 percent of foreign-born men (who were mostly unskilled) voted, whereas 78 percent of native men (generally more skilled) went to the polls in the Northeastern states.[14] In short, a widening income distribution encouraged the upper and middle classes in the North to curtail the franchise. But, partly due to political opposition from urban machines and partly due to a flourishing urban economy, both the threat posed by the immigrants

---

[13] Quoted in Kleppner (1982: 59).

[14] These estimates are again calculated using the method of ecological inference developed in King (1997).

Table 3.1. *Electoral Restrictions and Presidential Turnout in the United States in 1920*

Independent Variables	Level of Electoral Restrictions[a]	Turnout in 1920 Presidential Election
Constant	0.88	43.38
	(3.13)	(28.39)
Wage ratio in 1919[b]	−0.08	6.07
	(0.87)	(7.84)
Percentage of farming	−0.11	1.19*
population in 1919	(0.08)	(0.70)
Wage ratio*	0.04*	−0.49**
Farming population	(0.02)	(0.19)
Number of observations	48	48
R^2	0.421	0.473
Adjusted R^2	0.382	0.437

[a] Sum of residency, literacy and tax requirements. The index ranges from 0 to 6.
[b] Ratio of managers' salary to domestic service wages.
Estimation: Ordinary least squares.
Standard error in parenthesis.
** $p < 0.005$; * $p < 0.01$.

and the reaction of the upper classes to that threat were still much more subdued in the North than in the agrarian South.

To assess the extent to which both the type of assets and income inequality explain the extent of democracy, Table 3.1 displays the result of regressing on the ratio of managerial salaries to domestic service wages and the proportion of the farming population as well as their interaction of two dependent variables: the level of electoral restrictions in 1920 and the turnout in the presidential election of 1920. I have codified the extent of electoral restriction (years of residency, existence of a tax requirement and existence of a literacy test) on a scale of 0 to 6, following the information in Kousser (2000).[15] The first column shows that electoral restrictions are driven upward by the combination of growing wage dispersion and an agrarian economy. By contrast, electoral restrictions actually disappear in agrarian but highly equal economies. Likewise, in completely industrialized economies, the level of

---

[15] The coding is based on the sum of residency, literacy and tax requirements. Each requirement is scaled from 0 to 2. For the residency requirement, 2 is given to states requesting a minimum of 24 months of residency in the state. For literacy, the state scores 2 if there is a requirement, 0 otherwise. For tax, the state scores 2 if there is a statewide requirement, 1 if there is a local requirement and 0 if there is no requirement.

restrictions remains practically flat even when income inequality increases. Similar results are obtained for the level of turnout in the second column. Here the wage ratio is not statistically significant, and, as an independent variable, the proportion of rural population affects electoral participation marginally. The combination of both variables, however, has a substantial impact on turnout: the difference in the estimated turnout between, on the one hand, industrialized states or agrarian and equal areas and, on the other hand, unequal agrarian states, is over 40 percentage points.

Conclusions

This chapter has built, jointly with Chapter 2, a cumulative body of evidence that provides strong support for the theory developed earlier. The empirical strategy that has been followed includes the gathering of several types of evidence, both statistical and historical, across extensive periods of time. On the one hand, in Chapter 2, I analyzed transitions from and to democracy as well as the probability of revolutions and civil wars in two different samples of countries: one containing country data from 1950 to 1990 with direct measures of inequality; and a second one, from 1850 to 1980, using indirect measures, such as percentage of family farms, that, for the postwar period, are well correlated with the Gini index of income inequality. On the other hand, in this chapter I have examined more textured evidence for two countries, the United States and Switzerland, having substantial internal variation in levels of democratization in past centuries.

The econometric evidence marshaled in Chapter 2 confirms that, as pointed out by modernization theorists, there is a strong association between democratic stability and the level of per capita income. Still, the statistical results of the chapter lead us to conclude that per capita income is simply proxying for other (theoretically more robust) variables. First, the level of per capita income at which a democracy becomes consolidated has changed with the historical period under analysis: before 1940, 90 percent of those countries with per capita income above $4,000 (in constant prices of 1985) were democratic; after 1950, only 50 percent above that threshold were democratic.[16] To give just one example: Norway adopted universal suffrage with a per capita income of $1,500; in the postwar sample, the proportion of democratic countries in that range is less than 0.2. The same pattern can be found at the domestic level. Before 1830 extensive democratic

---

[16] For a more detailed discussion of the implications of this fact, see Boix and Stokes (2002).

Conclusions

practices prevailed only in the poorest cantons of Switzerland – the extension of suffrage was negatively correlated to wealth across the country.

The introduction and consolidation of democracies appears to be related mainly to the level of inequality and asset specificity in each country, even after conditioning on the preexisting political regime and using controls for country heterogeneity. Highly unequal countries remain primarily authoritarian, and, whenever they go through a democratic phase, they revert very quickly to dictatorial rule. Similarly, countries with a high proportion of immobile assets, such as agrarian wealth or oil fields, are unlikely to become democratic unless they enjoy a particularly equal distribution of income. The negative impact of oil and other fixed assets on democracy not only has the virtue of accommodating the paradox of wealthy dictatorships that haunts recent research on the development-democracy relationship. It also explains why the probability of having democratic transitions at high income levels in the postwar period is negative: countries that develop through industrialization and the corresponding emergence of nonspecific assets become democracies; the few countries that remain dictatorships despite considerable wealth are authoritarian precisely because of the type of wealth they have.

The nature and distribution of assets also match the historical evolutions of Switzerland and the United States. Democracy flourished practically unchallenged in the equal and agrarian Alpine cantons and Plains states. In contrast, in the American South and in the pre-nineteenth-century western cantons, the landowning elites restricted the franchise to themselves. With industrialization and the growth of financial centers, representative government was extended in the American Northeast and around the Swiss lakes despite relatively wide income differentials.

Finally, the joint interaction of asset specificity and inequality accounts for the outburst of political violence. Employing information culled for the last 150 years, I found that civil wars are likely events in societies with high levels of inequality and fixed assets, even after controlling for other variables such as per capita income, regime type, level of economic concentration, fuel exports and ethnic and religious fragmentation. Contrary to Marx's predictions, revolutions never happen in dynamic, growing societies. They take place in the "periphery" of the international economic system, where classes are locked in a zero-sum game.

4

Theoretical Extensions: Growth, Trade, Political Institutions

Using a rather simple set of assumptions, the first chapter shed light on the conditions that underlie different types of political regimes: the extent of inequality, the degree of capital mobility, the political resources of the classes or sectors involved in the struggle to determine the constitutional framework of the country, and, in part, uncertainty about political conditions. Chapters 2 and 3 then corroborated the validity of the theory through statistical and historical analysis.

In this chapter, I employ again the basic model of Chapter 1 to discuss its theoretical implications for two types of issues. In the first three sections, I examine how changes in the economy affect the chances of democracy. In the first section I find economic growth to be a necessary but not sufficient condition to generate a democratic outcome. The possibility that low taxes may spur faster economic growth may entice the poor to commit to moderate levels of redistribution. This should, in turn, reduce the wealthy's opposition to universal suffrage and hence facilitate the introduction of democracy. Still, the positive impact on democracy of potential growth hinges on the institutional capacity of the poor to abide by their promise to keep taxes low. This result sheds new light on the literature on the postwar consensus, which claims that the success of democracy in postwar Europe lay on striking a broad class compromise. While accepting the thrust of the argument, I show that its import is more limited than its defenders claim and that social pacts are necessary only to generate democratic outcomes in a rather constrained set of historical circumstances. In the second section, I briefly discuss how social mobility across classes may raise the likelihood of a democratic outcome. In the third section, I explore how trade openness and democracy are related. I show that both the optimistic and the pessimistic accounts scholars have presented about the effects of trade liberalization on democratic outcomes can be right. Whether or not higher trade openness fosters (or at least is associated with) democracy is ultimately a function of which factors or sectors are benefited or damaged by lower trade barriers.

Finally, in the fourth section I take up the much-debated issue of whether different constitutional arrangements have different effects on democratic stability. Holding the structural or economic parameters of the model constant, I consider how variations in electoral rules, the balance of power between the executive and the legislative branches and federalism may alter the chances of a democratic outcome. In opposition to most current theoretical work, I show that electoral rules and separation-of-power mechanisms do not generally alter the probability of a democratic success. By contrast, the decentralization of tax decisions, either through outright political separation or through the introduction of a confederate arrangement, may, under certain conditions, bolster the chances of democracy.

Economic Growth and Credible Commitment

Throughout the discussion in Chapter 1 on the conditions for democratization, I assumed a static economy, that is, an economy in which there was no present or future growth. I now explore how the occurrence of economic growth, either in the current period or in the future, may alter the likelihood of democracy. I find that, although equality of conditions and capital mobility are still central to the choice of political regime, the dynamic path of the economy can become important to the survival of democracy given certain institutional conditions.

Following Franzese's (1998) abridged rendition of Alesina and Rodrik's (1994) model of redistributive taxation, we can represent the distortionary impact of the tax rate τ on (savings and capital accumulation and therefore on) the growth rate γ as follows:

$$\gamma = \gamma(\tau); \text{with } \gamma' < 0, \gamma'' < 0 \tag{1}$$

That is, as the tax rate increases, the growth rate declines and does so at a faster pace as the tax rate becomes higher. (In the section on economic reform and democracy in Chapter 6, I examine the possibility that higher taxes may bolster the chances of a democratic regime through two channels: financing types of expenditure [public goods] that have a positive effect on the growth rate; and funding programs [mainly of human capital formation] that lead to a decline in income inequality and hence in the underlying redistributive tensions.)

131

In this dynamic model, with a given growth rate, we can represent the utility of any agent as:

$$U^i = \sum_{t=0}^{\infty} \frac{1}{(1+r)^t}(1+\gamma(\tau))^t \left[(1-\tau)k_j^i + \tau - \frac{\tau^2}{2}\right] \tag{2}$$

That is, the utility of any individual i in the dynamic path equals the present value of the net disposable income in each period conditional on the growth rate (itself affected by the tax rate).

Consider now how this changes the calculations of the agents involved in the choice of a constitutional regime. For the sake of simplicity, consider here two types of agents only, the wealthy and the poor, who weigh their gains over an infinite number of periods.[1]

The possibility of achieving higher growth rates, and a higher disposable income, alters, in the first place, the level of the tax rate. Since taxes affect growth negatively, the lower class may now be willing to reduce τ from the value it would take if only one period was played to maximize its welfare. The median voter, who belongs to the poor, would reduce τ to the level in which any losses in transfers accruing from that reduction would be more than compensated for by a faster growth rate. The decision to reduce τ would be, on the one hand, a function of the discount rate $\delta = 1/(1+r)$. For δ sufficiently close to unity, the incentives to reduce τ would be high. The tax rate would decrease, on the other hand, as its distortionary effects on the growth rate became steeper.[2]

These intertemporal calculations in turn affect the choice of political regime. More precisely, a downward shift in the tax rate only has consequences in the set of cases in which the wealthy are willing to impose a repressive regime, that is, whenever $\hat{y}_w^i < k_w^i - \rho^i$. For all other situations, that is, for those cases in which the wealthy do not have any incentive to engage in repression, and democracy is a foregone conclusion, the decision to reduce τ (relative to its one-shot value) to maximize growth would have economic consequences. But it would have no political effects since changing τ would not alter the calculations of agents on the regime to be established.

---

[1] To make the model more tractable, I also restrict their choice to two outcomes (democracy and dictatorship), with neither of the two classes uncertain about its opponent's political resources.

[2] This result runs parallel to Przeworski's (1985) analysis of the foundations of the material basis of consent of capitalism, where workers are shown to willingly moderate their wage demands to maximize the level of capital accumulation, the growth rate and future wages.

Whenever the constitutional regime is up for grabs, the poor weigh what they would get if τ was set at the level of the one-stage game and what they would get for a lower τ, $\tau^* < \tau$. That is, they compare what they would obtain without a tax reduction:

$$\delta^t(1 + \gamma(\tau))^t(y_p) \tag{3}$$

to what they obtain by lowering the tax to a level τ^* such that the wealthy agree to introduce democracy and the poor get:

$$\delta^t(1 + \gamma(\tau^*))^t(\widehat{y}_p^i) \tag{4}$$

Whenever the second expression (4) is higher, the poor would rather commit to a lower tax. In turn, the wealthy agree to a democracy whenever $\delta^t(1 + \gamma(\tau))^t \widehat{y}_w^i < \delta^t(1 + \gamma(\tau = 0))^t k_w^i - \rho < \delta^t(1 + \gamma(\tau^*))^t \widehat{y}_w^i$. Here $\widehat{y}_w^i$ denotes the after-tax income of the wealthy with a low tax τ^*.

Figure 4.1 describes the parameters of the game. The different tax rates are plotted in the horizontal axis. The payoffs under the different political regimes (authoritarian or democratic) for the two types of individuals (poor and wealthy) are plotted in the vertical axis. Under an authoritarian regime, there are no taxes and the income of neither the wealthy nor the poor changes since it is unaffected by either transfers or the distortionary consequences of taxes. Accordingly, it can be thought of as a reservation level, with the income of the wealthy equal to $\Delta y_w - \rho$ and the income of the poor equal to Δy_p, and represented by a straight line. The parameter Δ represents $\delta^t(1 + \gamma(\tau))^t$. Under a democracy, the income of the wealthy is $\Delta \widehat{y}_w$. The final disposable income declines with the tax as a result of transfers and the deadweight loss of the tax.

For a low tax rate, the disposable income of the wealthy in a democratic regime is higher than under an authoritarian system. For any tax rate higher than τ_A, however, $\delta^t(1 + \gamma(\tau^*))^t \widehat{y}_w^i < \delta^t(1 + \gamma(\tau))^t k_w^i - \rho$, which makes the wealthy better off under an authoritarian regime. In turn, the income of the poor under a democracy, $\Delta \widehat{y}_p$, takes the following form. For a low tax rate it declines relative to the initial level of income (a situation with no taxes) due to the distortionary effects of the tax on the growth rate, which are not fully compensated for by the transfer obtained from the rich. At tax rate τ_{D1}, the level of transfers pushes the final disposable income above the "reservation income" of the poor. Above the tax rate τ_{D2}, the fall in transfers (due to the fall in the disposable income of the wealthy) and the fall of the disposable income of the poor (due to the deadweight loss imposed by the tax) again reduces the poor's final disposable income below the pre-tax income.

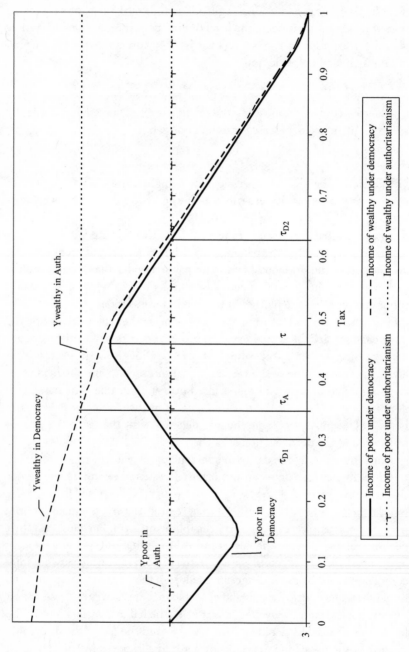

Figure 4.1 Economic Growth and Democratic Pacts.

The structure of payoffs of both social actors gives us the solution of the game. It is easy to see that, under a democratic regime and for a one- period game, the median voter would set the tax at τ. In that case, since the tax τ is higher than the repression cost ρ, the wealthy would not accept it. In an iterated game, however, a democratic outcome may become feasible. Both wealthy and poor share a common space, from τ_{D1} to τ_A, in which it is to the advantage of all to establish a democratic regime: the cost of repression there is higher than the net transfer for the wealthy; the poor, in turn, experience an increase relative to their "reservation income." Accordingly, if the game is repeated infinitely, and given a low discount rate, the poor can credibly commit to a tax marginally lower than τ_A to obtain a democratic transition.[3]

Again, besides the discount rate, the existence of a space where a democratic pact is feasible is a function of the level of repression costs and the distortionary impact of taxes. As in the basic model, a reduction in the cost of repression raises the disposable income of the wealthy in an authoritarian regime. Similarly, an increase in the distortionary effects of taxes over the growth rate speeds the fall of the post-tax post-transfer income of the wealthy under a democratic regime. In those two cases, and as represented in Figure 4.2, the threshold τ_A moves to the left of τ_{D1}. Democracy then becomes impossible because the poor and the wealthy do not share a range of tax rates that could convince both of them to move to democracy.

The introduction of growth considerations has a clear interest for our predictions of a democratic outcome. In economies in which poor individuals discount heavily, their incentives to promise nonpunitive taxes are relatively low and democracy is less likely. More importantly, the type of production structure and the corresponding growth rate in each society should lead to very different political outcomes. In economies where the productivity rate is relatively low, such as agrarian societies or economies based on rudimentary technologies, the possibility for sacrifices among the lower classes is almost nonexistent. Their discount rate would have to be extremely low for the lower classes to credibly commit to a low tax. In other words, with very low growth rates, the game between both sides of society just reproduces the zero-sum nature of the original model. Only very equal societies can successfully establish a democratic regime.

---

[3] Once more, this is not possible in a one-shot game since after commiting to τ_A and achieving a democratic transition, the poor would always have an incentive to set the tax rate equal to τ.

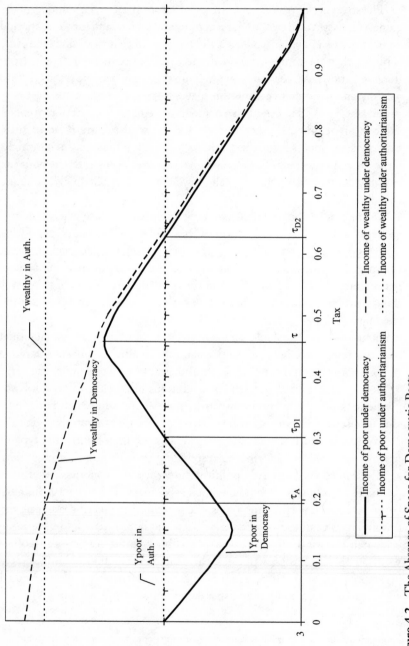

Figure 4.2 The Absence of Space for Democratic Pacts.

As growth rates become potentially higher, a temporal sacrifice for the sake of future gains becomes much more likely. Unless they are extremely myopic, the poorer segments of society, knowing that their income will be much higher in the future, now entertain the possibility of accepting a lower tax, prompting the moneyed classes to embrace democracy. Thus, industrialization, even if it leads (temporarily or even permanently) to a wider disparity of incomes, enhances the chances of a democratic regime. A democracy with low or moderate taxes can exist since workers and capitalists can more easily split total income in the future.

The Need for Credible Commitment

The benefits of a high growth rate constitute a necessary but not sufficient condition to boost the chances of democracy. The emergence of a democratic regime under conditions that would result in a dictatorship in a one-period game relies on the continuing coordination of poor and wealthy. It is only because the poor choose τ^* and forgo some immediate benefits that the rich find accepting a democratic regime to their advantage. Should the poor decide to impose a higher tax ($\tau > \tau^*$) once in office, the rich would shift back to a repressive strategy. Again, the poor decide to restrain themselves once they calculate that they are better off in a temporal path. Democratic equilibrium relies on the repeated interaction of both sides over an infinite number of draws.

The interest that the poor may have in following a self-restraining tax strategy would be undermined, however, if they lacked any sort of institution or organization to coordinate among themselves and comply with their promise. I have assumed throughout the discussion that the poor constitute a set of agents with infinite lives. This is clearly not the case. Once we allow for individuals with limited lives and thus with some uncertainty about whether they will still be alive in the next period, the equilibrium that results from successive iterations may well collapse. If the poor cannot credibly commit to a low-tax strategy in the future, there will be, in turn, no incentive for the rich to accept a democratic system. Accordingly, to sustain their commitment, workers need to be organized in institutions that constrain them to comply with their promises. Strong unions and parties that discipline voters and that, qua institutions, have a substantial interest in the welfare of future generations (their discount rate δ is, as it were, lower than that of an individual), increase the chances of democratic success.[4] Similarly, the presence of well-structured social-democratic forces rather than radical left-wing (that is, communist) parties should ease the transition to democracy.

Integrating (and Amending) the Literature on Postwar Consensus

This discussion accommodates one of the central insights of the literature on postwar consensus as stated in Przeworski and Wallerstein (1982) and, more recently, in Eichengreen (1996b). It also underlines recent work showing that broad social compacts have been central to successful transitions to the market economy in former communist regimes (Bresser Pereira, Maravall and Przeworski 1993).[5] The combination in postwar Europe of social peace and sustained growth can be seen as a result of there having been a set of institutions that bound capital and labor together to overcome what had been a very fragile political environment in most European countries in the interwar period. Domestic structural conditions in the late 1940s were not that different from those in the 1920s, yet no democratic breakdowns happened after World War II. The institutional arrangements that were put in place in several small economies in the mid-1930s, and then in Austria and in medium-size nations after the war, guaranteed the success of the capital–labor bargain that stabilized Europe in the third quarter of the twentieth century.

Nonetheless, the model developed so far challenges the conclusions of the institutionalist interpretation of the postwar consensus in one respect. According to this approach, institutions are *always* needed to sustain democratic peace and high growth rates. It should be apparent, however, that in this book institutions that lock in cooperative outcomes are necessary (to the success of democracy) in only one case: whenever both parties are balanced enough to fight over the constitutional regime. When the poor are too weak, no promise of moderation followed by an institutional arrangement would make the wealthy deviate from the authoritarian path. Similarly, when the working class is so powerful that the upper classes automatically

---

[4] This paragraph borrows from Franzese's analysis of time-inconsistency problems in the choice of welfare states (1998: 8) as well as from an animated discussion we had while sharing a pizza (in the United States, a better symbol than a cake of what political economy is all about).

[5] It can also put in a theoretical context the fact that, *ceteris paribus*, powerful yet moderate social-democratic parties have been important contributors to the success of a peaceful transition to democracy (Luebbert 1991).

decide to accept democracy, the poor have no incentive to commit to lower taxes to achieve a democratic regime. (Again, whether the poor may still be interested in a lower tax to boost the growth rate is a different matter.)

Institutions are beneficial therefore for what we may call "transitional" stages of political development. In the transition from a stage of development in which a powerful class of capitalists (or landowners) can hardly be challenged to one in which a growing middle class and increasingly well-organized lower class make democracy irresistible, societies may face a period of relatively balanced contenders, considerable turbulence and relative indeterminacy in political outcomes. In that scenario, the existence of institutional bargains may ease the transition to democracy. At medium levels of development democratic outcomes have been claimed to be empirically less predictable simply using measures of per capita income (Huntington and Domínguez 1975).[6] A similar pattern can be found for different levels of inequality. Democratic breakdowns are more likely in unequal societies. Transitions to democracy occur only in countries with low Gini indexes. By contrast, at medium levels of inequality the two types of transitions (from and to democracy) take place. If the model discussed here is right, we should find that the success of democracy at those intermediate levels is strongly tied to the presence of particular institutions, such as unions or churches, that facilitate a bargain among actors and monitor their commitment to it.

Finally, notice that my treatment of a dynamic bargain among different political agents explains why the (relative) breakdown of certain institutions, like corporatism, which was pervasive in Europe until the 1980s, should not threaten democracy or even welfare state arrangements, as some institutionalists claim. It should not do so precisely because, under the existing balance of power among groups, those institutions have now become superfluous to the maintenance of civil peace.[7]

---

[6] According to the data in Przeworski and Limongi (1997, Table 1), at medium levels of development, the yearly probabilities of transition to and from authoritarianism are relatively similar, at around 2 to 3 percent. This contrasts with the distribution of regime transition for other levels of development. In underdeveloped countries, most crises result in an authoritarian outcome: the probability of a transition from democracy to authoritarianism stands at 12 percent annually; the probability of a transition to democracy is only 0.6 percent. In turn, in developed countries, most transitions end in a democratic outcome.

[7] A similar point can be made about the fact that Eichengreen (1996b) and others cannot account for the economic performance and political success of the United States in the postwar period. Since they make that success conditional on the presence of a given set of institutions, the American case appears as an anomaly in their work. But it is *not* an

Social Mobility and Democracy

In the basic model, I have assumed that each individual has the same capital and therefore belongs to the same economic class for life.[8] Once we relax this assumption and we allow for some degree of interclass mobility, that is, for the possibility that an individual could change class or social status, the likelihood of a democratic regime increases.

To show how the existence of social or interclass mobility enters into the choice of political regime, let us denote the probability that any individual may be wealthy in each period t as p_w^i (with $p_{wt}^i \geqslant 0$). The distribution of p_w^i among individuals then summarizes the level and type of social mobility in a given population. A completely static or immobile society is one in which a set of individuals has $p_w^i = 1$ and is therefore wealthy all the time while the rest of society has a $p_w^i = 0$ and remains poor forever. This social structure was implicit in the basic model in Chapter 1. By contrast, an economy in which all individuals had the same probability of being wealthy would be an equal society. Although in each period only a part of the population would be wealthy (except if $p_w^i = 1$ for all), and thus there would always be economic differentiation, in expectation all individuals would have the same income. Given an infinite number of periods, or at least a sufficient number of periods to lead everybody to the same income by the end of the game, redistributive pressures would be mild at best and democracy would be in place permanently. In short, social mobility fosters democracy by easing social conflict.

The possibility of social or class mobility raises both a question and an insight. I briefly outline them here and then deal with them more thoroughly in later chapters. The question has to do with establishing what determines the emergence and sustainability of social mobility. In an economy characterized by a fixed amount of assets (be they land, or money or even the demand for educated people), it is not hard to see that those individuals who secure most of the wealth in the first round of the game (perhaps simply

anomaly once we restrict the need for institutions to a given set of circumstances. Several (alternative or complementary) explanations are possible to understand the American case: first, the balance of power is such that democracy is uncontestable; second, growth rates are high enough to lure the P segment into voting for lower taxes; third, and perhaps a more realistic explanation, turnout rates are low, and parties are weak, so that tax rates are close enough to the preferences of the average-income voter and political conflict is limited. Thus, institutional bargains of a European kind are not even entertained.

[8] Allowing for growth to occur leads to changes in capital but not in the relative position of actors (unless individuals experience different growth rates in their income).

as a result of luck) will be very unlikely to forgo it in the following round. They will rather try to block any future changes in the ownership of assets through political means. In short, they will be inclined to establish an authoritarian system to sustain their initial advantage. Thus, authoritarianism is not just a mechanism to limit the amount of redistribution through taxes. In a society with fixed resources, it is also a means to shape the distribution, among individuals, of the probability of being wealthy.[9]

By contrast, social mobility would be easier to sustain in an economy where assets grow – either in a spatial sense (as in frontier societies that allow the currently poor to move to still-unoccupied lands) or in a temporal sense (as a result of productivity gains). A growing pool of assets is likely to raise the probability of all becoming rich ($p_w^i \to 1$ for all) and thus increases the chances of achieving social peace and democracy.

Income Volatility and Taxes in a Democracy

The introduction of social mobility generates an additional insight into the final tax rate that voters approve. On the one hand, if there is complete social mobility, the tax rate should be zero. As shown earlier, given the same probability $p_w^i = 1$ for all individuals, and excluding the possibility that the wealthy would distort mobility for future periods, an economy has full equality of income (over a sufficiently extended period of time). Since taxes have some distortionary effects on output, and given that all individuals have the same final income, none of them has an incentive to vote for any (redistributive) tax.

On the other hand, social mobility may spur taxes in the following manner. Assume that all individuals in the economy are risk averse. As is well known, with risk aversion, individuals suffer a fall in their welfare whenever their income, although unchanged on average, increases in its variability. Since social mobility increases income volatility, it results in a loss in utility among voters. A straightforward way to minimize that welfare loss consists in voting for a tax to transfer income from the wealthy to the poor in each period. By equalizing after-tax after-transfer income, all voters wipe out any income volatility and maximize their welfare.

To sum up, as class or income mobility increases, both income equality and the likelihood of a democratic outcome rise. Yet taxes and transfers do not necessarily decline or disappear. They may well go up – precisely to

[9] This question is discussed in the third section of Chapter 6.

neutralize the higher levels of risk that are associated with an open economy. I will return to this finding to explore the political sources of the structure of the public sector in Chapter 5. There I will show that the size of the state is explained by political demands rooted in both the nature and the distribution of assets as well as in the existence of economic risk.

Trade and Democracy

Predictions among researchers about the impact of trade openness on the choice of political regime are extremely mixed. Trade liberalization has been seen as generally incompatible with democracy because it imposes considerable losses on key economic sectors. Trade openness has recently been pursued by authoritarian regimes and by policy makers who are sufficiently isolated from public opinion (Haggard 1990; Fernandez and Rodrik 1991; Stokes 1999). Yet the fact that trade and democratic regimes were hand in hand in such disparate societies as nineteenth-century England and ancient Greece has not gone unnoticed by some authors (Rogowski 1989).

In the context of the model employed in this book, it is straightforward to show that trade openness affects the choice of a political regime conditional on what factors or sectors are abundant in the economy. To see the varying effects of trade, assume two types of countries, A and B. In both countries, there are two types of agents: skilled workers, who use a relatively well-developed technology and therefore earn high wages, and unskilled workers, who operate a primitive technology and receive low wages. The countries vary, however, in the distribution of types. Whereas in country A skilled workers are the scarce factor (and unskilled workers are the abundant factor), in country B skilled workers constitute the abundant factor. In country A, unskilled workers, who are the abundant factor, clearly benefit from an expansion in trade. As the demand for unskilled workers goes up, their wages increase and wage compression takes place. With inequality declining, previous redistributive tensions ease and the probability of democracy goes up. In country B, by contrast, any decline in tariffs hurts the poor class. As the demand for skilled workers, who are the abundant factor, increases, wage dispersion goes up, political pressures for redistribution grow and an authoritarian backlash becomes more likely.

To sum up, trade affects the choice of political regime depending on the distribution of factors in a given economy in the following way. Whenever the poor class constitutes the abundant factor in the economy, trade openness leads to a process of wage compression that eases redistributive

142

tensions and hence favors the introduction of democracy – Britain in the nineteenth century. Conversely, whenever the poor are the scarce factor in the economy, trade openness reduces their income, intensifies income inequality and makes authoritarianism more likely – most Latin American countries for a substantial part of the twentieth century.

Notice that, by the same logic, labor outflows (of unskilled workers) will drive domestic wages up, diminish distributional tensions in the countries of origin, and therefore precede a democratic transition. In Denmark, Norway and Sweden, strong migratory flows to the United States led to a significant reduction in wage inequality in the late nineteenth century (O'Rourke and Williamson 1999), probably contributing to the peaceful extension of the franchise in the early decades of the twentieth century.[10]

Political Institutions

In line with the recent formal literature that stresses the equilibrium-inducing role of institutions, the presumption among many researchers on democratization has been that a "well-written" constitution contributes in a substantial manner to securing democratic stability. However, formal models have only been used to account for varying equilibria within already well-established democratic regimes. No explicit formal theories have been advanced to link certain institutions to the stability of regime. That institutions matter has been explored only empirically: witness the relatively recent debates on the impact of presidentialism (Shugart and Carey 1992; Linz and Valenzuela 1994) or the much older one on proportional representation and the breakdown of democracies in interwar Europe (Hermens 1941). Moreover, all the institutionalist models that stress the stabilizing consequences of certain constitutional structures, such as, say, proportional representation, have generally been developed without modeling the pre-existing social and economic conditions in which institutions operate.

By contrast, given the relatively tight model employed in this book about the underlying distribution of interests and therefore about the rational course of behavior for all actors, it is possible here to explore, more precisely, how different institutional arrangements may affect the calculations of different actors and therefore the chances of democratic consolidation.

---

[10] A similar process may be taking place one hundred years later – as a substantial number of Mexican and Central American laborers migrate to the United States, the chances of a democratic outcome increase in their countries of origin.

Broadly speaking, whether institutions play any role in ensuring democratic outcomes depends mainly on whether they modify the underlying balance of power among any of the contending parties. If they do not, that is, if they are what may tentatively be called "weak" institutions, they have no influence on the stability of democracy. Weak institutions are simply those rules employed to aggregate preferences. If individuals have any incentives (deriving from the preexisting distribution of resources) to impose a dictatorship or to engage in rebellious action against the government, no change in the way preferences are aggregated can bridle the interests of the social agents. Take again the two-classes model developed in Chapter 1. If the wealthy impose constitutional rules that deliver a policy outcome unacceptable to the median voter, the poor will reject them. Anticipating the reaction of the poor, the wealthy will then have to employ some force to sustain the institutional system working to their advantage. In short, any "weak" institutions that are out of equilibrium with the underlying distribution of interests cannot survive in the long run. Electoral rules are the most obvious case of a weak institution. Similarly, and with the exception of one circumstance that I spell out at the end of the subsection on the separation of powers, the choice of presidentialism or parliamentarism does not modify the chances of democratic survival.

By contrast, if institutions do alter the balance of power among political actors, that is, if they are "strong" institutions, they may affect the chances of having a stable democracy. A strong institution is any structure that reallocates resources among agents (for example, by giving the control of the police to the winner) and therefore reinforces (or weakens) a preexisting distribution of endowments. As will be discussed later, a politically decentralized structure is likely to be the closest arrangement to a strong institution.

Voting Mechanisms and the Case of Proportional Representation

Under both majoritarian and proportional representation systems, and given a one-dimensional policy space (around taxes) and well-behaved utility functions, the solution will always be, on average, the tax rate preferred by the median voter.[11] In a plurality system, politicians will converge on the

---

[11] The identity between the solutions under both systems is based on the assumption that electoral districting is such that the national median voter at election time remains so in parliament (through the voter's representative). This is what happens if the whole country is a single district (as in the case of direct presidential elections or pure proportional representation elections). The assumption is broken if electoral districts are carved in such a

median voter's ideal point (Shepsle 1991). In a proportional representation system, although politicians may not converge on the median voter, actual policy (in parliament) will depend on the median parliamentarian (Laver and Schofield 1990). It is also safe to predict that the median parliamentarian will be close to the median voter (Huber and Powell 1994). Accordingly, the stability of a democratic regime is not fundamentally affected by the electoral system in place.[12]

Table 4.1 shows some evidence on the minimal effect of electoral systems. Disaggregated by type of electoral system, it indicates the total number of annual observations of democracy, the total number of cases of democratic breakdown and the probability of democratic breakdown (calculated as the ratio of the latter to the former). It also reports, in parenthesis, the same data for parliamentary democracies – this is done to explore the claim made by the literature that democratic stability is particularly jeopardized by the combination of presidentialism and a legislature elected through proportional representation (Mainwaring 1993). For each type of electoral regime, the results are tabulated by level of per capita income in U.S. dollars of 1985, the average level of urbanization and industrialization, the percentage of family farms and Gini index. For the first three indicators, the period of analysis extends from the last third of the nineteenth century to the end of the twentieth century. For the last indicator, the sample of observations encompasses the period from 1950 to 1990.[13]

Overall, proportional representation regimes exhibit a slightly higher proportion of democratic breakdowns than majoritarian systems – but, as I show later, in Table 4.5, the difference is not statistically significant. Nor do the consequences of choosing different electoral laws exhibit any clear

---

way that the median voter ceases to be decisive in the policy-making process. This latter possibility, which can also take place by manufacturing majorities through a certain type of separation of powers, is discussed in more detail in the next subsection and in note 16 below.

[12] Part of the literature mistakenly models the aggregation of preferences in majoritarian and proportional representation parliaments through different mechanisms. Whereas they apply the median voter theorem to Westminster types of parliaments, they maintain that proportional representation structures are more conducive to the representation of minorities (which are left aside in a plurality system). This conflates, however, the institution of proportional representation with the practice of consociationalism – the former may be a necessary condition, but it is never a sufficient one, for the latter to exist. Once a parliament has been chosen, and in the one-dimensional policy space I am assuming, the median voter's bliss point constitutes an equilibrium in both systems.

[13] For a complete description of the data set, see Chapter 2.

Table 4.1. *Observed Probability of Democratic Breakdown by Electoral Laws and Economic Conditions, 1850–1990*

	Legislature Elected Through Proportional Representation (In parenthesis: Parliamentarian regimes)			Legislature Elected Through Majoritarian Laws (In parenthesis: Parliamentarian regimes)		
	Annual Observations	Observed Failures	Probability of Breakdown[a] (%)	Annual Observations	Observed Failures	Probability of Breakdown[a] (%)
Per capita income US $ of 1985 (1850–1990)						
0–1,999	270 (99)	11 (2)	4.07 (2.02)	194 (160)	14 (10)	7.22 (6.25)
2,000–3,999	505 (315)	14 (6)	2.77 (1.90)	325 (292)	2 (2)	0.62 (0.68)
4,000–5,999	247 (189)	3 (0)	1.21 (0.00)	184 (144)	0 (0)	0.00 (0.00)
6,000–7,999	177 (138)	1 (0)	0.56 (0.00)	110 (98)	0 (0)	0.00 (0.00)
8,000 and over	305 (299)	0 (0)	0.00 (0.00)	220 (150)	0 (0)	0.00 (0.00)
TOTAL	1,504 (1,040)	29 (8)	1.93 (0.77)	1,033 (844)	16 (12)	1.55 (1.42)
Average percentage of nonagricultural and of urban population (1850–1980)						
0–24.9	64 (38)	6 (2)	9.38 (5.26)	86 (59)	5 (4)	5.81 (6.78)
25–49.9	450 (297)	10 (3)	2.22 (1.01)	334 (272)	6 (4)	1.80 (1.47)
50–74.9	427 (358)	5 (2)	1.17 (0.59)	299 (234)	0 (0)	0.00 (0.00)
75–100	7 (7)	0 (0)	0.00 (0.00)	73 (67)	0 (0)	0.00 (0.00)
TOTAL	948 (680)	21 (7)	2.22 (1.03)	792 (632)	11 (8)	1.39 (1.27)
Percentage of family farms (1850–1980)						
0–24.9	271 (30)	16 (1)	5.90 (3.33)	70 (70)	2 (2)	2.86 (2.86)
25–49.9	326 (255)	8 (4)	2.45 (1.57)	345 (319)	10 (8)	2.90 (2.51)
50–74.9	259 (235)	4 (2)	1.54 (0.85)	469 (316)	2 (1)	0.43 (0.32)
75–100	277 (277)	1 (1)	0.36 (0.36)	16 (16)	0 (0)	0.00 (0.00)
TOTAL	1,133 (797)	29 (8)	2.56 (1.00)	900 (721)	14 (11)	1.56 (1.53)
Gini index (1950–90)						
Above 50 percent	44 (10)	2 (0)	4.55 (0.00)	14 (14)	0 (0)	0.00 (0.00)
35–50 percent	175 (88)	4 (0)	2.29 (0.00)	176 (127)	3 (2)	1.70 (1.57)
Below 35 percent	111 (111)	0 (0)	0.00 (0.00)	137 (100)	0 (0)	0.00 (0.00)
TOTAL	330 (209)	6 (0)	1.81 (0.00)	327 (241)	3 (2)	0.92 (0.83)

[a] Ratio of observed failures to annual observations.

pattern when we separate the observations according to per capita income. At low levels of per capita income, the probability of democratic breakdown in majoritarian systems is twice as high as in proportional representation regimes. Yet between $2,000 and $4,000 the impact of each electoral regime is the opposite: proportional representation fares worse. At higher levels of per capita income, the type of electoral system has no impact on the survival of a democracy. Electoral systems do not differ in any systematic manner conditional on the structure of rural property and the underlying structure of economic assets. Finally, for high and middle levels of inequality, the proportion of democratic crises is higher in proportional representation systems – the result, however, seems to be driven by presidentialism. For low levels of inequality, the type of electoral law does not matter. In short, the electoral system seems to be mostly irrelevant for regime stability.

From a theoretical point of view, different mechanisms of representation may have a (slight) effect on the survival of democracies. Under proportional representation, the median parliamentarian (representing the median voter) does not vary over time. As a result, $\tau^* = \tau_m$ every year, where τ_m denotes the tax set up by the median voter. By contrast, in non–proportional representation systems, and given partial divergence among competing parties (Alesina and Rosenthal 1995), τ^* will equal τ_m *on average* over time but will vary from election to election. Now, if either the wealthy or the poor are risk averse, the introduction of proportional representation should make a democracy more stable since the agents' expected utility will not be inherently diminished by repeated swings in the outcome.

Separation of Powers

Consider now how a change in the constitutional balance of power between the different branches of government may affect the likelihood of having a stable democracy. For the sake of the discussion we may distinguish between two ideal types of constitutional arrangements: a presidential system, in which the executive and the legislative branches are elected separately and have, broadly speaking, equal weight in the policy-making process;[14] and a parliamentary system, in which the executive is ultimately accountable to parliament.

In a parliamentary system, the only parameter that is relevant is the position of the median voter (and how she is affected by the underlying

---

[14] For the sake of simplicity I assume that there are only two separate branches.

distribution and nature of assets). Parliamentary systems vary with the electoral system in place and the distribution of preferences across districts. These parameters have already been discussed in the previous subsection.

The Consequences of Presidentialism in a Democratic Constitution   In presidentialism, if the ideal policy points of both the president and the median representative in congress are identical, the system of separation of powers is in itself irrelevant to the generation of democratic stability – although it may have many other effects, such as inducing greater political accountability, reducing rent-seeking behavior and so on. Either the ideal point of both policy makers is acceptable to the social agents (that is, the wealthy are willing to accept democracy and the poor have no incentive to revolt) or it is not. If the branches of government differ in their bliss points, then the issue at hand is which of the two branches ultimately determines policy and then what is the relationship between that policy decision and the policy preferred by the median voter. If the branch that has the final say over taxes (either because it has veto power, as in the case of the executive, or because it can override the veto, as in the case of congress) coincides with the country's median voter, the system is democratic.

Separation of Powers as a Mechanism to Limit Democracy   If, as a result of the constitutional structure, the branch that eventually sets the tax rate does not coincide with the preferences of the majority of the population, one cannot speak of a democratic outcome in a strict sense.[15] This type of constitutional arrangement simply masks the existence of either an authoritarian or a semidemocratic regime. Consider these two possibilities in turn.

The system of separation of powers has often been employed to block a democratic outcome. Most of the constitutional debates of nineteenth-century Europe hinged on the proper division of powers between the monarch and parliament. Whereas European liberals defended the primacy of parliament, conservative parties defended a constitutional system in which the executive, in office either by right of birth or, at most, "chosen" only by the wealthy, had the right to veto legislation and could not be overridden by parliament. In Wilhelmine Germany, for example, the Kaiser was

[15] In the basic model of Chapter 1, with two classes and the median voter belonging to the poor, this type of constitutional arrangement would lead to $\tau = 0$, which is equal to the solution in an authoritarian regime.

not obligated to accept the budgetary proposals of the universally elected Reichstag. The dominance of a nonelective executive was founded on the resources and incentives of the monarchy and its allies. The political regime in place was without any doubt an authoritarian one.

A variation of this example is one in which the system of separation of powers is established to partially distort a democratic regime. This is achieved by putting each constitutional branch in the hands of one social sector and requiring that final legislation be the result of a compromise between the two policy makers. Under this arrangement, if the presidency were controlled by, say, the wealthy, congress would represent the remaining classes. (A similar case would be a bicameral system in which the upper and the lower houses represented different economic interests.) The tax rate is then set within the range delimited by the tax preferred by each sector. This semidemocratic regime can be self-sustaining only under the following conditions. First, the poor must find the semidemocratic regime preferable to engaging in revolutionary action. Second, the semidemocracy must be cheaper than either an authoritarian regime or a democracy for the wealthy to establish. For this to happen, the costs of repression borne by the rich must fall more rapidly than the increase in the tax rate that takes place from going from an authoritarian regime (where $\tau = 0$) to a semidemocratic regime (where τ is positive). If the repression costs remain the same or drop only slightly after shifting to a semidemocratic regime, the wealthy have no incentive to introduce semiopen institutions: they now pay taxes and bear the costs of violence against the poor.

The combination of both conditions (leading to semidemocracy as a rational strategy) happens very occasionally. It must be for this reason that, historically, the introduction of a "balanced" system of separation of powers has been established as a means to tie, in a credible manner, different classes (say, the wealthy and the middle class) to a political regime that excludes other social sectors (such as the working class) – this was the standard procedure in nineteenth-century Europe.[16]

---

[16] Notice that a system with gerrymandering or with a biased representation of a particular sector (say, rural districts) in parliament achieves the same result. It displaces the median parliamentarian or policy maker away from the median voter toward an ideal policy that is more acceptable to those with enough political resources to alter the democratic game. But again, the stability of that solution depends on the structural parameters of the game. As inequality decreases or as the resources of the underrepresented increase, there should be a constitutional change directed at realigning the median policy maker with the median voter.

Notice that a very similar mechanism is employed to sustain a federal structure, which involves tackling an analogous problem of credible commitment, in this case among different territories. A federal system consists in a pact in which each subnational unit relinquishes its tax and regulatory sovereignty to the federation in exchange for a guarantee that it will be allowed to retain both substantial control over its interests and enough power to affect the decisions of the whole polity. To secure the federal pact, that is, to avoid that any of the parties to the compact may be expropriated by the rest, the decision-making power is effectively split in a way such that different territories are given control over different branches of government or legislative chambers. Since policies must always be compromised, none of the territories (especially the most populous) can empty the federal pact of its true value. I will come back to this solution later.

In short, the system of separation of powers generally matches a particular distribution of economic assets and political resources (again, the particular case of federalism is treated later). Different ways to organize the relationship between presidents and parliaments cannot prop up or reduce the likelihood of a democratic outcome, unless those different institutions come with particular resources (such as the control of the army by the president or monarch) that alter the powers of its holders. Any prolonged crises that are attributed to conflicts between powers (and, by derivation, to the system of separation of powers) are in fact the result of underlying parameters, that is, of conflicts between agents at the societal level. Or, to put it the other way around, disputes between powers that do not lead to a political crisis (such as a civil war, revolution or democratic breakdown) take place in countries with a level of equality and a degree of asset specificity such that the stability of the current constitutional regime is guaranteed.

Presidentialism and the Rising Stakes of the Political Game   In an influential essay in the neoinstitutionalist literature, Linz (1994) has argued exhaustively that, other things being equal, a presidential system is more likely to jeopardize democracy than a parliamentarian regime. First, since presidential elections consist in the selection of only one candidate, they generate a sharp zero-sum game in which the winner takes all and the loser is effectively deprived of all power and even of the capacity to influence legislation that parliamentary structures afford to opposition parties. Accordingly, minorities are excluded from the political game, and any kind of consensual or consociational politics is impossible to develop. With a substantial part of the population shut out from government, the legitimacy of the constitutional regime should be fragile. Second, presidential elections, by excessively raising the stakes of the electoral and political game, increase the level of political tension among candidates and of ideological polarization among electors. Finally, and related, in a presidential system political conflict becomes so intense that the odds that any of the candidates will behave "properly" during the electoral campaign or will accept the outcome after the election will be very low. Electoral manipulation will be pervasive, the loser will contest the results and the winner will immediately develop all sorts of illegal strategies to secure reelection in the future. Perhaps more importantly, the institution of the presidency endows its incumbent with substantial resources to capture all sorts of societal resources and to enlarge his power base.[17]

As I discuss shortly, neither of the two first claims, that is, that presidentialism generates a system of "majoritarian" politics and that it polarizes both the party system and the electorate, seems to be inherent to presidential regimes. On the contrary, both of them can equally occur in parliamentarian constitutions. As for the third argument, it is flawed if we unconditionally apply it to all presidential regimes. Still, it is valid in certain cases: given a particular type and distribution of assets, notably when capital is fixed and unequally distributed, presidential regimes may be more likely than parliamentarian regimes to engender a dynamic of conflict resulting in a coup.

To examine whether presidential systems intensify the power of the majority, let us start by assuming a simple scenario with two candidates running for presidential office and each one of them promising a certain tax rate (and its associated level of redistribution). In a world with full information (and full participation), they should converge on the same ideal policy – the one preferred by the median voter. No matter who wins, the tax preferred by the median voter will be implemented. In other words, the majority of the population effectively imposes its preferred solution over the minority. Now, this scenario and the political solution it generates are in no way unique or specific to presidentialism. In parliamentary regimes the same result will occur, for precisely the same reasons. Parliament will end up voting for the median voter tax, that is, the tax preferred by the majority. Notice also

---

[17] Linz (1994) also lists several other defective characteristics of presidentialism, such as the presence of a "dual democratic legitimacy" (of both the executive and congress) and the temporal rigidity of the presidential mandate. For the purposes of the discussion that follows, these defects can be subsumed in the three problems already listed.

that whether or not the tax approved under a presidential system will be a politically stable equilibrium, that is, whether the net taxpayers will accept the democratic outcome, will depend on the underlying distribution and specificity of assets. If taxes are too high (and the political resources at the disposal of the wealthy considerable), a coup will take place. Otherwise, democracy will remain in place. But, once more, that result in no way differs from what will happen under parliamentarianism: whether or not the tax rate voted by parliament will be acceptable to the net taxpayers will simply be a function of the structural characteristics of the economy and the distribution of political resources. In short, both regimes are characterized by the same results given the same underlying distribution of preferences.[18]

A similar result emerges when we examine the (central) claim that presidentialism breeds higher levels of political polarization than parliamentarianism. For a process of polarization to take place in the electoral game, always keeping the distribution of voters' preferences constant, there must be either uncertainty about the distribution of voters or reputational problems among politicians. In those circumstances, either the contenders actually diverge in their policy promises or the winner, once in office, deviates from her electoral promise (to vote τ_m) and imposes a different tax. If the tax is excessive as a result of the victory of a left-wing candidate, the likelihood of a coup will increase. But here again, there seems to be nothing inherent in a presidential regime that increases the level of uncertainty or the credibility problems in the political arena (vis-à-vis a parliamentarian constitution). If presidentialism is indeed threatening to democracy, the sources of the threat have to lie elsewhere.

Consider the nature of the third claim about the dangers of presidentialism – namely, that it raises the stakes of the game to such a level and gives presidents so much power that it jeopardizes the electoral process. A presidential system probably makes it easier for a single politician to behave as a harsh rent seeker and, in fact, from the perspective of the owners of the assets, as a bandit, than does a parliamentarian regime. Once she has won the presidential election, the incumbent, unencumbered by the opposition and being only partly (or discontinuously) accountable to all the other branches of government, may successfully seize most assets of the nation and impose a dictatorship. Correspondingly, to preempt the actions of the president,

---

[18] As indicated in note 12 above for majoritarian and proportional representation systems, it would be a mistake to model the aggregation of preferences and the positioning of candidates differently in parliamentarian and presidential regimes.

the congressional opposition or the armed forces, supposedly behaving as a moderating power, may decide to launch a coup. By contrast, parliamentary regimes make it harder for a prime minister to turn into a tyrant. Cabinets resemble company boards, and the prime minister is tied by the coalition of policy makers that has put him in office.

Still, the capacity of the president to accumulate power and properties is conditional on the nature of assets in the country. As discussed in Chapter 1, whenever assets are very country specific (and probably concentrated in a few hands), the threat of expropriation looms large. In those circumstances, a strong executive simply gives its holder an excellent opportunity to grab those assets. But if assets are mobile or spread out among the population, presidential systems are, no matter how powerful they make the executive branch, harmless.

If this discussion is correct, we should expect presidential systems to be especially dangerous in underdeveloped countries with highly concentrated economies (in one sector or product) yet to exhibit similar rates of democratic breakdown to parliamentarian regimes in developed or equal economies. In Table 4.2 I display the number of annual observations of presidentialism and parliamentarism and the number and frequency of democratic breakdowns by per capita income, percentage of family farms, proportion of urbanized and manufacturing population, and income inequality. As already noticed in Przeworski et al. (2000), presidential systems have a higher rate of failure on average – an annual probability of democratic breakdowns of 4 percent against an annual probability of 1 percent in parliamentarian regimes. The distribution of presidential breakdowns is, however, skewed. For low and medium level of per capita income, presidential regimes have a slightly higher annual rate of failure than parliamentarian regimes – the very high rate for the segment between $4,000 and $6,000 picks up the wave of authoritarian coups in the Latin American subcontinent in the 1960s. Yet for high levels of development, there have been no failures under a presidential system.[19] A similar result follows for the average level of urbanization and industrialization. At low levels of industrialization, presidential regimes are more brittle than parliamentarian systems. But their stability becomes similar as they become more industrialized. For different levels of inequality, the results are strongly in line with

---

[19] For previous empirical work on the differential performance of parliamentarian and presidential systems, see Przeworski et al. (2000) and, for non-OECD nations, Stepan and Skach (1994).

Table 4.2. Observed Probability of Democratic Breakdown by Presidentialism and Economic Conditions, 1850–1990

	Presidential Regimes			Parliamentary Regimes		
	Annual Observations	Observed Failures	Probability of Breakdown[a] (%)	Annual Observations	Observed Failures	Probability of Breakdown[a] (%)
Per capita income US $ of 1985 (1850–1990)						
0–1,999	223	15	6.73	284	15	5.28
2,000–3,999	242	9	3.72	611	8	1.31
4,000–5,999	98	3	3.06	333	0	0.00
6,000–7,999	51	1	1.96	236	0	0.00
8,000 and over	76	0	0.00	449	0	0.00
TOTAL	690	28	4.06	1,913	23	1.20
Average percentage of nonagricultural and of urban population (1850–1980)						
0–24.9	58	5	8.62	111	9	7.50
25–49.9	267	13	4.87	562	7	1.23
50–74.9	159	4	2.29	570	2	0.35
75–100	6	0	0.00	74	0	0.00
TOTAL	490	22	4.30	1,374	18	1.30
Percentage of family farms (1850–1980)						
0–24.9	303	20	6.60	109	4	3.67
25–49.9	97	6	6.19	588	14	2.38
50–74.9	177	3	1.69	555	3	0.54
75–100	0	0	0.00	293	1	0.34
TOTAL	577	29	5.03	1,545	22	1.42
Gini index (1950–90)						
Above 50 percent	38	3	7.89	24	0	0.00
35–50 percent	138	4	2.90	221	2	0.90
Below 35 percent	37	0	0.00	219	0	0.00
TOTAL	213	7	3.29	464	2	0.43

[a] Ratio of observed failures to annual observations.

our predictions. In countries with a small number of family farms, the rate of democratic breakdown is over 6 percent among presidential regimes – twice the rate in parliamentarian systems. In countries with a Gini index above 50 percent, presidential systems have an annual failure rate close to 8 percent. In moderately unequal states, the rate of democratic breakdown is close to 3 percent. By contrast, the number of crises in parliamentarian regimes is small. The type of executive ceases to have any impact in equal economies.

In short, adopting presidentialism is probably a bad idea in sub-Saharan Africa and a substantial part of Latin America. It may also be an error in postsocialist economies rich in natural resources. But it should have no deleterious consequences in developed economies with relative equality and highly mobile assets.

Political Decentralization

It is only in exceptional cases that a given income distribution at the national level is uniformly distributed across that territory. On the contrary, in most countries, each region or subterritory displays a different income distribution than the general distribution for the whole territory. (This necessarily means that *at least one* of the subterritories is more equal than the whole territory. It could also be the case that *all* the subterritories are internally equal – but that, due to their differences in average income, the general income distribution is unequal.)

In those circumstances, that is, whenever the distribution of assets at the national and subnational level is different, the chances that a democracy will prosper will vary with the level of tax centralization across subterritories. If income differences are high at the national level and there is a completely centralized tax system, redistributive tensions will be important and democracy will be contested by the populations concentrated in the richer areas. By contrast, redistributive tensions and therefore the occurrence of authoritarianism will decline if political and fiscal sovereignty is devolved to smaller units. With political decentralization, the chances of securing a democratic outcome will increase in those subterritories whose income distribution is more equal than the one at the general level. Logically, decentralization does not lead to more democracy in subterritories whose inequality is equal to or bigger than that in the territory as a whole.

The survival of relatively democratic regimes in the Northeastern and Western areas of the United States in the nineteenth century was dependant

155

on the maintenance of a de facto confederate system – where states enjoyed nearly complete sovereignty over taxes and the legality of slavery. With a very centralized state, those units would have been affected by the harsh inequalities of the South and a democratic system would have been harder to sustain.[20]

Table 4.3 shows the likelihood of breakdown of federal and nonfederal systems, tabulated by the same economic indicators employed in previous tables. It also reports the same data for federal and nonfederal systems that are parliamentarian between parentheses. By level of development, the evidence on the consequences of federalism is mixed: federal systems work much better under $4,000 yet their performance is clearly worse between $4,000 and $8,000. In terms of property and income distribution and level of industrialization, the results clearly show federalism to be a better mechanism to provide democratic stability. Federal systems have fewer transitions to authoritarianism for all levels of industrialization and urbanization. At high levels of inequality (a Gini above 50 percent or few family farms), the probability of breakdown is slightly higher in federal systems. For moderate inequality, democratic breakdowns fluctuate around 2 to 3 percent in nonfederal countries, yet decline quickly under a federal constitution. The most important result, however, is that once we exclude those cases with a presidential system, federalism clearly behaves as a democratic stabilizer. Almost no federal parliamentarian system has experienced a democratic breakdown. By contrast, nonfederal countries are much more affected by noninstitutional conditions: they become stable only when inequality and asset specificity decline.

This insight applies equally well to the international order. Differences in per capita income across the globe are truly extraordinary. Figure 4.3 shows the distribution of world population according to average per capita income of the country where they lived in 1993 – the figure simply reproduces estimates made by Milanovic (1999). The world Gini index was 66 percent in that year (Milanovic 1999) – equal to the maximum value in the data set collected by Deininger and Squire (1996) for national Gini indexes. In a unified country, such wide disparities of income would engender harsh political tensions and lead to the introduction of an authoritarian system or to violent revolutionary explosions. According to the estimations undertaken earlier, in Chapter 2, in a country with a Gini index of 66 percent,

---

[20] Indeed, it was the assertion of the federal government, under an administration opposed to slavery, that led to the American civil war.

Table 4.3. Observed Probability of Democratic Breakdown by Federalism and Economic Conditions, 1850–1990

	Nonfederal Systems (In parenthesis: Parliamentarian regimes)			Federal Systems (In parenthesis: Parliamentarian regimes)		
	Annual Observations	Observed Failures	Probability of Breakdown[a] (%)	Annual Observations	Observed Failures	Probability of Breakdown[a] (%)
Per capita income US $ of 1985 (1850–1990)						
0–1,999	397 (203)	25 (13)	6.30 (6.40)	97 (67)	3 (0)	3.09 (0.00)
2,000–3,999	690 (518)	14 (7)	2.03 (1.35)	163 (93)	3 (1)	1.84 (1.08)
4,000–5,999	283 (246)	1 (0)	0.35 (0.00)	148 (87)	2 (0)	1.35 (0.00)
6,000–7,999	191 (173)	0 (0)	0.00 (0.00)	96 (63)	1 (0)	1.04 (0.00)
8,000 and over	340 (316)	0 (0)	0.00 (0.00)	185 (133)	0 (0)	0.00 (0.00)
TOTAL	1,901 (1,456)	40 (20)	2.10 (1.37)	689 (443)	9 (1)	1.30 (0.23)
Average percentage of nonagricultural and of urban population (1850–1980)						
0–24.9	125 (78)	11 (7)	8.80 (8.97)	39 (28)	1 (0)	2.56 (0.00)
25–49.9	599 (426)	18 (7)	3.01 (1.64)	234 (143)	1 (0)	0.43 (0.00)
50–74.9	447 (377)	1 (1)	0.22 (0.27)	284 (195)	5 (1)	1.76 (0.51)
75–100	63 (63)	0 (0)	0.00 (0.00)	17 (11)	0 (0)	0.00 (0.00)
TOTAL	1,234 (944)	30 (15)	2.43 (1.59)	574 (377)	7 (1)	1.22 (0.27)
Percentage of family farms (1850–1980)						
0–24.9	340 (109)	18 (4)	5.29 (3.67)	69 (0)	5 (0)	7.25 (0.00)
25–49.9	575 (485)	16 (11)	2.78 (2.27)	96 (89)	2 (1)	2.08 (1.12)
50–74.9	299 (266)	5 (3)	1.67 (1.13)	429 (285)	1 (0)	0.23 (0.00)
75–100	236 (236)	1 (1)	0.42 (0.42)	57 (57)	0 (0)	0.00 (0.00)
TOTAL	1,450 (1,096)	40 (19)	2.76 (1.73)	651 (431)	8 (1)	1.25 (0.23)
Gini index (1950–90)						
Above 50 percent	47 (24)	2 (0)	4.26 (0.00)	15 (0)	1 (0)	6.67 (0.00)
35–50 percent	270 (165)	6 (2)	2.22 (1.21)	89 (63)	0 (0)	0.00 (0.00)
Below 35 percent	162 (151)	0 (0)	0.00 (0.00)	93 (67)	0 (0)	0.00 (0.00)
TOTAL	479 (340)	8 (2)	1.67 (0.59)	197 (123)	1 (0)	0.51 (0.00)

[a] Ratio of observed failures to annual observations.

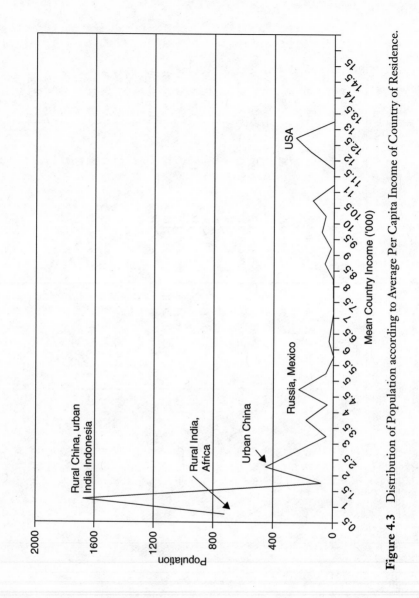

Figure 4.3 Distribution of Population according to Average Per Capita Income of Country of Residence.

Table 4.4. *Regional Gini Coefficients in 1993*
(Distribution of Persons by $PPP Income Per Capita)

Africa	47.2
Asia	61.8
Eastern Europe and Former Soviet Union	46.4
Latin America and Caribbean	55.6
Western Europe, North America and Oceania	36.6

Note: The regional Gini index is calculated by treating each individual equally – simply as an inhabitant of that region.
Source: Milanovic (1999: 19).

the annual probability of a transition to democracy is 0 and the annual probability of an authoritarian coup is 0.76.[21] By contrast, today's system of separate nations makes sure that the "South" does not effectively impose redistributive mechanisms on the "North." The lack of truly unified supranational institutions in fact secures the maintenance of stable democracies in the developed world as well as in certain developing countries. If all countries were to unite under a single political authority, democracy, which appears to be sustainable in separate countries with different income levels (provided each one of them is internally homogeneous and politically independent), would simply collapse.

Notice that, by the same logic, the regional or continental distribution of income should be a good predictor of the chances of building supranational democratic bodies in each area. Table 4.4 displays the Gini index for several regions in the world in 1993 – data are again taken from Milanovic (1999). The level of income inequality ranges from a Gini of 61.8 in Asia to a Gini index of 36.6 in the joint area of Western Europe, North America and Oceania. It is clear why Western Europe has been the only region where there has been a sustained process of political integration in the last four decades.

Political Institutions and Democratic Stability

To test the potential impact of different constitutional frameworks on democratic stability, both alone and conditional on the type and distribution of assets, Table 4.5 reports the likelihood of transitions from democracy

---

[21] The estimation is done by equating per capita income to the 1993 world average income of $3,100.

Table 4.5. *Annual Probability of a Democratic Breakdown as a Function of Constitutional Structures, 1950–90*

	Model 1	Model 2	Model 3	Model 4
Constant	−1.098*	−1.337**	−1.195**	−0.859
	(0.576)	(0.494)	(0.489)	(0.654)
Per capita income	−0.448**	−0.103*	−0.309***	−0.406***
(in thousand $)	(0.178)	(0.054)	(0.078)	(0.203)
Proportional representation [a]	0.015			−0.177
	(0.331)			(0.403)
Proportional representation*	0.270			0.292
Per capita income	(0.182)			(0.205)
Parliamentarism [b]		−0.040		0.067
		(0.278)		(0.307)
Parliamentarism*		−0.168*		−0.174*
Per capita income		(0.099)		(0.100)
Federalism [c]			−0.666**	−0.774**
			(0.316)	(0.361)
Federalism*			0.225***	0.191*
Per capita income			(0.086)	(0.107)
Religious fractionalization [d]	−0.448	−0.247	−0.003	−0.614
	(0.461)	(0.458)	(0.434)	(0.492)
Ethnic fractionalization [e]	0.783*	0.740**	0.650*	0.946**
	(0.403)	(0.370)	(0.351)	(0.424)
Log-likelihood	−145.09	−146.18	−151.13	−138.82
Prob > Chi-square	0.0000	0.0000	0.0000	0.0000
Pseudo R^2	0.1941	0.2048	0.1956	0.2289
Number of observations	1615	1618	1633	1615

[a] Dummy variable. Proportional Representation = 1.
[b] Dummy variable. Parliamentarism = 1.
[c] Dummy variable. Federalism = 1.
[d] Level of religious fractionalization, measured as a Hirsch-Herfindhal index of fractionalization based on the data on religious membership in LaPorta et al. (1998).
[e] Level of ethnic fractionalization, measured through an index built by LaPorta et al. (1998) by averaging five different sources in Easterly and Levine (1997).
Estimation: Probit model.
Standard errors in parenthesis.
***$p < 0.01$; **$p < 0.05$; *$p < 0.01$.

into authoritarianism for parliamentarism, electoral systems and federal arrangements for the period 1950–90. Parliamentarism is a dummy variable coded 0 for the presence of presidential systems. Proportional representation is also a dichotomous variable that takes the value of 1 if the electoral

Table 4.6. *Annual Predicted Probability of Democratic Breakdown by Type of Constitution, 1950–90*

A. Predicted Probability of Democratic Breakdown by Type of Executive and Per Capita Income [a]

	Per Capita Income (1985 $)					
	1,000	3,000	5,000	7,000	9,000	11,000
Parliamentary regime	0.060	0.018	0.004	0.001	0.000	0.000
Presidential regime	0.089	0.060	0.039	0.025	0.015	0.009

B. Predicted Probability of Democratic Breakdown by Territorial Structure and Per Capita Income [b]

	Per Capita Income (1985 $)					
	1,000	3,000	5,000	7,000	9,000	11,000
Federal	0.043	0.030	0.020	0.013	0.008	0.005
Nonfederal	0.101	0.029	0.006	0.001	0.000	0.000

[a] Simulation based on Table 4.5, Model 1. All other variables are set at their median value.
[b] Simulation based on Table 4.5, Model 2. All other variables are set at their median value.

system is based on proportional representation. They have been built based on Cox (1997), IDEA (1997), Linz and Valenzuela (1994), Shugart and Carey (1992) and the Keesing's Contemporary Archives. Federalism is also a dichotomous variable taken from Downes (2000). To maximize the number of observations, I have first employed a model with per capita income only. I employ other explanatory variables later.

In Table 4.5, Model 1 shows that neither the coefficient for proportional representation alone nor the interaction with per capita income is significant. In turn, Model 2 indicates that, although presidential regimes alone have no statistically significant impact on the stability of democratic regimes, the coefficient of presidentialism interacted with development is significant. A correct interpretation of the results requires the simulation of the joint effect of development, presidentialism and their interaction. This is done in Table 4.6.A, which shows that for countries with a per capita income of $1,000, the probability of a democratic breakdown is 9 percent if there is a presidential regime versus 6 percent in a parliamentarian regime. For a per capita income of over $10,000 the likelihood of a democratic breakdown is practically zero under both regimes.

Model 3 in Table 4.5 tests the impact of federalism. Again, a simulation (in Table 4.6.B) shows that at very low levels of development (less than $2,000), unitary democracies are twice as likely to collapse as federal democracies. But the rates of democratic breakdown converge very quickly above that level of per capita income.[22]

Table 4.7 extends the same analysis to the period 1850 to 1980 interacting the type of constitution with the percentage of family farms and with the index of occupational diversification, that is, the average of nonagricultural population and urban population. Again, a proper understanding of the effect of different institutional systems requires its simulation, which is reported in Table 4.8. Except for low levels of family farms and urbanization, where proportional representation seems to stabilize democracies, the type of electoral system has no impact on the probability of democratic breakdown (Table 4.8.A).

The type of executive has a small impact on the stability of democracies. For the lowest levels of family farms and urbanization, parliamentarian democracies turn out to be more fragile. Otherwise, presidential regimes exhibit a higher rate of authoritarian transitions, particularly at medium levels of industrialization and urbanization (Table 4.8.B). These results contradict in part our theoretical expectations. Notice, however, that the higher level of democratic breakdowns among parliamentarian regimes in countries with a small percentage of family farms is driven by the observations before 1945. Once we regress the same model on post–World War II observations, presidential regimes are more conducive to authoritarianism in unequal and preindustrial societies.

Finally, the probability of a democratic breakdown is about twice as high in unitary systems than in federal systems for unequal economies. Federalism acts even more strongly to reduce authoritarian coups in agrarian societies (Table 4.8.C).

Independence and Federalism

Since both the territorial dimension and organization of a nation seem to affect the type and stability of its political regime, I turn now to explore, on the one hand, the conditions that lead to the choice of either a confederate arrangement or a system of sovereign nations (granting tax independence to their members) and, on the other hand, how the creation of a system of

---

[22] The interaction of ethnic fragmentation with each institutional arrangement generates statistically insignificant coefficients. These results, which are not shown here, seem to put into question the idea that proportional representation and federalism may be better adapted to cope with ethnic representation.

Political Institutions

Table 4.7. *Annual Probability of a Democratic Breakdown as a Function of Constitutional Structures, 1850–1980*

	Model 1	Model 2	Model 3
Constant	0.672	−1.043***	−0.314
	(0.680)	(0.352)	(0.290)
Percentage of family farms[a]	−0.033**	−0.012**	−0.014***
	(0.013)	(0.006)	(0.005)
Index of occupational diversification[b]	−0.044***	−0.009~~~	−0.031~~~
	(0.014)	(0.008)	(0.007)
Proportional representation[c]	−1.589**		
	(0.755)		
Proportional representation* Percentage of family farms	0.020~~~		
	(0.014)		
Proportional representation* Index of occupational diversification	0.031**		
	(0.016)		
Parliamentarism[d]		0.629~~~	
		(0.501)	
Parliamentarism* Percentage of family farms		−0.004~~~	
		(0.009)	
Parliamentarism* Index of occupational diversification		−0.020*	
		(0.011)	
Federalism[e]			−1.353**
			(0.679)
Federalism* Percentage of family farms			−0.011~~~
			(0.009)
Federalism* Index of occupational diversification			0.043***
			(0.014)
Log-likelihood	−131.43	−158.01	−147.59
Prob > Chi-square	0.0000	0.0000	0.0000
Pseudo R^2	0.1567	0.1461	0.1659
Number of observations	1755	1840	1823

[a] Area of family farms as a percentage of the total area of holdings. *Source:* Vanhanen (1997).
[b] Arithmetic mean of percentage of nonagricultural population and percentage of urban population. Urban population is defined as population living in cities of 20,000 or more inhabitants. *Source:* Vanhanen (1997).
[c] Dummy variable. Proportional Representation = 1.
[d] Dummy variable. Parliamentarism = 1.
[e] Dummy variable. Federalism = 1.
Estimation: Probit model
Standard errors in parenthesis.
*** $p < 0.01$; ** $p < 0.05$; * $p < 0.01$
~~~ $p < 0.01$ in joint test of interactive terms and its components.

Table 4.8. *Annual Predicted Probability of Democratic Breakdown by Type of Constitution, 1850–1980*

A. Predicted Probability of Democratic Breakdown by Electoral System and Economic Conditions[a]

	Percentage of Family Farms					
	0	20	40	60	80	100
Proportional representation	0.10	0.06	0.04	0.02	0.01	0.00
Majoritarian	0.33	0.13	0.04	0.01	0.00	0.00
	Mean Percentage of Nonagricultural Population and Urban Population					
	0	20	40	60	80	100
Proportional representation	0.10	0.06	0.03	0.02	0.01	0.00
Majoritarian	0.43	0.14	0.03	0.00	0.00	0.00

B. Predicted Probability of Democratic Breakdown by Type of Executive and Economic Conditions[b]

	Percentage of Family Farms					
	0	20	40	60	80	100
Parliamentary regime	0.13	0.07	0.04	0.02	0.01	0.00
Presidential regime	0.10	0.07	0.04	0.02	0.01	0.01
	Mean Percentage of Nonagricultural Population and Urban Population					
	0	20	40	60	80	100
Parliamentary regime	0.21	0.08	0.02	0.01	0.00	0.00
Presidential regime	0.09	0.06	0.04	0.03	0.02	0.01

C. Predicted Probability of Democratic Breakdown by Territorial Structure and Economic Conditions[c]

	Percentage of Family Farms					
	0	20	40	60	80	100
Federal	0.08	0.03	0.01	0.00	0.00	0.00
Nonfederal	0.14	0.08	0.05	0.03	0.01	0.01
	Mean Percentage of Nonagricultural Population and Urban Population					
	0	20	40	60	80	100
Federal	0.01	0.02	0.03	0.05	0.09	0.13
Nonfederal	0.25	0.10	0.03	0.01	0.00	0.00

[a] Simulation based on Table 4.7, Model 1. All other variables are set at their median value.
[b] Simulation based on Table 4.7, Model 2. All other variables are set at their median value.
[c] Simulation based on Table 4.7, Model 3. All other variables are set at their median value.

independent or loosely tied countries in a given area actually expands the range of democratic outcomes. To do so, I discuss these questions with a model in which there are only three choices – authoritarianism, democracy and independence – in the first part of this subsection. I then take up the possibility of federal arrangements in the second half of this subsection.

The Choice of Independence To endogenize the choice of political regime and the size of a country as a joint decision, Figure 4.4 depicts an independence game with two regions or countries (whether they are regions or countries depends on the status quo – a unified state or an already separated system), A and B.[23] Each region has two types of voters, wealthy and poor. In region A, the median voter is a wealthy individual. In region B, the poor constitute the majority of the population. In a unified country formed by the two regions, the poor are the majority of the population. In the first stage of the game, the wealthy in region A decide whether or not to support independence (already in place if A is a sovereign state). If they decide to go for independence, the poor in region B must decide whether to acquiesce to independence or to engage in armed opposition (to prevent the split or to conquer region A) – whether they can succeed is (as in Chapter 1) a probabilistic event. If the wealthy decide to accept a unified state, they have, in turn, to choose the type of regime. At this point, the set of decisions mirrors the basic model in Chapter 1. The wealthy can either go for democracy or authoritarianism, and the poor can react to the latter by revolting or acquiescing.

Besides the distribution of wealth across social sectors (as well as the level of asset specificity), three parameters determine the decision of each agent: π, or the trade losses suffered from separation; ρ^d, or the costs of repression in a unified state borne by the wealthy; and ρ^i, or the costs of separating (or, alternatively, of maintaining an independent state) sustained by the wealthy. For the sake of simplicity, assume that the costs of separation

---

[23] This analysis builds upon recent theories of political integration developed by Alesina and Spolaore (1997) and Bolton and Roland (1997), among others. (Bolton, Roland and Spolaore [1996] offer a nonformal survey of these theories.) In line with Alesina and Spolaore (1997), I allow for variation in the type of political regime (democratic or authoritarian) governing each country – something that is not explored in Bolton and Roland (1997). In turn, I follow the latter in linking the political conflicts over the size of nations to differences in income distribution at the national and subnational levels. Finally, I depart from both in that I examine the joint choice of political regime and the size of country.

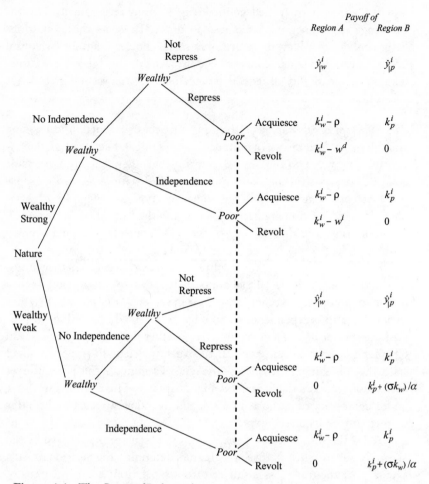

Figure 4.4 The Game of Independence.

ρ^i include the trade losses π. As before, the costs of repression can be either high or low (ρ^j_d and ρ^i_j with $j = h, l$). Again, whereas the wealthy know the costs, the poor can assess them only with some uncertainty.

The solutions mirror the basic model, but the possibility of democracy increases substantially (particularly in region A and, depending on the distribution of types, probably in region B too). For sufficiently low levels of inequality and asset specificity, leading to $\widehat{y}^i_w > k^i_w - \rho^i_l > k^i_w - \rho^d_l$, the wealthy accept a unified state (or in fact acquiesce to a process of political integration to realize trade gains) and a democratic regime. For low,

166

but not sufficiently low, levels of inequality and asset specificity, the solution depends on how costly independence is when compared to domestic repression. Whenever the costs of independence and domestic repression are both high and larger than the tax rate, that is, $\widehat{y}_w^i > k_w^i - \rho_h^i = k_w^i - \rho_h^d$, the wealthy accept a unitary democratic state. If the costs of separation or repression differ, then the solution adopted by the wealthy differs correspondingly. For $k_w^i - \rho_l^d > \widehat{y}_w^i > k_w^i - \rho_h^i$, the wealthy pursue an authoritarian strategy: authoritarianism is cheaper than the tax rate under a democracy and independence is the most expensive strategy. As noted in Chapter 1, the poor acquiesce to the repression since they calculate that, for such low levels of inequality, the costs to the rich must be low. For the reverse situation, that is, $k_w^i - \rho_l^i > \widehat{y}_w^i > k_w^i - \rho_h^d$, the wealthy embrace independence.[24] Two factors determine the corresponding costs of domestic repression and separation. As trade losses increase, the chances of separation decline; or, to put it in a way closer to the existing literature on political integration, as the level of economic integration rises at the world level, the wealthier regions have a higher incentive to split from the poorer areas. But the status quo (that is, the starting point) matters as well. Independence is more easily defended than achieved. Nations aspiring to independence have to exert more effort than already independent nations to succeed in achieving full political sovereignty. It is harder for Catalonia to become independent than for Portugal to remain free.

As the levels of inequality and asset specificity increase, the cost of taxation becomes higher under democracy than under any other alternative, that is, $k_w^i - \rho_h^d \lessgtr k_w^i - \rho_h^i > \widehat{y}_w^i$. If the poor region has no incentive to revolt,[25] the wealthy choose either an authoritarian solution or an independence strategy depending on which one is cheaper. Once the poor region gains from opposing the repressive or independence strategy of the rich region, war is unavoidable. If the costs of domestic repression are low, the wealthy will impose an authoritarian regime. If the costs of independence are low, a separation strategy will prevail. In both cases, even if the poor occasionally revolt, the wealthy will eventually prevail. As discussed in Chapter 1, if the repression costs are high, the wealthy will choose a mixed strategy between a unitary democracy, independence and authoritarianism to minimize the revolutionary impulses of the poor.

---

[24] If $k_w^i - \rho_l^d = k_w^i - \rho_l^i > \widehat{y}_w^i$, the wealthy are indifferent between independence and authoritarianism.

[25] This happens if $q\left(k_B^i + \sigma k_A^i\right) < k_B^i$.

Asset Specificity and Independence   Recent empirical work on the causes of secession has confirmed the higher propensity of wealthier regions to secede – at least within postsocialist countries (Treisman 1997; Hale 2000). Still, independence movements have also tended to run strongly in regions that, although exhibiting an average per capita income lower than the country to which they belong, are well endowed with natural resources. What may be called the Scottish paradox, the Norwegian resistance to the process of European integration and, more generally and more extremely, most of the decolonization process of the 1960s do not disconfirm, however, the model of the book. The likelihood to secede is positively correlated with the country specificity of assets. As discussed in the context of sectoral models of politics in Chapter 1, landowners and farmers are prone to bear high taxes at the hands of both industrialists and laborers, precisely as a result of the immobility of their assets. Likewise, any area with highly region-specific assets should expect to suffer confiscatory measures at the hands of the median voter located in less asset-specific parts of the country (or metropolis). The inhabitants (or at least the elites) of the area with fixed resources, such as oil, diamonds or copper, will be likely to launch independence movements to block the process of transfer to either other regions of the country or the metropolis – even if, again, their average income is lower than the average income of the metropolis.

Federalism   So far I have examined the origins of different territorial systems by looking at a choice between separation, or complete tax autonomy, and a unitary state. A question that remains to be considered is the extent to which the intermediate system of federalism, in which a fraction of the tax rate is decided by each region or subterritory, may enhance democracy.

For a federation to be a viable alternative two conditions must be met. On the one hand, both the wealthy and the poor, who now can choose between independence, an authoritarian regime, a federal democracy and a unitary democracy, must find a federal arrangement to their advantage. Generally speaking, the wealthy regions will support a federal constitution if the sum of the tax in a federal regime and the police costs of maintaining this system (lower than those borne either to maintain an authoritarian system or to separate, but higher than the zero costs of a full unitary democracy in which the median voter belongs to the poor region) is lower than both the tax in a unified democracy and the costs of domestic repression and independence. If the latter are lower, the wealthy nation will again choose to establish an authoritarian regime or to become a separate state. If the cost of maintaining a federal system wipes out the reduction in taxation that comes from having a federal arrangement, the wealthy region will embrace a unitary democracy. The poor regions will in turn concede a federal system if, unable to impose a unitary democracy (or to revolt and expropriate from the rich), they are better off than under independence.

On the other hand, a federation can bolster the likelihood of a democratic outcome only if it is based on conditions or institutions that credibly secure the autonomy of each state against the confiscatory temptation of the rest of the country. There are at least three mechanisms that reinforce the stability of a federal pact. First, the strength of federal arrangements increases with the number (and balanced resources) of federated states: with a multiplicity of roughly equal members, none of them will be able to impose its will over the rest of the federation. Second, federal institutions ease redistributive tensions only if their subunits are endowed with enough political or military resources (in the form of a national guard, police, and so on) to sustain the federal or confederate arrangement they entered. Finally, and for reasons pointed out earlier in the discussion on separation of powers, successful federations rely on a bicameral system where equally important chambers represent different territories differently. With each chamber securing partial control over political resources and with political decisions requiring their joint consent, all subnational units can have relative confidence in their ability to preserve their sovereignty in the future. The wealthy regions are able to impose a cap on the amount of redistribution. The poor regions know that there is a floor to the flow of transfers. Otherwise, that is, without any effective barriers to block the complete merger of separate nations, it would always be in the interest of the poorer regions to reestablish a unitary tax system to secure net transfers to them. Anticipating the weakness of a de jure but not de facto federal system, the wealthy regions would then struggle to become truly independent if that were at all possible.[26]

---

[26] Notice that this explains why in relatively decentralized systems, where federal safeguards are weak, there are sustained nationalist movements and recurrent political conflict. This is the case of Spain, where there is no chamber organized along territorial lines that truly secures the rights of autonomous communities against the center – the Senate is completely subordinated to the lower house. The regions that may be threatened by a reversion to centralism substitute credible federal institutions for the constant mobilization of resources and people against the center. In other words, nationalist movements are the reverse side of the threat posed by unchecked centralist politicians.

Conclusions

This chapter has extended the basic model presented in Chapter 1 in two directions. In its first three sections, it has relaxed the economic assumptions that underlie the theoretical model to introduce dynamics of (aggregate) growth, (differential rates of) social mobility and trade. The possibility of lowering taxes to spur higher growth rates opens up some space for a deal between contending social sectors to establish a democratic regime in exchange for a reduction in the level of fiscal pressure. This pact, however, is relevant only under two conditions: first, in situations in which neither of the two sides can impose its most preferred solution; second, whenever the parties in contention have the institutional capacity to credibly commit to such a deal. Social mobility also raises the likelihood of a democratic outcome in a more straightforward manner. Since increasing rates of social mobility tend to equalize the income of individuals over time, conflict over the distribution of resources declines and a democratic regime becomes acceptable to all. Finally, trade has conflicting effects on the stability of political regimes: whenever it compresses income differentials, by rewarding labor-abundant economies, democracy becomes easier to establish. By contrast, in capital- or land-abundant countries, trade openness leads to more inequality and hence more political clashes.

The last section of the chapter explores, instead, the extent to which designing different institutional settings can raise the chances of democratic consolidation. To date, neoinstitutionalists have explored the potential beneficial effects of proportional representation, parliamentarism or federalism without controlling for the distribution of interests and the levels of political mobilization in the countries under study. Yet the consequences of institutions can be determined only in the context of a fully specified model, that is, a model where preferences are described (and then allowed to vary for different types of constitutional designs). The results that follow from taking this integrated approach certainly deflate the expectations of the institutionalist literature. Proportional representation does not seem to foster democratic consolidation over any other electoral rule. Presidentialism may reduce the chances of democratization, but only under certain conditions (an economy with concentrated fixed assets) and for reasons not fully considered in the literature – it bolsters the rent-seeking capacity of politicians. Federalism, and particularly a system of sovereign nations, appears as the best solution to political conflict: as wealthy nations split or establish credible safeguards from poor areas, the chances of democracy increase.

170

5

Democracy and the Public Sector

As explored in detail in the previous chapters, the choice of political institutions is driven by their consequences in the distribution of income among citizens of the regime. Knowing that each political regime is a particular mechanism to aggregate the preferences of individuals for the ideal distribution of economic assets in a given society, all political actors develop appropriate strategies to secure their most favorable political regime, that is, the one that maximizes their welfare. The least well-off individuals support a democracy, since it gives them a chance to establish redistributive mechanisms to their advantage. By contrast, well-off citizens, who would have to bear a net loss of income under a democracy, support a constitutional structure in which only they can vote.

If the choice of a political regime is a function of its distributive implications, then the corresponding economic consequences and fiscal arrangements that come with a democracy and an authoritarian regime must differ. Under an authoritarian system, where all or a substantial part of the electorate is excluded from the decision-making process, the size of the public sector should remain small. By contrast, after a transition to democracy shifts the position of the median voter toward the lower side of the income distribution, the level of taxes and public spending should increase, in line with the model of optimal taxation presented in Chapter 1. Still, the size and structure of the public sector in a democracy are characterized by two additional traits. First, precisely because inequality is relatively low in a democratic regime, the extent of publicly enforced redistribution (derived from income differences) remains moderate, at least compared to the level of transfers that would take place if the redistributive demands that characterize highly unequal societies were to prevail in those economies. Second, the tax rate in a democracy varies with its level of electoral turnout – the

171

larger the number of low-income voters that vote, the higher the level of taxes and transfers will be.

To examine the impact of different political regimes on the size and composition of the public sector, this chapter is organized as follows. The first section outlines the political and economic mechanisms through which democracy leads to the expansion of public spending and the formation of the welfare state. To do so, it conceptually distinguishes between public investment, redistributive expenditure and insurance programs. It then shows why political regimes and their underlying distribution of assets mainly shape the latter two but only indirectly affect the level of public goods and public capital formation. The second section describes the battery of dependent variables (current revenue and public consumption of general government, total expenditure of central government, transfers and sub-sidies of central government and salaries of public employees of central government) to be tested, the set of independent variables employed and the estimation strategy. The third section reports the results of the test. Among other things, it shows that democracies and higher levels of electoral turnout lead, conditional on current economic conditions and the distribu-tion of preferences, to a larger public sector. Notice that this finding has two implications. First, it validates the premise on which the theory about regime choices was based – that is, it confirms that the expectations and calculations I assumed about the actors involved were correct. Second, and more generally, it indicates that the type of political regime matters for the welfare of citizens.

The Growth of the Public Sector

To model the causes underlying the growth of the public sector, I rely again on the basic model developed in Chapter 1, where economic agents, endowed with different levels of assets (such as skills and property), vote for a tax rate to finance the (primarily redistributive) activities of the state. Again, the tax rate will correspond to the ideal policy of the median voter. That is, policy makers will choose the tax rate that maximizes the well-being of the last voter needed to form a majority. As derived in Chapter 1, since pref-erences are related to pre-tax individual income (and hence single peaked), the level of the tax rate will depend on the difference between the average income and the income of the median voter. The larger the difference, the more interested in redistribution the median voter will become and the higher the tax rate will be. Still, in choosing the tax rate, the median voter (or the median parliamentarian) will be constrained by both the distortionary effect of taxes and the mobility of capital.

I enrich this model with two additional assumptions that have valuable implications for the analysis of the evolution of the public sector. In the first place, citizens set the tax rate with an eye on allocating the resulting public revenue in two ways. A proportion λ of the collected public revenue T, where $T = \Sigma \tau k_j$, is distributed among all individuals in equal parts, that is, $\lambda \tau$ is given to each individual, in the way in which all public revenue was allocated in Chapter 1.[1] The remaining part, $(1 - \lambda)T$, is spent on public investment, that is, on policies to pay for infrastructures, human capital formation and regulatory agencies that enforce the rule of law and secure property rights, therefore raising the productivity of factors.

In the second place, although the income of individuals depends mainly on their corresponding capital endowment, we can think of income as being affected, with a certain probability, by possible temporal fluctuations due to external shocks, changes in demand and so on. This can be denoted as $y_j = \alpha k_j$ where $\alpha \succ 0$. Notice that this parameter incorporates the discussion on mobility and, particularly, on income volatility developed in the second section of Chapter 4.

We are in a position to describe how the type of political regime shapes, alone and in interaction with the distribution of income and the preferences across the population and the evolution of economic conditions, the components of the public sector: the level of purely redistributive spending, the extent of spending on public investment and the size of "insurance" programs developed to cope with income volatility.

Redistributive Demands

The size and nature of the redistributive part of public spending evolves conditional on both the economic and political dimensions of each country. In highly unequal economies, such as those characterized by a strong cleavage between landowners and a mass of landless peasants, redistributive programs remain minimal. The presence of sharp income differentials generates strong redistributive pressures that should lead to very high taxes and transfers. But they do not translate into a larger public sector

---

[1] That is, in Chapter 1, $\lambda = 1$.

precisely because, in line with the political model of Chapter 1, the upper segment of the income ladder, anticipating the distributional consequences of democracy, blocks the extension of the franchise. With a restricted electorate, the distance between the average income and the median voter's income stays small or even negligible, and the public sector remains a small fraction of the economy.

By contrast, in societies with low to moderate levels of inequality, democratic regimes tend to prevail and taxes and transfers evolve with the demands of all or most voters. More precisely, the degree of redistributive effort varies with the level of electoral turnout. Differences in the likelihood of electoral participation across voters alter the position of the median voter and, therefore, the tax rate. Thus, for example, if turnout declines among the least skilled voters, the median voter becomes closer to the average income voter and the public sector shrinks even if the franchise is universal. In the limit, that is, if all voters abstain except for those with an income equal to or higher than the mean income, the size of the public sector in a democracy becomes similar to the one in an authoritarian system.

Controlling for the extent of differential turnout across social classes, democratic regimes have moderate levels of redistributive spending (that is, public spending directed to reduce income inequality). The reason is simple and has to do, again, with the political and economic basis of the constitutional regime in place. As shown in Chapters 1 to 3, democratic regimes take root only once the extent of inequality (and asset specificity) declines to the point at which political actors find it advantageous to subject themselves to the rule of the ballot box. But, naturally, if the underlying inequality of democracies is mild, their corresponding fiscal structure should not be excessively redistributive: we will not find there the extent of quasi-expropriatory taxation that a strict Meltzer-Richards model (the model employed in Chapter 1 to derive how taxes are set in a democracy) should lead us to expect in countries with medium to high levels of inequality governed by democratic institutions (Meltzer and Richards 1981). To put it differently, the fact that the constitutional definition of the median voter (and therefore, the median voter's position relative to the economic agent with the mean income) is endogenous to the type of income distribution explains why the Meltzer-Richards model of optimal taxation has not performed well in several empirical tests: in high inequality countries, the franchise is legally restricted to censor income differences; in low inequality countries, where everybody votes and the median voter truly coincides with the median subject of the income distribution, the interest to redistribute is moderate.[2]

Nonetheless, the fact that the structural basis of democracies curtails their redistributive bent (compared, at least, to the suppressed demands of authoritarian regimes) does not mean that redistribution does not take place in representative regimes. It does, conditional on the distribution of preferences and the underlying economic interests of the electorate (and, again, electoral turnout). The pressure to redistribute is small in nonindustrial yet relatively equal countries, that is, in farmer economies. In such "pre-modern" societies, where peasant families own roughly similar plots of land and are affected by similar risks, democratic institutions are feasible. The public sector remains, however, small because redistributive tensions are low. Moreover, even though they are not universal, communal arrangements to share risk, such as common lands or church-distributed benefits, and the use of extended families for the provision of food, shelter and care may be fairly extensive, hence substituting for the state.

In developed, industrialized societies, where both inequality and asset specificity are moderate, democracies are also stable constitutional arrangements. But with relatively heterogenous electorates, redistributive programs arise driven mainly by two types of distributional demands.[3] First, technological breakthroughs and the expansion of manufacturing and service-oriented jobs, which transform the old economic structure of either farming societies or landowning economies, change the distribution of income and economic risk as follows. Important pockets of low-income earners or even poor voters appear among the industrial working class. Similarly, the volatility of income becomes more concentrated in specific segments of the population. More precisely, unemployment spells and work-related accidents, which emerge as the downside of manufacturing-led productivity increases, become important among industrial workers, particularly those most unskilled. In other words, the process of industrialization and the formation of a broad class of wage earners result in stronger pressures for *intragenerational transfers*. Second, a general improvement in material conditions and in health technologies in particular prolongs life

---

[2] For a summary of studies testing the empirical value of the Meltzer-Richards model, see Holsey and Borcherding (1997: 575–76).

[3] For discussions of the process of economic modernization, see Flora and Alber (1981). For a critical examination, see Esping-Andersen (1990). For a first analysis of its impact on the public sector, see Wagner (1883), Wilensky (1975) and Baumol (1967).

expectancy and eventually leads to a shift in the demographic structure. As the profile of the population matures and the proportion of old cohorts expands, pressure for *intergenerational transfers*, in the form of pensions and health care programs, goes up. Broadly speaking, whereas the pressure for intragenerational transfers is a phenomenon contemporary to industrialization, the aging of the population occurs at a later stage in modern societies.

To sum up, this discussion predicts the following conditional relationship between political regime and economic conditions. Under authoritarian regimes, and independent of the type of economy, the level of redistributive spending should be minimal. Under democracies, the extent of redistribution will vary with the underlying economic and social structure. In farming economies, it will be low. As industrialization creates a urban working class and then generates the basis for an older population, public spending should go up.

Economic Development and the Provision of Public Goods

Whereas the pure redistributive component of public spending varies conditional on the interaction of political regime, the extent of electoral participation and the underlying array of economic interests, the level of public investment is mostly a function of economic conditions and the process of economic development.[4]

In deciding how to split any tax revenue between investment and transfers, the median voter votes for a proportion λ to be directed to public investment such that the marginal benefit she obtains (through her income) from the last unit being spent on public investment equals the net benefit she derives from transfers. In other words, λ will be chosen at a value at which the combined increase in the median voter's income due to public investment and to the expansion of total output (which implies a larger pool available for redistribution) equals the increase derived from the last unit received in transfers. Hence, the proportion to finance public investment will increase with the growing positive effect of the former on the productivity of capital and labor.

Broadly speaking, it seems safe to assume that the intensity with which public investment affects individuals' productivity and returns varies with

---

[4] Naturally, public investment has a redistributive component itself that I bracket here for the sake of simplicity. See, however, Boix (1998).

their level of income. At very low levels of (per capita) income, public investment increases the marginal productivity of labor either very slightly or not at all – extensive road building in subsistence farming economies hardly changes the level of development. However, beyond a certain income threshold, an increase in the provision of collective goods and public investment has strong effects on the productivity of factors. Accordingly, as the economy and per capita income start to grow, the incentive for policy makers to raise the supply of capital and public goods increases. Most public investment, generated to reap the benefits of development, takes place independently of the political regime in place (or, more precisely, of the actual location of the median voter on the income scale).[5] Still, the type of political regime may affect the extent of public investment partially in the following way. Assuming that authoritarian regimes exclude the poorest voters from the policy-making process, the median voter in a non-democratic system is richer than the median voter in a full democracy. Accordingly, at the same level of development (for the same distribution of income among individuals), the incentive to invest may be higher in an authoritarian regime than in a democracy. As incomes increase, however, and given that the marginal return for public investment may decline at high per capita income levels, the differences among regimes (resulting from differently located median voters) in public investment rates should decline.

Income Volatility, Economic Openness and Public Compensation

Finally, the tax rate and the size of the public sector also rises with the volatility of the income of the electorate. Assume that voters are averse to risk, that is, they prefer a stable income over a volatile income, even if both are, on average, equal, and that they vote the tax rate before they know their parameter α, that is, how volatile their income will turn out to be. As the fluctuation of income increases, as a result, for example, of the oscillation of

---

[5] It is true, however, that policy makers cannot automatically be assumed to behave as social planners. The implementation of optimal policies happens only under political or legal institutions that effectively restrain rent-seeking behavior among politicians. Democratic institutions, by easing the task of monitoring policy makers, may, on average, lead to a fuller provision of public goods. For a discussion of this point, see Olson (1993) and Przeworski and Limongi (1993). In Chapter 6, I explore the economic and political consequences of having politicians that seek rents. Here, however, politicians automatically react to the demand for productive expenditure as determined by the level of income.

world business cycles that cannot be directly controlled by the government of a small open economy, voters may be inclined to increase public spending as a mechanism to stabilize their economic position.

The effect of income volatility on the size of the public sector will be mediated by the type of political regime depending on its distribution across the population. If the distribution of income volatility (the parameter α) is uniform across individuals, public revenue and expenditure should increase independently of the type of political regime or extension of the franchise. If the risk of income fluctuation is biased across sectors, public-insurance schemes will vary with the regime in place. If the risk is concentrated among the poor, public expenditure will increase only under democratic regimes. If the risk is higher among asset owners, public expenditure will increase under authoritarian regimes.[6]

I already mentioned that the process of industrialization leads to a change in the distribution of risks and to their potential concentration in certain economic sectors. In exploring the consequences that the international economy has on the domestic political arena, a growing literature has shown in the last two decades that higher levels of trade systematically lead to a larger public sector among both developed and developing nations. The actual mechanisms that underlie the statistical relationship are still the object of considerable debate, but, for an important part of the literature, higher levels of trade integration (coupled with high sectoral concentration in the economy) are seen as leading to growing risks associated with the international business cycle, which in turn put pressure on policy makers to develop publicly financed compensatory programs in favor of the exposed sectors (Katzenstein 1985; Rodrik 1998). This result is directly incorporated into the model and then subject to empirical verification in the section that follows.

---

[6] Moene and Wallerstein (2001) have recently modeled the idea of risk as a variable that increases the demand for public-insurance programs. In their model, demands for insurance, which is characterized as a normal good, increase with (per capita) income. The problem with this approach is that although it explains why spending on insurance should rise with income (and therefore richer social sectors and voters and richer countries should have more insurance programs), it does not explain why this insurance should be *public* in its provision. Unless there is a market failure, richer voters should prefer privately funded and privately provided programs to publicly enforced schemes. Accordingly, the idea that risk is spread differentially across economic sectors and that its distribution shapes, in interaction with the franchise, the size of public programs, seems to be more plausible. For this latter type of approach, see Baldwin (1990) and, formally, Mares (2001).

Data and Methods

Sample

To determine the strength of the theories reviewed in the first section, I examine the size and composition of both general government and central government.

The size of *general government*, that is, of the sum of all levels of government, is assessed employing two measures:

1. Current receipts of general government as percentage of GDP. This measure, taken from the United Nations National Accounts, offers the best approximation of the size of the whole public sector, among both programs and levels of government. The data covers approximately 65 countries (22 are Organization for Economic Cooperation and Development members) from 1950 to 1990, with some variation in the years covered, and provides about 2,000 data points.
2. Final consumption expenditure of general government as percentage of GDP. This measure, taken from the World Bank, covers the period from 1960 to 1999 and gives over 4,600 country-year data points.

The size and internal composition of *central government* is examined employing the following data on public expenditure:

1. Total expenditure of central government as percentage of GDP.
2. Nonmilitary expenditure of central government as percentage of GDP.
3. Subsidies and transfers of central government as percentage of GDP.
4. Wages and salaries of central government as percentage of GDP.

All these measures are taken from the World Development Indicators data set and go from approximately 1970 to 1999 except nonmilitary expenditure, which starts in 1985.

Since employing data at the central government level may lead to biased results for federal systems such as India, Argentina and the United States or for purely decentralized ones such as Sweden, which uses the local sector to provide a substantial part of its social services, the results for central government have to be checked against the results for general government. Still, both central and general government data are relatively well correlated: the correlation between current revenue of central government and general government (both as percentage of GDP) is 0.84 in my sample;

179

the correlation between the current revenue of general government and nonmilitary spending of central government is 0.78.

Independent Variables

I consider the following independent variables:

(1) *Political Institutions*, which include:

(a) "Democratic Regime," which indicates whether each country was a competitive democracy in the five previous years and thus ranges from 0 (no democracy ever) to 1 (democracy always). To measure the presence of a democratic regime, I employ the index described in Chapter 1.

(b) "Level of Turnout in Democracies." According to the model in the first section, who actually votes should matter as much as (or even more than) who is legally entitled to vote: changes in the level of turnout may shift the position of the median voter and hence affect the tax rate. Since individual data on participation is unavailable for all the countries in the sample, this hypothesis can only be tested using national levels of participation. Nonetheless, and holding other things constant, given that the individual probability of voting has been shown to increase with income, it is plausible to conclude that as national turnout declines, abstention takes place mostly among the poorest voters.[7] Hence, at lower levels of participation, the difference between median voter income and average income should decline and the size of the public sector should shrink. The variable "Turnout in Democracies" is calculated as an interactive term of "Turnout" and "Democratic Regime." "Turnout" is defined as the proportion of those voting over all those citizens who are over the legal voting age and is taken from IDEA (1997). It has been calculated for each year on the basis of data from elections that have taken place in the five years previous to the year of the dependent variable observation.

(c) The following three variables capture the extent to which different constitutional arrangements distort the representation of the median voter's preferences: (i) a dummy variable for the presence of presidential regimes; (ii) a dummy variable coding whether a proportional representation electoral system is used or not; and (iii) a dummy variable that captures the existence of a federal system. The first two variables have been built based

---

[7] For evidence that, in the absence of mechanisms of political mobilization, such as parties or unions, turnout is positively related to income, see Rosenstone and Hansen (1993) and Franklin (1996).

on Cox (1997), IDEA (1997), Linz and Valenzuela (1994), Shugart and Carey (1992) and the Keesing's Contemporary Archives. The variable on federalism follows Downes (2000).

(2) *Economy*, which includes the set of variables that measure the effects of economic conditions on the size of government:

(a) The log value of real per capita income, which proxies for the shifts in the distribution of preferences associated with economic development and is expected to have a positive effect on the size of the public sector: it should increase the demand for public goods, and, since it tracks the growth of industrial and postindustrial societies and the demographic maturation of countries, it should be correlated with the growth of unemployment-related expenditures, health spending and old-age pensions. For the regressions on public revenue, with data starting in 1950, I employ constant dollars of 1985, Chain Index, expressed in international prices, taken from the Penn World Tables. For the remaining estimations, which continue until 1994, I take data on per capita income (in constant dollars of 1990) published by the World Bank.

(b) Two variables that approximate more directly the preference structure of the electorate: the average share of the agricultural sector over GDP, taken from the World Bank and expected to enter negatively in the model; and the percentage of population 65 years of age or older, a variable that tracks the shift of the median voter to an older age, taken from the World Bank.

(c) The level of income inequality, measured through the Gini index, as defined in Chapter 2.

(3) Although underlying economic conditions, such as the demographic profile, the number of industrial workers or the level of inequality, may shape alone the type of the public sector, the thrust of the model predicts that the size of government will vary conditional, to a large extent, on the political regime in place. Excluding the provision of public goods, the public sector will remain small in authoritarian regimes. In democratic regimes, instead, the size of the public sector will increase as governments meet the demands for transfers fostered by economic and demographic changes. To capture this prediction, I introduce the interactive term *Economy*Political Institutions* in which economic conditions are alternatively measured through per capita income, share of agriculture, percentage of old-age population and Gini index, and where political institutions are either political regime or level of turnout. The expectation is that the interactive term will have a positive impact on the size of government.

181

(4) *Trade*, which may increase the risks associated with the international business cycle and hence the political pressures for publicly financed compensatory programs in favor of the exposed sectors. According to Rodrik (1998), external risk, measured as fluctuations in the terms of trade, is positively associated with income volatility, measured through fluctuations in real GDP: a 10 percent increase in external risk comes with a 1.0–1.6 percent increase in the standard deviation of the growth rate of GDP.[8] Trade openness, which has been found to be a strong predictor of the public sector (Cameron 1978; Rodrik 1998; Garrett 1998, 2001; Adserà and Boix 2002), is measured through the log value of the ratio of trade (sum of imports and exports) to GDP and is taken from the Penn World Tables.

(5) Finally, I have controlled for the ratio of fuel exports over total exports and the proportion of nonfuel primary exports over total exports. Both measures are taken from World Bank Tables.

Following Beck and Katz's procedure (1995), I have estimated the pooled cross-sectional time-series model through ordinary least squares, adjusting the standard errors for unequal variation within panels and correcting for autocorrelation.[9]

Empirical Results

As we will see, Tables 5.1 through 5.6 report the impact of the main variables of the model – economic development or modernization, trade openness, political regime, turnout and the interaction of political and economic variables – on the different measures of size of the public sector. Tables 5.1 and 5.2 show the two measures of general government: current public revenues for the period 1950–90 and public consumption of general government for the period 1960–99, respectively. Table 5.3 reports

---

[8] Using the Summers-Heston data base (which includes 147 nations for the period 1950–90 and 4,546 observations), Adserà and Boix (2002) also show that the volatility of the business cycle (calculated as the standard deviation of changes in the growth rate in five-year periods) increases with trade openness. More specifically, for each logged unit of trade openness, the volatility of the business cycle goes up by 0.60 (and is statistically significant at the 1 percent level). The result is robust to the introduction of control variables such as per capita income, economic structure and weight of fuel and primary exports.

[9] All estimations have been implemented through Stata's xtpcse procedure. Autocorrelation has been modeled as a first-order process with a common coefficient for all panels. Results do not change with panel-specific autoregressive terms. Moreover, the following tests have been developed to ensure the robustness of results: country-by-country and year-by-year deletions, introduction of dummies by regional areas, and lagged dependent variable. Results were robust to these procedures except where noted.

the results for total expenditure of central government from 1970 to 1999. Table 5.4 displays the results for nonmilitary expenditure of central government from 1985 to 1997. Finally, Tables 5.5 and 5.6 look at two components of expenditure: transfers and subsidies of central government, which is a good proxy for the development of welfare state programs, and public wages of central government.

For each dependent variable I report four models. The first model regresses the dependent variable on per capita income, trade openness, democratic regime and the interaction of regime and income. The second model substitutes turnout in democratic regimes for political regime (turnout is equated to 0 in authoritarian regimes) and the interaction of electoral participation and per capita income for the previous interaction of political regime and per capita income.

The third model explores the mechanisms of development in more detail. As discussed in the theoretical section, economic development or, more generally, modernization constitutes a complex phenomenon that alters the distribution of risk and income across sectors and generations. In the third model, I attempt to unpack the effects of development using more direct measures that capture the change in the underlying distribution of preferences due to the growth of a manufacturing working class (leading to larger intragenerational transfers) and the aging of the population (resulting in an expansion of intergenerational transfers). This is done by adding two factors, the share of the primary sector in the economy and the proportion of old population, and their interaction with democratic regime, to the initial model estimated in the first model. Since observations for those measures are more scarce than per capita income data, the data set dwindles to between one half and two thirds of the initial sample. Although the results are in line with the initial model, it is important to have in mind these data constraints when examining the estimations. Given that per capita income, size of the primary sector and old population are strongly correlated for most years – the size of the primary sector and proportion of old population explain at least about 85 percent of the variance in the log of per capita income – I drop the level of per capita income in the third model.

The fourth model runs the size of the public sector on the Gini index, political regime and electoral participation as well as the interactions of the inequality index with both political regime and turnout. It also includes controls for per capita income and trade openness. This model is not displayed for nonmilitary spending (Table 5.4) because the number of observations is very low.

Public Revenue of General Government

Democracy and Underlying Economic Conditions. Consider first the estimates in Model 1, Table 5.1. Both economic development and trade openness, which are strongly significant from a statistical point of view, affect the size of government positively. Political regime alone depresses public revenues. But this has to be put in relation to the strong effect of the interactive term of democracy and per capita income: as discussed previously, the impact of socioeconomic modernization is to a large extent conditional on the political regime and level of participation.[10]

To interpret the results of Model 1, Table 5.1, and particularly the effect of the interactive term, I simulate in Figure 5.1 the evolution of current public revenue as a proportion of GDP when real per capita income rises under both a democratic polity and an authoritarian regime. Trade openness has been set equal to the sample mean of 62 percent of GDP. The structure of the simulation in Figure 5.1 suggests the following stylized facts. In the first place, the level of development has, again, an unconditional impact on the size of the public sector. At low levels of development, the public sector is small. Democratic India, the authoritarian regimes of sub-Saharan Africa or Central America or even the limited democracies of nineteenth-century Europe fit into this pattern. The state then grows with per capita income. Regardless of the political regime in place, the size of public revenue increases by almost 10 percentage points from very low to medium levels of development, and then by another 5–7 percentage points from medium to high levels of development.

In the second place, the nature of the political regime does not affect, on its own, the size of the government. For that to be true, the public sector should always be larger under a democratic system at all income levels. The results show, instead, that democratic regimes in truly underdeveloped economies are not taxing more than authoritarian regimes. At extremely low levels of development, public current revenue is, in fact,

---

[10] The United Nations National Accounts do not include data on the size of the public sector in former socialist countries. Using data from the IMF (several years), I have run the same regressions in Table 4.1, including total revenues of general government in Hungary (1981–89), Poland (1984–88), Yugoslavia (1971–89) and Romania (1972–89). No data are available for China, East Germany, the USSR and other non-European socialist countries. These regressions, with and without a dummy variable for "planning economies," generate estimates very similar to the results obtained without any planning systems. The dummy for planning economies indicates that the size of the public sector is about 20–25 percentage points of GDP larger in socialist economies.

Table 5.1. *Public Revenue of General Government as Percentage of GDP, 1950–90*

	(1)	(2)	(3)	(4)
Constant	−22.60***	−20.41**	7.84**	−91.55***
	(6.88)	(8.22)	(3.42)	(14.37)
Per capita income (Log)[a]	3.95***	4.14***		7.48***
	(0.93)	(1.05)		(0.78)
Trade openness (log of sum of	3.86***	2.54***	3.32***	3.36***
exports and imports over GDP)[b]	(0.55)	(0.58)	(0.68)	(0.75)
Democratic regime[c]	−25.56***	0.38	−5.19**	32.54***
	(7.74)	(1.43)	(2.48)	(9.59)
Democratic regime* Log of	3.38***			
real per capita income	(1.02)			
Level of turnout in		−0.43***		0.35***
democratic regimes		(0.13)		(0.12)
Level of turnout* Log of		0.06***		
real per capita income		(0.02)		
Share of agricultural sector			−0.18***	
in GDP[d]			(0.04)	
Democratic regime* Share of			0.06	
agricultural sector			(0.07)	
Percentage of population			1.34***	
65 years or older			(0.34)	
Democratic regime*			0.62*	
Proportion of old population			(0.36)	
Fuel exports as percentage of			0.08***	
all exports			(0.02)	
Gini index				0.86***
				(0.28)
Democratic regime* Gini index				−0.66***
				(0.21)
Level of turnout* Gini index				−0.007***
				(0.003)
Number of observations	1998	1400	1029	621
R^2	0.3758	0.4663	0.6653	0.7443
Model Chi-square	366.26	415.26	1033.94	502.90
Prob > Chi-square	0.0000	0.0000	0.0000	0.0000

[a] Constant US$ of 1985. *Source:* Penn World Tables.

[b] Trade openness: Log of the sum of exports and imports over GDP. *Source:* Penn World Tables.

[c] Democratic regime: Five-year average of democratic institutions. Variable goes from 1 (democracy in previous five years) to 0 (nondemocracy in previous five years). Average calculated on index developed in Chapter 1.

[d] Share of agricultural sector: Percentage of GDP from agricultural sector. *Source:* World Bank Tables.
Estimation: Ordinary least squares estimation, with panel corrected standard errors, and correction for autocorrelation and for heteroskedastic disturbances between panels.
Standard errors in parenthesis.
*p < 0.10; **p < 0.05; ***p < 0.01.

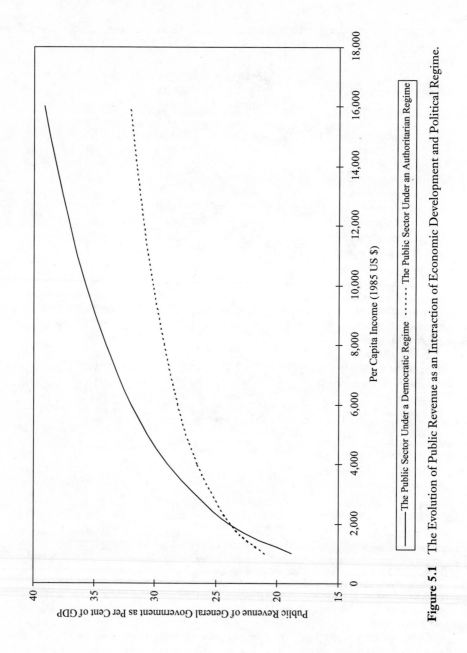

Figure 5.1 The Evolution of Public Revenue as an Interaction of Economic Development and Political Regime.

Per Capita Income (1985 US $)

Public Revenue of General Government as Per Cent of GDP

—— The Public Sector Under a Democratic Regime ····· The Public Sector Under an Authoritarian Regime

somewhat higher in nondemocratic regimes. At a per capita income of $500 (in 1985 prices), public revenue is about 4 percentage points of GDP lower in democracies than in authoritarian regimes. This is due to several factors. First, the demands for transfers associated with development have not affected democratic states. Second, authoritarian regimes, with their comparatively richer median voters (in relation to democracies), have slightly more incentive to spend on capital formation. Finally, authoritarian states may be more expensive due to their need to finance their repressive apparatus.[11]

As socioeconomic modernization takes off, democratic institutions lead to larger governments. The former generates a set of demands and needs that democratic politicians have to respond to. Once real per capita income goes over $1,000, the public sector expands at a faster rate under democratic regimes. With a per capita income of $6,000, public revenue is about 4 percentage points higher in a democratic country. For a per capita income of $12,000, public revenue would hypothetically be 6 percentage points higher in a democracy. The historical experience of recent democratic transitions fits these results quite nicely. Consider the paradigmatic case of Spain, where democracy was reestablished in the late 1970s. In 1974, Spain had a per capita income of $7,291 (in 1985 prices) and its current public revenue amounted to 22.8 percent of GDP. Ten years later, although per capita income had remained stagnant (it was $7,330 in 1984), current public revenue had risen to 32.7 percent. Among non-OECD nations, in the Philippines, for example, current public revenue went up from 14 percent of GDP to 19 percent of GDP after the restoration of democracy in the late 1980s without per capita income changing in that period.

Turnout and the Public Sector. Model 2 in Table 5.1 examines the effect of turnout, which determines the median voter, alone and in interaction with per capita income. The coefficients are significant and strongly confirm the theoretical model. Figure 5.2, using the coefficients in Table 5.1, Model 2, simulates the impact of different levels of turnout under different conditions of development. In underdeveloped countries, participation has no impact. For mid-income nations, however, turnout becomes substantially important. For high levels of per capita income, the size of the public sector varies from 37.5 percent of GDP in countries where only two fifths of the

---

[11] Regressing military spending as a percentage of GDP on per capita income and regime, dictatorships spend 2 percentage points of GDP more than democracies (the coefficient is statistically significant at $p < 0.1$).

187

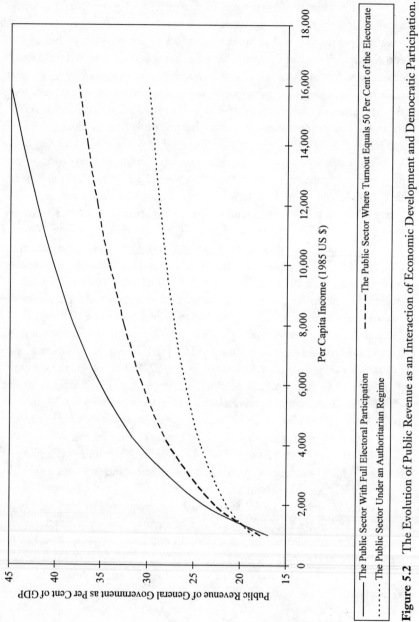

Public Revenue of General Government as Per Cent of GDP

Per Capita Income (1985 US $)

——— The Public Sector With Full Electoral Participation

– – – The Public Sector Where Turnout Equals 50 Per Cent of the Electorate

·········· The Public Sector Under an Authoritarian Regime

Figure 5.2 The Evolution of Public Revenue as an Interaction of Economic Development and Democratic Participation.

population vote (the cases of the United States or Switzerland) to about 45 percent where everybody votes.[12]

Although I have not reproduced the results in Table 5.1, I have also tested the impact of presidentialism, proportional representation and federalism. Federalism has no impact on the size of the public sector. From a theoretical standpoint, the impact of proportional representation on the size of the public sector is unclear. On the one hand, it has been pointed that whereas in plurality systems politicians can target a few marginal districts with very narrowly designed redistributive programs, parties need to please a large number of voters (across the entire country) under proportional representation (Persson and Tabellini 1998). Yet, on the other hand, provided that the population is similarly distributed across the country, all parties should be expected to (partly) converge on the median voter under the two systems and thus implement similar policy programs.[13] In Boix (2001), I have shown that the public sector is slightly larger in countries governed under proportional representation laws – by about 1.7 percent of GDP.[14] By contrast, presidentialism has a significant negative effect on the size of the public sector. Under presidential systems public revenue is around 4 percent of GDP lower than under parliamentarian regimes. Although presidentialism significantly depresses participation (by over 12 percentage points in my estimates), its effect does not wane once we control for turnout. The separation-of-powers structure that comes with presidentialism seems to impose a bias toward the status quo on current policy that slows the growth of government.[15]

[12] For recent evidence on the impact of turnout on the size of transfers using the sample of OECD nations, see Franzese (2001).

[13] It is true that whereas under proportional representation the median parliamentarian will always be close to the median voter, under plurality one should expect more variability in government composition. But over time, that is, on average, policy location should be the same given similar electorates.

[14] The coefficient of proportional representation oscillates in size when we exclude specific years or countries. Proportional representation seems to affect the size of government mostly in an indirect way: by reducing barriers to entry and diminishing the incentive to vote strategically, it boosts political participation – a well-known result in the literature on electoral turnout (Franklin 1996) – and therefore makes government more responsive to citizens' demands. Controlling for economic development, degree of party competition and other institutional characteristics (presidentialism and federalism), turnout is around 9 percentage points higher in proportional representation systems in the data set used in this book.

[15] For a different interpretation of the impact of presidentialism, see Persson and Tabellini (1998). Using a much smaller sample (a cross-section of about 50 countries), Persson and

Mechanisms of Development. Model 3 in Table 5.1 attempts to unpack the effects of "development" by examining the impact of the primary sector and demographic structure on the public sector. The size of the primary sector in the economy has a substantial weight on the evolution of the size of the public sector. A decrease of one percentage point of the agricultural sector in the GDP implies an increase of public revenue of 0.18 points of GDP. With all the other variables at their mean level, public revenue would amount to around 27 percent in a country with no agricultural sector and about 16 percent in a country with two thirds of the economy in the primary sector. Modernization, which changes the types of productive activities most of the population is engaged in and bolsters an urban working class, accounts for much of the emergence of a significant public sector. Notice also that, as predicted in the model, the process of industrialization translates into a bigger government at a faster pace under a democracy: the public sector grows by another 0.06 points for each percentage drop in the size of agriculture – the coefficient is, however, not statistically significant.

Confirming the standard literature on the determinants of the welfare state in OECD nations, the proportion of old population has a strong positive effect on the size of government. For each percentage point of old population, the public sector goes up 1.34 percentage points of GDP. With the other variables at their mean, public revenues increase 20 percentage points of GDP if we go from a minimum of 2.5 percent of the population older than 65 to the sample maximum of 17.5 percent. The impact of an aging population becomes even more intense under a democratic regime. Each percentage point of old population increases the size of public revenues by another 0.62 percentage points of GDP.

Finally, Model 3 also includes the proportion of fuel exports over total exports. Moving from an economy without oil to one in which all exports are oil, public revenue goes up 8 percentage points of GDP.

Inequality and the Public Sector. The model of optimal taxation that underlies the constitutional choice in Chapter 1 was initially developed in the economics literature to predict the level of taxes as a result of income

---

Tabellini estimate that presidential systems depress public expenditure by about 10 percent of GDP. They attribute this negative effect to the fact that, by sharpening the extent of potential conflict among politicians, a separation-of-powers system enables voters to discipline politicians and therefore to reduce the level of rents. Their theoretical explanation is, however, unconvincing. The size of rents appropriated by politicians through the budget cannot account for this differential between presidential and parliamentarian regimes.

differences and the corresponding intensity of redistributive demands. Yet, as noted earlier, the model has not been very successful from an empirical point of view. By endogenizing the choice of median voter, this book explains why the model is only partly useful to predict tax and spending levels. Excessive levels of inequality lead to authoritarian solutions and therefore to low public spending. Low inequality opens up the space for democracy and redistribution – but redistribution remains under bearable limits. Moreover, among democracies the impact of inequality is mediated by electoral participation (and the position of the real median voter). All in all, the extent of differences between the median voter and the average-income voter should have a positive but relatively mild effect on public spending.

Model 4 in Table 5.1 shows that democracy and turnout are indeed the strongest determinants of public revenue. Within that result, the Gini index is positive and statistically significant. As income distribution widens, political demands for redistribution go up. The interactive term of the Gini index and democracy is negative and thus is apparently contrary to the model. But this has to be put in the context of the very high coefficient of democratic regime (32.5), which compensates for the negative coefficient of the interactive term. Once again, the level of political participation boosts public revenue substantially. The interactive term of turnout and the Gini index has a negative impact on the public sector and is statistically significant. The size of this coefficient implies that only at very high levels of income inequality (over a Gini index of 62) do higher levels of participation translate into a slight drop in government size – for the maximum value of the Gini index in the sample (66), it falls by less than 1 point when one goes from low to high levels of turnout.[16]

Public Consumption of General Government

Table 5.2 examines the causes of variation in final public consumption of general government for the period 1960–99. Final consumption is

[16] The waning effects of higher participation on government size at very high levels of income inequality may be attributed to the following fact. For very high levels of inequality, that is, in societies with a very skewed distribution of income in favor of the rich, any reasonable level of turnout will lead to having a median voter with a low income. Therefore, any increase in participation will not change significantly the already substantial distance between the median and average income. By contrast, for much more equally distributed income structures, participation will correspondingly increase the distance between the median voter income and average income and will therefore affect more strongly the size of the tax burden.

Table 5.2. *Public Consumption of General Government as Percentage of GDP, 1960–99*

	(1)	(2)	(3)	(4)
Constant	6.16***	−0.28	13.66***	−12.97***
	(1.95)	(2.86)	(1.98)	(4.77)
Per capita income (Log) [a]	0.03	0.59		1.67***
	(0.28)	(0.40)		(0.19)
Trade openness (log of sum of	2.20***	2.66***	1.49***	0.65*
exports and imports over GDP) [b]	(0.27)	(0.40)	(0.36)	(0.34)
Democratic regime [c]	−6.97***	−0.97	−6.05**	10.55***
	(2.41)	(0.86)	(1.68)	(2.66)
Democratic regime* Log of	0.92***			
real per capita income	(0.32)			
Level of turnout in		−0.02		0.09
democratic regimes		(0.05)		(0.06)
Level of turnout* Log of		0.004		
real per capita income		(0.006)		
Share of agricultural sector			−0.13***	
in GDP [d]			(0.03)	
Democratic regime* Share of			0.08*	
agricultural sector			(0.04)	
Percentage of population 65 years			−0.30*	
or older			(0.17)	
Democratic regime*			0.68***	
Proportion of old population			(0.18)	
Fuel exports as percentage of			−0.01	
all exports			(0.01)	
Gini index				0.23**
				(0.10)
Democratic regime* Gini index				−0.21***
				(0.06)
Level of turnout* Gini index				−0.002
				(0.001)
Number of observations	4627	2773	3064	763
R^2	0.1723	0.3061	0.2660	0.6442
Model Chi-square	134.97	109.91	173.78	223.16
Prob > Chi-square	0.0000	0.0000	0.0000	0.0000

[a] Constant US$ of 1985. *Source:* Penn World Tables.
[b] Trade openness: Log of the sum of exports and imports over GDP. *Source:* Penn World Tables.
[c] Democratic regime: Five-year average of democratic institutions. Variable goes from 1 (democracy in previous five years) to 0 (nondemocracy in previous five years). Average calculated on index developed in Chapter 1.
[d] Share of agricultural sector: Percentage of GDP from agricultural sector. *Source:* World Bank Tables.
Estimation: Ordinary least squares estimation, with panel corrected standard errors, and correction for autocorrelation and for heteroskedastic disturbances between panels.
Standard errors in parenthesis.
*$p < 0.10$; **$p < 0.05$; ***$p < 0.01$.

substantially affected by trade openness – a result that confirms the estimates of Rodrik (1998). Interestingly, Model 1 shows that economic development has no impact on public consumption alone. But its effect is strong in interaction with democracy.

Model 3 reveals that while a reduction in the weight of agriculture propitiates an increase in public consumption, public consumption is in fact higher in agrarian economies with a democratic system. In other words, in underdeveloped nations redistribution takes place not through transfers (and the construction of a welfare state) but through public employment and direct expenditure. Not unexpectedly, the proportion of old population is associated (in nondemocratic countries) with a fall in public consumption. This should probably be interpreted as a result of a process of demographic change that forces a shift in the structure of the state toward welfare programs based on transfers. Model 4 shows that inequality increases public consumption alone – but the effect is always secondary to the impact of regime and turnout.

Total Expenditure of Central Government

Tables 5.3 and 5.4 examine total expenditure and nonmilitary expenditure of central government respectively. Model 1 in Table 5.3 shows that the growth of total expenditure is driven, on the one hand, by trade openness and, on the other hand, by the interaction of democracy and development. Development alone has no impact on expenditure and democracy alone depresses it. Models 2 and 3 in Table 5.3 confirm what we learned in Table 5.1. Turnout in developed nations boosts the size of the public sector – although results are not very strong statistically. Similarly, the growth of an industrial sector and an aging population increase total spending (Model 3). The effect of old population becomes particularly intense under a democratic system.

The estimations fit our theoretical expectations particularly well for nonmilitary expenditure of central government. As shown in Table 5.4, Model 1, trade openness and the interaction of democracy and per capita income have a very strong impact on the size of the state. Under an authoritarian state, nonmilitary spending does not change with economic development. By contrast, with democracy, the level of nonmilitary spending of central government doubles from about 10 percent of GDP to almost 20 percent of GDP as per capita income moves from $1,000 to $10,000. An expansion in the level of turnout in developed countries raises spending considerably

Table 5.3. *Total Expenditure of Central Government as Percentage of GDP, 1970–99*

	(1)	(2)	(3)	(4)
Constant	0.45	−5.22	6.34	−29.93***
	(4.45)	(5.62)	(5.80)	(13.15)
Per capita income (Log) [a]	0.80	1.01		2.18***
	(0.64)	(0.83)		(0.58)
Trade openness (log of sum of	5.06***	5.86***	5.59***	4.08***
exports and imports over GDP) [b]	(0.58)	(0.63)	(0.87)	(0.98)
Democratic regime [c]	−11.96**	−3.60*	−8.48*	15.30
	(5.27)	(2.19)	(4.61)	(9.69)
Democratic regime* Log of	1.52**			
real per capita income	(0.71)			
Level of turnout in		−0.07^		0.25
democratic regimes		(0.13)		(0.17)
Level of turnout* Log of		0.02^		
real per capita income		(0.01)		
Share of agricultural sector			−0.12*	
in GDP [d]			(0.07)	
Democratic regime* Share of			0.07	
agricultural sector			(0.10)	
Percentage of population			0.43^	
65 years or older			(0.34)	
Democratic regime* Proportion			0.67^	
of old population			(0.54)	
Fuel exports as percentage of			−0.02	
all exports			(0.03)	
Gini index				0.46
				(0.32)
Democratic regime* Gini index				−0.33
				(0.21)
Level of turnout* Gini index				−0.006
				(0.004)
Number of observations	2626	1795	2000	598
R^2	0.2797	0.3771	0.1947	0.5111
Model Chi-square	160.47	235.49	155.70	135.67
Prob > Chi-square	0.0000	0.0000	0.0000	0.0000

[a] Constant US$ of 1985. *Source:* Penn World Tables.

[b] Trade openness: Log of the sum of exports and imports over GDP. *Source:* Penn World Tables.

[c] Democratic regime: Five-year average of democratic institutions. Variable goes from 1 (democracy in previous five years) to 0 (nondemocracy in previous five years). Average calculated on index developed in Chapter 1.

[d] Share of agricultural sector: Percentage of GDP from agricultural sector. *Source:* World Bank Tables.

Estimation: Ordinary least squares estimation, with panel corrected standard errors, and correction for autocorrelation and for heteroskedastic disturbances between panels.

Standard errors in parenthesis.

*$p < 0.10$; **$p < 0.05$; ***$p < 0.01$

^ In joint test of per interactive term and its components, it is statistically significant (Prob > chi2 = 0.0000).

Empirical Results

Table 5.4. *Nonmilitary Expenditure of Central Government as Percentage of GDP, 1985–97*

	(1)	(2)	(3)
Constant	−0.12	2.93	−11.76*
	(5.70)	(7.34)	(6.43)
Per capita income (Log)[a]	−0.54	−0.32	
	(0.93)	(1.05)	
Trade openness (log of sum of	6.59***	5.70***	7.27***
exports and imports over GDP)[b]	(0.78)	(0.84)	(1.05)
Democratic regime[c]	−28.04***	−2.86	−2.93^
	(7.74)	(3.06)	(4.50)
Democratic regime* Log of	3.89***		
real per capita income	(0.93)		
Level of turnout in		−0.35**	
democratic regimes		(0.15)	
Level of turnout * Log of		0.05***	
real per capita income		(0.02)	
Share of agricultural sector			0.04
in GDP[d]			(0.09)
Democratic regime*			−0.04
Share of agricultural sector			(0.12)
Percentage of population			1.13**
65 years or older			(0.47)
Democratic regime*			0.29^
Proportion of old population			(0.49)
Fuel exports as percentage of			−0.04
all exports			(0.03)
Number of observations	1107	855	871
R^2	0.5160	0.5538	0.4847
Model Chi-square	272.32	283.16	366.69
Prob > Chi-square	0.0000	0.0000	0.0000

[a] Constant US$ of 1985. *Source:* Penn World Tables.

[b] Trade openness: Log of the sum of exports and imports over GDP. *Source:* Penn World Tables.

[c] Democratic regime: Five-year average of democratic institutions. Variable goes from 1 (democracy in previous five years) to 0 (nondemocracy in previous five years). Average calculated on index developed in Chapter 1.

[d] Share of agricultural sector: Percentage of GDP from agricultural sector. *Source:* World Bank Tables.

Estimation: Ordinary least squares estimation, with panel corrected standard errors, and correction for autocorrelation and for heteroskedastic disturbances between panels. Standard errors in parenthesis.

*$p < 0.10$; **$p < 0.05$; ***$p < 0.01$

(Model 2). Agriculture and old population change in the way expected from a theoretical point of view.

Subsidies and Transfers of Central Government

Table 5.5 focuses on the expenditure programs that constitute the core of the welfare state. The process of development changes the size of subsidies and transfers slightly. Trade openness plays a much smaller role than for total revenues and expenditure. A possible interpretation of this result is that domestic compensation does not seem to take place through the welfare state but through public consumption, public employment and probably public capital-formation programs.

Figure 5.3 simulates the evolution of this set of expenditures as an interaction of development and democracy. Under an authoritarian regime, the size of transfers and subsidies is close to 0. By contrast, under a democratic regime, and once development occurs, the size of the program grows nearly by a factor of two to about 18 percent of GDP for high levels of development. It is worth comparing this simulation to the results in Figure 5.1. In that case, the size of the overall public sector grew even under an authoritarian regime – although at a lower pace than under a democratic regime. When we put the two estimates together, the theoretical model put forward in the first section fits well the empirics. The public sector grows as a result of economic modernization regardless of the political regime in place through higher expenditure in public goods and investment. But in the area of transfers, such as pensions, universal health care or unemployment benefits, it does so only after democracy is introduced. The results in Table 5.5 and Figure 5.4 are important because they reject the rather widespread theory among economists and some political scientists (Przeworski et al. 2000: 162–65) that the public sector covaries with development because poor countries do not have the resources to sustain a strong state whereas rich nations do. This explanation does not hold in view of the striking effect of democratization on core programs of the welfare state.

Figure 5.4 simulates the results in Model 2 in Table 5.5. Again, participation matters. In authoritarian regimes, the level of transfers and subsidies is practically flat. At high levels of development, they represent about 12 percent of GDP when turnout is 50 percent and close to 20 percent of GDP when there is no abstention.

In Model 3, the proportion of old population has a very significant effect on transfers and subsidies. Each point of old population increases them

Empirical Results

Table 5.5. *Subsidies and Transfers of Central Government as Percentage of GDP, 1970–99*

	(1)	(2)	(3)	(4)
Constant	−5.95***	−8.11**	−6.22*	−26.06***
	(2.27)	(3.68)	(4.70)	(8.28)
Per capita income (Log)[a]	1.28***	1.58***		2.30***
	(0.34)	(0.55)		(0.29)
Trade openness (log of sum of	0.58**	0.74**	1.95***	0.37
exports and imports over GDP)[b]	(0.26)	(0.30)	(0.63)	(0.45)
Democratic regime[c]	−16.38***	−0.09	−1.84**	10.36
	(2.80)	(1.65)	(4.57)	(6.62)
Democratic regime* Log of	2.50***			
real per capita income	(0.39)			
Level of turnout in democratic		−0.18**		0.31***
regimes		(0.13)		(0.09)
Level of turnout* Log of		0.03***		
real per capita income		(0.01)		
Share of agricultural sector			−0.03	
in GDP[d]			(0.08)	
Democratic regime* Share of			0.01	
agricultural sector			(0.09)	
Percentage of population			1.32***	
65 years or older			(0.52)	
Democratic regime* Proportion			0.16^	
of old population			(0.52)	
Fuel exports as percentage of			−0.02	
all exports			(0.03)	
Gini index				0.26
				(0.18)
Democratic regime*				−0.19
Gini index				(0.13)
Level of turnout*				−0.006***
Gini index				(0.002)
Number of observations	2359	1660	1784	554
R^2	0.2545	0.2859	0.0928	0.4796
Model Chi-square	750.64	657.68	798.03	347.57
Prob > Chi-square	0.0000	0.0000	0.0000	0.0000

[a] Constant US$ of 1985. *Source:* Penn World Tables.
[b] Trade openness: Log of the sum of exports and imports over GDP. *Source:* Penn World Tables.
[c] Democratic regime: Five-year average of democratic institutions. Variable goes from 1 (democracy in previous five years) to 0 (nondemocracy in previous five years). Average calculated on index developed in Chapter 1.
[d] Share of agricultural sector: Percentage of GDP from agricultural sector. *Source:* World Bank Tables.
Estimation: Ordinary least squares estimation, with panel corrected standard errors, and correction for autocorrelation and for heteroskedastic disturbances between panels.
Standard errors in parenthesis.
*$p < 0.10$; **$p < 0.05$; ***$p < 0.01$
^ In joint test of per capita income, democratic institutions (or turnout) and the interactive term, statistically significant (Prob > chi2 = 0.0000).

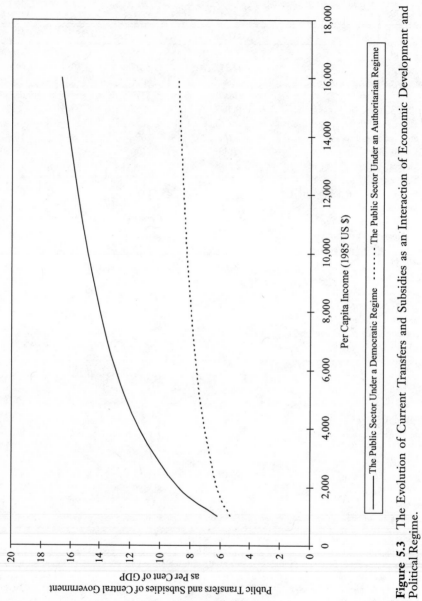

Figure 5.3 The Evolution of Current Transfers and Subsidies as an Interaction of Economic Development and Political Regime.

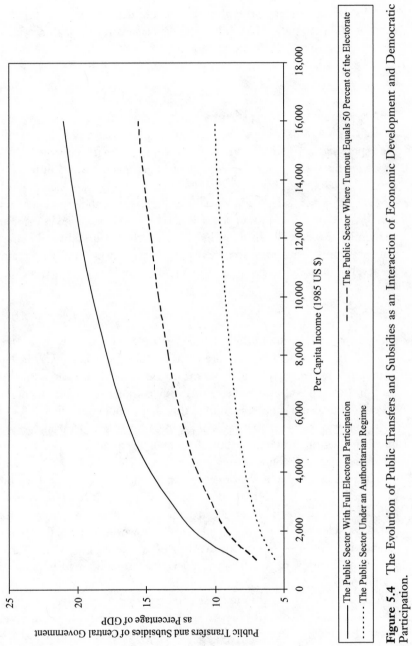

Figure 5.4 The Evolution of Public Transfers and Subsidies as an Interaction of Economic Development and Democratic Participation.

by 1.17 percentage points. We must conclude that the growth in public revenue and nonmilitary expenditure takes place mainly through programs directed toward the elderly population.

Wages and Salaries of Central Government

Table 5.6 examines the explanatory value of the different models of public sector growth for the expenditure on public employment. The results are especially instructive when they are compared with previous tables. Trade openness has a slight effect on public employment expenditure. The level of development has a negative but statistically not significant effect. With development, democracies reduce the size of public wages. Again, it is possible that the forms of redistribution that are practiced in agrarian economies are gradually displaced by the new demands for universal welfare state programs – this seems to receive confirmation from Model 3. Finally, the level of turnout increases the size of public employment (Model 2).

Conclusions

This chapter has explored the role that the type of political regime, conditional on the distribution of preferences among citizens, plays in determining the size of the public sector. In the process of examining that relationship, it has also furnished a relatively complete specification of the overall political and economic sources that shape public spending.

In line with the idea that taxes and expenditure are set through a political mechanism whereby politicians match the preferences of the enfranchised, we have found strong empirical evidence showing that a substantial part of the public sector varies conditional on the political regime in place. In authoritarian regimes, generally imposed to block redistribution, taxes remain low. Conversely, in democratic regimes the public sector grows considerably. Its expansion takes place, however, as a function of the extent of electoral participation, the distribution of economic risk across voters and the type of redistributive demands across different population segments.

As electoral turnout goes up, taxes and transfers rise correspondingly. The interpretation of this chapter is that, by shifting the median voter toward low-income sectors, a higher level of electoral participation intensifies the existing redistributive tensions in the political system and effectively forces politicians to expand public programs.

Table 5.6. *Wages and Salaries of Central Government as Percentage of GDP, 1970–99*

	(1)	(2)	(3)	(4)
Constant	4.54***	3.37**	9.88***	3.15
	(1.31)	(1.59)	(1.33)	(3.93)
Per capita income (Log)[a]	−0.03	−0.05		0.12
	(0.18)	(0.22)		(0.15)
Trade openness (log of sum of	0.70***	1.01***	−0.06	1.11***
exports and imports over GDP)[b]	(0.18)	(0.20)	(0.25)	(0.28)
Democratic regime[c]	2.65	−2.53***	−0.71	0.40
	(1.82)	(0.67)	(0.93)	(1.97)
Democratic regime* Log of	−0.44*			
real per capita income	(0.23)			
Level of turnout in		0.07**		−0.09*
democratic regimes		(0.03)		(0.05)
Level of turnout* Log of		−0.01***		
real per capita income		(0.00)		
Share of agricultural sector			−0.05***	
in GDP[d]			(0.01)	
Democratic regime* Share of			−0.00	
agricultural sector			(0.02)	
Percentage of population			−0.25**	
65 years or older			(0.10)	
Democratic regime*			0.00	
Proportion of old population			(0.10)	
Fuel exports as percentage of			−0.01	
all exports			(0.01)	
Gini index				−0.04
				(0.08)
Democratic regime*				−0.01
Gini index				(0.04)
Level of turnout*				0.002
Gini index				(0.001)
Number of observations	2218	1575	1667	509
R^2	0.2915	0.4035	0.2670	0.5281
Model Chi-square	47.37	49.92	50.45	30.55
Prob > Chi-square	0.0000	0.0000	0.0000	0.0001

[a] Constant US$ of 1985. *Source:* Penn World Tables.
[b] Trade openness: Log of the sum of exports and imports over GDP. *Source:* Penn World Tables.
[c] Democratic regime: Five-year average of democratic institutions. Variable goes from 1 (democracy in previous five years) to 0 (nondemocracy in previous five years). Average calculated on index developed in Chapter 1.
[d] Share of agricultural sector: Percentage of GDP from agricultural sector. *Source:* World Bank Tables.
Estimation: Ordinary least squares estimation, with panel corrected standard errors, and correction for autocorrelation and for heteroskedastic disturbances between panels.
Standard errors in parenthesis.
*$p < 0.10$; **$p < 0.05$; ***$p < 0.01$

The unequal distribution of risk emerges as well as a key factor in the expansion of spending in industrial democracies. Whereas risks are generally common to most individuals in agrarian societies, modern technological shocks lead to the differentiation of the population according to skills and to the corresponding concentration of risks, such as industrial accidents and joblessness, in particular segments of the population. With the decline of extended families, the traditional means of supporting workers in economic downturns, that is, informal help from relatives, disappear. In democratic arenas, these changes translate into strong political pressures, normally channeled through organized labor (that is, social-democratic movements), to establish publicly financed, collective insurance schemes.

The underlying distribution of income also shapes the size of the public sector. As discussed throughout this chapter, the extent of direct redistributive pressures, of the kind predicted by the political model of taxation employed in the book and related to the distance between median and average income, should be (controlling for levels of turnout) mild at most. Since democracies flourish only in societies with moderate levels of inequality, median voters do not impose excessive taxes on high-income earners. In other words, by looking at democracies, it should be difficult or perhaps even impossible to find empirical evidence that corroborates a positive relationship between more inequality and higher taxes. Again, this does not discredit the model of taxation we have employed: it simply validates this book's main goal of endogenizing the political game that determines the median voter. Even if the empirical evidence for a positive relationship between inequality and taxation is weak, it is important to stress that the nature of income distribution seems to be directly relevant to explaining public spending in one type of program: public spending on pensions (and health). As the population becomes older, that is, as the median voter ages, the pressure for intergenerational transfers increases sharply.[17]

Finally, the size of the public sector is also shaped by factors that operate independently of the political regime in place. The opportunities granted by a potentially growing economy spur public intervention. To cope with

---

[17] The conditional effect of regime type matches Rodrik's (1998) findings that political regimes have redistributive effects on the size of factor shares in the economy. As later confirmed in Przeworski et al. (2000: 168–75) for a larger sample, the share of labor in national income hovers around 30 percent in poor countries, regardless of the political regime in place. By contrast, in countries with per capita income above $4,000, that is, in economies with an industrial workforce, its size varies with regime: whereas it remains depressed under authoritarian systems, it rises to about 45 percent in democracies.

Conclusions

market failures that haunt the provision of key infrastructures and to set up a regulatory framework that boosts private investment, states may step in and increase tax collection. Similarly, a higher degree of economic openness, which constrains the ability of states to manage the domestic business cycle, spurs the generation of public programs to compensate their losers.

6

The State, the Threat of Expropriation and the Possibility of Development

The previous chapters of the book described the choice of political regimes as mainly the result of the underlying economic conditions and political resources of social classes and sectors in each country. In other words, the democratic or authoritarian character of the state reflected the existing balance of power between different political agents and sectors – a balance that was shaped, in turn, by the distribution and nature of assets and political resources among societal agents. Politics was understood as the emergence and management of conflict in society.

In that model, politicians played a rather subdued role from a theoretical point of view. They were seen as simply reflecting the interests of social groups and, at most, of tacitly solving the coordination problems that beset any group engaged in collective action. But their preferences (and corresponding strategies) did not deviate from the preferences of their electors (and from the strategies that any other elector in office would have pursued). In short, political elites, either in government or in opposition, lacked autonomy vis-à-vis citizens.

Although that simplified conception of the relationship between politicians and citizens gave us substantial theoretical and empirical leverage, the linkage between politicians and their constituencies is generally imperfect. Politicians are unlikely to behave as pure agents in pursuit of the interests of their principal (the broad public in a democracy or the enfranchised class in an authoritarian regime). Instead, as stressed in recent literature on political accountability, political elites may exploit deficient levels of information among citizens as well as incomplete mechanisms of control in the hands of the citizens to pursue their own goals and to appropriate rents and assets for themselves. To put it differently, besides the central "horizontal" conflict between social sectors that characterizes the process of political transitions and that I discussed in the preceding chapters, there is also a "vertical" conflict between rulers and their constituencies that we need to pay attention to.

With this goal in mind, the first section examines the extent to which politicians may pursue and achieve their own goals qua politicians, that is, as agents with objectives that are different from or even opposed to the broader goals of the social sectors they represent. More specifically, the central aim of this section is to determine whether and how political elites, conditional on the regime in which they operate and on the initial nature and distribution of assets, may change the underlying distribution of assets to their advantage. The section starts by showing that democracies are relatively self-sustaining equilibria: because democracies are characterized by accountability mechanisms that minimize the level of state corruption and hence the transfer of assets to policy makers, the initial conditions that favored the democratic transition are unlikely to be altered by political maneuvering. By contrast, in authoritarian regimes, where citizens monitor policy makers with difficulty, the level of rent appropriation is much higher. After a relatively prolonged period of authoritarian rule, the concentration of economic assets and political resources should increase and should be more extreme than under a regime based on electoral competition. Within right-wing authoritarian regimes, the extent of rent appropriation will vary with the internal constitution of the state: it is much greater in "pure" dictatorships (that is, in those with an uncontested ruler) than in "parliamentary" or "committee-like" nondemocracies (such as eighteenth-century Britain), where policy makers monitor each other to some extent. Rent appropriation by state elites may occur in left-wing or communist dictatorships as well. As a matter of fact, the section will show that the type of society in which revolutionary episodes occur (again, economies unequal and rich in fixed assets) and the confiscatory practices of the new elites explain in a straightforward manner the cycle of military takeover and revolution that often besets Third World countries.

Besides fleshing out the political or bureaucratic means through which the underlying distribution of assets may change, the introduction of (partially) autonomous politicians and the analysis of how they may transfer wealth to themselves have a central theoretical advantage. They give us the necessary tools to examine how the underlying economic and political conditions that trigger a political transition to democracy arise. In other words, they offer a way to endogenize the structural causes behind the process of democratization. This is the task of the second part of the chapter.

I undertake it in two steps. I start by reflecting, in the second section, on the capacity of reformist or enlightened policy-making elites to implement reforms that reduce inequality and subsequently foster democracy. The conclusions are overall pessimistic. In unequal societies democracy cannot be established without comprehensive reforms aimed at reducing income differentials, yet domestic actors can rarely implement those reforms because the reforms are blocked by those opposing democracy in the first place. In short, the introduction of rapid structural reforms seems to be of limited value for widening the space for democracy. Accordingly, after concluding that most political transitions are wedded to relatively long processes of economic change and development, I turn, in the third section, to discussing the long-run parameters that may account for national and historical variation in inequality and factor mobility.

The State and the Threat of Expropriation

As rightly pointed out by the "state-centered" literature of two decades ago, the state or, more precisely, the elite controlling the state must be modeled as having its own set of goals, which may be partly (or completely) at odds with the interests of societal actors. Nonetheless, besides providing a much-needed reminder of the independent role of state elites, the highly influential conception of the state as an autonomous actor in politics has proven to be virtually useless from an empirical point of view.

On most occasions, statist scholars simply emphasize the need to take into account the autonomy of the state to explain political outcomes, as when Nordlinger notes that the "state's policy preferences are its own" and that "they are also decidedly distinctive" (1988: 882) – a rather shallow claim. At most, they describe state elites alternatively as Weberian types wedded by the logic of administrative rationality, as a set of bureaucrats in pursuit of greater administrative and political power or as policy makers maximizing national security.[1] With such a vague description of the preferences of state actors, the explanatory value of the state-centered literature has necessarily remained minimal.

To model the political conflict that takes place in the allocation of goods and power between state and citizens, we must turn to the more recent literature on political accountability. Here that vertical dimension of conflict is treated as a political game played between a principal (the public) and

[1] See Skocpol (1979), Evans, Rueschemeyer and Skocpol (1985) and Nordlinger (1988).

an agent (the politician or policy maker) in which the former delegates to the latter a given set of instruments to execute certain goals (Przeworski, Stokes and Manin 1999). In the game, the interests of both parties may be at odds. Even while acting partly on the interests of their potential electors (either the wealthy, the middle class, the workers or a particular economic sector), policy makers are likely to pursue their own political agenda: they may be interested in enriching themselves while in office; or, even if they are honest, their ideas about what enhances the welfare of the public may differ from what the public itself wants. With self-interested politicians and state elites, the delegation of decision-making and policy-implementation responsibilities automatically opens up the space for significant inefficiencies and corruption among politicians. As a result, it generates the possibility that the state, through a process of rent appropriation, could both reshuffle the distribution of assets (in favor of the state elite) and thwart growth (since it erodes a secure framework for property rights needed to sustain investment).

The ability of politicians to exploit the public varies with the distribution and nature of assets in the economy, the type of political institutions through which they relate to the public, and the information citizens have about the state of the world, the policies to be pursued and their welfare consequences. I explore these questions in the rest of this section. I first consider the case of democracies as generators of political accountability (in the first subsection). I then discuss the appropriation of rents by politicians in right-wing dictatorships (in the second subsection). After a brief analysis in the third subsection of the effects that asset concentration (independent of political regime) has on corruption, I conclude with a description of the evolution and consequences of left-wing authoritarian regimes in the last subsection. Again, the insights of this section about the relationship between social actors and state elites will be applied in the following two sections to sketch out a model of economic and political development.

Democratic Accountability

As shown in seminal papers by Barro (1973) and Ferejohn (1986), the solution to the delegation problem described earlier, in which politicians may be tempted to exploit the lack of information citizens may have about policies and their consequences either to pursue their own agenda or to appropriate rents, lies in the public's establishing a control mechanism, such as regular elections, to discipline the policy maker. Provided that electors vote retrospectively, that is, that they look backward to the results provided by the incumbent before casting their ballots, elections force policy makers to be accountable to the public. The credible threat of losing their offices in the next period compels policy makers to deliver good services and refrain from extracting rents. Moreover, the degree of information that citizens possess curbs the opportunities politicians may have to engage in political corruption and mismanagement. As citizens have more precise knowledge about both the policies adopted by politicians and the environment in which they are implemented, policy makers have less room to deviate resources to themselves. Provided that competitive elections are in place to punish the incumbent, rent appropriation should also decline.

Political accountability is lower and corruption should be higher in dictatorships than in democracies. Even though authoritarian regimes eventually rely on the active support of specific social sectors and/or some tacit tolerance or minimal consent across the population, dictators employ repressive methods to remain in power. Thus, the cost of overthrowing a dictatorship is higher than the effort citizens need to make to get rid of an incumbent through democratic elections. The use of repression and the cost to change a dictatorial regime make the threat of removal of an authoritarian government lower on average than that of a democratic cabinet. Authoritarian elites have then more leeway to appropriate income than do democratically elected politicians. Similarly, the public will accept lower levels of government performance under a dictatorship than in a democracy because they discount the costs they would have to incur to otherwise bring down the regime.

I here offer some empirical data on the differential levels of corruption and rent-seeking under democratic and nondemocratic regimes – and for different levels of information among the public. Table 6.1 shows the mean index of corruption, which taps both the demand for bribes from business by political and administrative authorities as well as practices such as patronage, nepotism and job reservation, and the average index of risk of expropriation by the government according to political regime and the level of newspaper circulation over 100 nations from 1980 to 1990. Both indicators have been developed by the Political Risk Services Group and are published in its "International Country Risk Guide." The index of corruption ranges from 0 to 6. The threat of expropriation goes from 0 to 10. A higher number indicates a government that is, respectively, cleaner and less threatening to private property. The circulation of daily newspapers

Table 6.1. *The Level of Rent Appropriation by Political Regime and Newspaper Readership, 1980–90*

	Democracies		Dictatorships	
	High Newspaper Circulation[c]	Low Newspaper Circulation[d]	High Newspaper Circulation[c]	Low Newspaper Circulation[d]
Lack of corruption[a]	5.48	3.57	3.48	2.70
Lack of risk of expropriation[b]	9.60	7.85	8.05	6.12
Proportion of cases (in %)	12	32	2	54

[a] Range from 0 to 6.
[b] Range from 0 to 10.
[c] Equal or above 0.3 daily copies per person.
[d] Below 0.3 daily copies per person.
Sources: Indexes of corruption and risk of expropriation taken from Political Risk Services Group. Level of newspaper circulation taken from World Bank (2000).

per person, which measures the quality of informational controls, is built with data on newspaper circulation reported in World Bank (2000). The measure ranges from 0 in Mauritania to around 0.6 daily copies per person in Japan and Norway. High circulation is a circulation equal to or above 0.3 newspapers per person.

As is apparent from Table 6.1, democracies with a well-informed electorate are systematically less corrupt and less exposed to expropriatory action than badly informed democratic publics and, particularly, dictatorships. This positive correlation between democracy and newspaper circulation and good governance holds, in statistical tests performed in Adserà, Boix and Payne (2001), after controlling for economic development, political instability, religion, legal and constitutional structure, size of the public sector, trade and financial openness, weight of agriculture and minerals in the economy and electoral turnout.

In short, democracy brings political accountability. This has, in turn, key implications for the political and economic equilibria of the model. The risk that, under a democratic government, the existing distribution of assets could be changed through the gradual appropriation of assets and rents by politicians toward a more skewed distribution of wealth in their favor seems low. In other words, democracy has a set of mechanisms that make it a self-sustaining equilibrium.

(Naturally, democracies are not exempt from the possibility that certain exogenous shocks, such as military invasions or the discovery of oil fields that increases the proportion of fixed assets, could change their underlying distribution and type of assets and increase the incentives leading to the introduction of an authoritarian regime. Consider, for example, the evolution of the late Roman Republic. Its systematic territorial expansion raised the stakes of political power to unprecedented levels, endowed several political entrepreneurs with vast resources and, through civil wars fought by generals enriched by external conquests, finally led to the collapse of its relatively representative institutions.)

Rent Appropriation in Authoritarian Regimes

Defined precisely by the lack of electoral mechanisms to control policy makers, authoritarian regimes should (and, as shown in Table 6.1, do) engage in higher levels of rent appropriation than democracies. As will be developed in the third section, on inequality and capital mobility, dictatorships are born to sustain (and often to expand) the expropriatory strategies that tyrants (be they kings or military officers) carry out as they achieve power.

What is missing in the literature on the relationship between political regimes and political accountability (and hence economic growth), however, is the appreciation that authoritarian regimes come or are institutionalized in different forms with distinct consequences for the extent of rent appropriation and, what is of most interest to us here, for the internal political dynamics of the regime. These institutional differences correspond to the extent to which power is concentrated at the elite level. On the one hand, there are "parliamentary" or "committee-like" dictatorships in which the members of the ruling class have a relatively equal say in the decision-making process. On the other hand, there are authoritarian regimes where a single ruler practically monopolizes all political decisions.

Britain's system of government in the eighteenth century is a good example of the former case. Since 1688 landowners virtually assumed complete control of Parliament to the exclusion of all other social actors (Powell 1973). Yet within the parliamentary system, there were political factions and a balanced system that preserved a certain plurality and equality among its members. With such an internal plurality in place, the risk of rent appropriation from the ruling class or the state elite is lower than in a centralized or one-person dictatorship. If the decisions on how to allocate resources or regulate the economy depend on a committee or assembly, every actor (either alone or, more probably, in a coalition with other actors) holds a certain capacity to veto other actors' moves. This proposition subsumes North and Weingast's insight (1989) that the independent status of the English Parliament and its ability to check the Crown (with a credible threat of removal) helped the government to secure property rights. Nonetheless, instead of viewing parliaments (and by extension, democracy) as the only mechanism to make a credible commitment, it broadens their hypothesis in the following sense. Property rights are, generally speaking, strengthened by the existence of a balance of power among several actors that makes it impossible for one of them to expropriate from all the others. The institutionalization of this balance of power in a committee or assembly (or, as I consider later, in a territorial manner through a system of sovereign and equal nations or a federal arrangement) simply reinforces the preexisting political equilibrium that gives guarantees to investors.[2]

In response to North and Weingast's work (1989), it has been retorted, in a strict Marxian vein, that the finding that Parliament played a role in protecting property rights in seventeenth-century England is "not particularly surprising given that only the propertied enjoyed political rights" (Przeworski et al. 2000: 209). The insight was already made in a pointed manner by Barrington Moore when he described eighteenth-century England as ruled by a "committee of landlords" that allowed the landed upper classes to operate a sweeping transformation of the English countryside in the century that followed the Glorious Revolution (Moore 1966: 19). But just focusing on the capacity of the landed interests to defend themselves from the expropriatory threat of organized peasants and workers misses a key point of the lesson offered by the British model. Besides sheltering the wealthy from the rest of society, the primacy of Parliament also protected landowners from themselves and from the king.

By contrast, in one-person dictatorships, the tyrant represses the lower classes while *at the same time* attempting to transfer assets from the rich to himself. After becoming president of Nicaragua in 1937, Anastasio Somoza, who owned no land before staging the coup that put him in power, started to amass a considerable fortune for his family. By the 1970s the Somozas owned 46 coffee farms, 7 sugar plantations, 51 cattle farms, 400 tobacco farms, 60 percent of all beef-packing plants and 100 percent of the fishing

---

[2] This insight runs parallel to the discussion on presidentialism in Chapter 4's subsection on the separation of powers.

and cigar industries in the country, and they held almost a monopoly over coffee and beef exports and domestic milk production.

The distinction between unconstrained or absolutist monarchies and pluralistic or proto-parliamentarian states receives empirical confirmation across countries and historical periods. It is underpinned by work of DeLong and Shleifer (1993) on the economic performance of Western European countries from 1000 to 1800. In those areas in which monarchs had considerable leeway and could behave, in Olsonian terms, as "stationary bandits," urban population growth (taken as a proxy for economic growth) was more modest than in nonabsolutist countries.

Similarly, a comparison between monetary policy within the Spanish kingdom in the seventeenth century confirms that the differential impact of various types of nondemocratic regimes also accounts for intrastate variation. Until the abolition of an autonomous Catalan government by Philip V in 1714, Catalonia and Castile had very different political institutions. Whereas in Castile the old Cortes rarely met and when they did they automatically assented to all royal decisions, the Catalan parliament, controlled by the nobility, the clergy and the upper layer of some urban centers, kept virtual sovereignty over taxes and monetary policy throughout the seventeenth century (Elliott 1986). These two types of governments had divergent economic effects. To solve recurrent financial needs sparked by continuous wars in Europe, Spanish kings resorted to massive devaluations of the Castilian currency by coining with an alloy that contained ever-growing proportions of copper. As a result, good silver coin, which was the only currency valid for foreign trade, could be bought only by paying an ever-increasing premium – of 50 percent in 1650, 200 percent in 1670–75 and 275 percent in 1680. The monetary mismanagement of the mid-seventeenth century coincided with a 25 percent fall in the population of Castile between 1651 and 1682. By contrast, after the 1640 Catalan uprising against Madrid ended with a reaffirmation of the local autonomous institutions, the Catalan pound hardly changed in its value against silver. Monetary stability and, its companion, economic prosperity were so remarkable that in 1683 the historian and lawyer Feliu de la Penya published his book *The Phoenix of Catalonia* to symbolize the hope of an economic renaissance. As Pierre Vilar notes, in Catalonia "as in England, the 18th century began in the 17th century" (Vilar 1976: 235).

The differential expropriatory threat posed by distinct types of dictatorships also finds support in contemporary times. Table 6.2 displays the average level of lack of corruption and lack of expropriation risk by political

Table 6.2. *The Level of Rent Appropriation by Types of Authoritarian Regime and Democracy, 1980–90*

	Democracies	Dictatorships with Legislature	Dictatorships without Legislature
Lack of corruption[a]			
Top quartile of per capita income ($6,226–$33,946)	5.22	4.69	3.17
Second quartile of per capita income ($2,756–$6,225)	3.64	3.21	3.03
Third quartile of per capita income ($1,135–$2,755)	2.54	2.30	1.50
Bottom quartile of per capita income ($299–$1,134)	2.01	2.48	2.55
Lack of risk of expropriation[b]			
Top quartile of per capita income ($6,226–$33,946)	9.20	8.18	4.17
Second quartile of per capita income ($2,756–$6,225)	7.07	6.38	4.89
Third quartile of per capita income ($1,135–$2,755)	5.75	5.72	3.58
Bottom quartile of per capita income ($299–$1,134)	5.56	5.43	4.95

[a] Range from 0 to 6.
[b] Range from 0 to 10.
Per capita income comes expressed in 1990 constant dollars.
Sources: Indexes of corruption and risk of expropriation taken from Political Risk Services Group. Classification for democracies, dictatorships with legislature and dictatorships without is taken from Przeworski et al. (2000).

regime in the period 1980–90. Again, the two indexes are taken from information developed by the Political Risk Services Group. Results are shown for democracies and, following Przeworski's coding, for dictatorships with and without a legislature. The averages are further split according to quartile groups in level of per capita income. In line with the predictions, corruption and, particularly, the likelihood of expropriation are much higher in unified dictatorships than in internally pluralistic regimes.[3] Thus, personalistic authoritarian regimes that persist over long periods of time should, on average, lead to higher levels of wealth inequality and, hence, to a lower probability of democratic transitions.

[3] The different level of expropriatory risk between dictatorships with and without a legislature is statistically robust to the introduction of controls.

213

Asset Concentration and Rent Appropriation

Before turning to the effects of revolutionary regimes, consider the ways in which the internal structure of the economy may change the ability of policy makers to appropriate rents. As wealth becomes more concentrated, the cost of confiscation must decline. This claim is examined in the upper panel of Table 6.3 – by looking at corruption and expropriatory risk for different levels of export concentration. As already discussed in Chapter 2, the index of export concentration is a Hirsch-Herfindhal index based on 239 three-digit standard international trade classification categories of exports as estimated by UNCTAD and varies from 0.06 (a highly diversified economy) to 1 (whenever only one product is exported). Authoritarian regimes score lower values (and therefore have more corruption and less secure property rights) than democracies in almost all cases. But within each regime, the degree of corruption and insecurity increases as the economy becomes more concentrated.

In turn, the bottom panel of Table 6.3 examines the two indexes by regime and level of inequality. Regime type again matters for both corruption and expropriatory risk. The distribution of income also affects the cleanliness and security of countries. As inequality declines, both corruption and the risk of expropriation fall (particularly among democracies). For very high levels of inequality, the level of graft is identical between democracies and dictatorships.

Revolution and the Expropriation of Assets

Let us now turn to explore the economic and political dynamics of left-wing or revolutionary regimes. The evolution of left-wing dictatorships is a function of the way in which the poor, or at least those that engage in the revolt against the wealthy, decide to administer the expropriated assets. The revolutionary party or class can divide them in roughly similar shares, creating an equal society and therefore establishing the conditions to achieve a stable democratic regime. Alternatively, it may decide to put the assets under the unified control of the new postrevolutionary authority.

Three types of reasons may impel the winner not to divide the expropriated assets. First, purely self-interested considerations, such as maximizing wealth or power, may incline the revolutionary elite, that is, the segment of society that organized the poor into revolutionary action, to take control of the existing wealth. In this case, revolutionaries are bandits who crudely manipulate the revolutionary impulses of the masses to their own

Table 6.3. *The Level of Rent Appropriation by Concentration of Wealth and Political Regimes, 1980–90*

A. By Level of Export Concentration[a]	Democracies	Dictatorships
Lack of corruption[b]		
Top quartile of export concentration (countries with index from 0.560 to 0.997)	2.73	2.32
Second quartile of export concentration (countries with index from 0.366 to 0.559)	3.17	2.36
Third quartile of export concentration (countries with index from 0.201 to 0.365)	4.24	2.71
Bottom quartile of export concentration (countries with index from 0 to 0.200)	4.87	2.92
Lack of risk of expropriation[c]		
Top quartile of export concentration (countries with index from 0.560 to 0.997)	6.55	5.29
Second quartile of export concentration (countries with index from 0.366 to 0.559)	6.68	5.39
Third quartile of export concentration (countries with index from 0.201 to 0.365)	7.40	5.70
Bottom quartile of export concentration (countries with index from 0 to 0.200)	8.81	6.47
B. By Degree of Income Inequality	**Democracies**	**Dictatorships**
Lack of corruption[b]		
High income inequality (countries with Gini over 50 percent)	2.80	2.90
Medium income inequality (countries with Gini between 35 and 50 percent)	3.85	2.73
Low income inequality (countries with Gini below 35 percent)	5.61	3.39
Lack of risk of expropriation[c]		
High income inequality (countries with Gini over 50 percent)	7.00	5.98
Medium income inequality (countries with Gini between 35 and 50 percent)	7.61	6.55
Low income inequality (countries with Gini below 35 percent)	9.46	7.07

[a] Range from 0 to 1. Hirsch-Herfindhal index of export concentration based on 239 three-digit standard international trade classification categories of exports as estimated by UNCTAD.
[b] Range from 0 to 6.
[c] Range from 0 to 10.

Sources: Indexes of corruption and risk of expropriation taken from Political Risk Services Group. Classification for democracies, dictatorships with legislature and dictatorships without is taken from Przeworski (2000).

advantage. Second, the new state elite may decide not to redistribute for efficiency considerations. If exploitation of the assets exhibits economies of scale or requires high fixed investments, the state may consider it advisable to centralize their management completely. Likewise, the new elite may also hold the belief that the division of assets would lead to excessive consumption and relatively low levels of investment, hence condemning the country to a perpetual state of underdevelopment. The revolutionary elite would then rather embrace a Stalinist strategy, based on centralizing all property, reigning in consumption and heavily allocating the surplus to investment, to move the country from a stage of primary exports to an industrial society. Third, the revolutionary elite may prefer to centralize the property and management of assets in application of strict "Maoist" principles: since the rates of investment and productivity among individuals may vary (due to genetic or cultural traits), splitting all the assets among the poor may lead over time to the reemergence of inequalities and therefore to the defeat of the revolutionary goals. To prevent that outcome, the revolutionary elite would rather retain full control over all assets and allocate the returns (wages) among individuals in a centralized and strictly equalizing manner.

Empirically there is little evidence that left-wing coups and regimes have been followed by equalizing agrarian reforms or by the division among the population of other fixed assets such as mines and oil fields. In what is likely to be the most comprehensive study of agrarian reforms conducted in the developing world after 1945, Powelson and Stock (1990) conclude that only those implemented in South Korea, Taiwan and the Indian state of Kerala benefited the peasants. The first two instances were de facto imposed by the United States. Agrarian reforms that followed revolutionary episodes, such as in Mexico, Cuba and Nicaragua, resulted in the introduction of property mechanisms (either based in the primacy of communal lands or in the collectivization of farms) that distorted production and often depressed output. In state-led reforms, such as those pushed through by military officers in Peru and Egypt, or anticolonial movements in Algeria, Somalia, Tanzania and Zambia, bureaucratic officials eventually appropriated most of the agricultural surplus and again precipitated a fall in productivity.[4]

---

[4] Other agrarian reforms, led mostly by authoritarian rulers, hardly changed the structure of property. These include Paraguay, Venezuela, Colombia and Ecuador, which consisted in the distribution and colonization of previously unoccupied land. In Bolivia landowners successfully weathered the popular mobilization of the 1950s (de Janvry 1981). The agrarian

The Cycle of Corrupt Left-Wing Dictatorships If the new political authority pushes for the complete centralization of the ownership and management of property, to maximize either its own wealth or, holding more
enlightened views, national output, the root of the problems that caused
the revolutionary explosion to begin with will persist. Over time, and particularly if the process of industrialization does not take place or ends in
failure, a split will reappear between the political elite, who manages and
eventually secures de facto ownership of the assets, and the rest of the population. This division will reproduce the old, prerevolutionary economy
where capital owners were pitted against the laborers. The only difference
will be that the role of new "capitalists" will be now played by the revolutionary elite. As a result, after a while, the very tensions that led to the
expropriation of the old owners' assets will emerge again and violence will
inevitably flare up.

Thus, in economies with high levels of fixed assets, we should expect to
observe the following "cyclical" pattern to take place over time. A tyrant
or a king will be dethroned either through a "left-wing" takeover executed
by progressive officers or, in a highly mobilized society, by a popular revolution. After taking control of the state, the revolutionary elite will lay
out extensive plans for the rational exploitation of natural resources and
the development of the economy.[5] However, corrupt practices and the
mismanagement associated with nonmarket strategies will gradually sink
in. The old left-wingers will naturally become identical to the right-wing
tyrannies they deposed. This in turn will set in motion another wave of popular anger, coups and civil wars, followed by the election of new predatory
elites.

Such recurrent cycles of sudden outbursts of violence followed by the
reassertion of authoritarian rule characterize those countries built around
highly specific assets. In several Middle Eastern countries, such as Iraq,
Libya and Syria, pan-Arabist and "tiermondiste" socialists who expropriated the wealth of sheiks and foreign companies in the 1950s and 1960s

reforms of Guatemala in 1952–54, Chile in 1967–73 and Pakistan in 1971 were either blocked
or reversed by subsequent coups.

[5] Historically, the existence of vast amounts of natural resources has often led to nationalization of the resources across the world. The best cross-national predictor of the size of the
public business sector (as a percentage of GDP) is the proportion of fuel and other mineral
exports. In the late 1980s, for example, the correlation between the two variables was 0.484
(and 0.600 if we exclude Sudan). Estimations are based on data taken from Garrett (1998)
and World Bank (1999).

ended up imposing bluntly repressive and corrupt governments and now face new contestation from so-called Islamic fundamentalists, who, should they win, would end up behaving in a similar manner. In several African mining states, a long string of coups and internal wars has pitted different elites and social sectors against each other for the control of gold, diamonds and fuel, leading on occasion to the collapse of the state structure in countries like Sierra Leone and to some extent Zaire. A similar pattern of military takeovers, internal conflagration and adulterated agrarian reforms has characterized Haiti's, several Central American states', some periods of oil-rich Venezuela's and most of Bolivia's history since they became independent in the early nineteenth century.[6]

Expropriation and Industrialization   To overcome the trap of poverty and cyclical political chaos that chains highly unequal and asset-specific countries, the revolutionary elite may, as indicated earlier, attempt to control the nationalized assets and then devote a large portion of profits to investment in order to unleash an industrial economy. Again, it is unclear why the revolutionary elite should spawn a long process of state-led investment, particularly given that it implies a reduction in current consumption. Two forces generally impel political elites to industrialize: first, a natural desire to catch up with more modern economies; second, and more importantly, security concerns, that is, the need to modernize to prevent neighbors from amassing resources to defeat them in future wars.[7] Still, the propensity to invest in industrializing strategies goes down as the returns from natural resources go up. In countries abundant in oil or very valuable minerals, the state postpones industrial investment programs since the profits from selling manufactures appear low in comparison and relatively uncertain. In other words, after a revolutionary shock, industrialization is more likely to happen in agrarian economies specialized in "food crops" (rice, corn, wheat) than in countries with highly valued export crops (such as coffee) or mines. Notice that it is in those countries less prone to shift to

---

[6] Notice that according to this book the existence of "lootable" assets does not necessarily lead, as claimed by recent researchers (Collier and Hoeffler 2001), to a situation of permanent instability; rather, it leads to prolonged periods of stability interspersed with violent outbursts.

[7] For example, the proximity of Germany stimulated the Soviet Union to launch ambitious industrialization plans in the interwar period. By contrast, and other things being equal, the geographic distance of Beijing from Delhi and the Himalayan chain may have reduced India's incentive to massively modernize its economy.

new economic activities where the cycles of repression and revolution just described are more intense.

If the process of industrial investment goes on and new types of assets are created, such as human capital in segments of the population, financial capital and so on, then by definition the postrevolutionary structure of state control and enforced equality disappears.[8] The state elite may then have to decide between restoring revolutionary purity, through either sustained purges or a massive "cultural" revolution, and embracing a new economy that implies the formation of countervailing groups outside the state. In the latter case, the old revolutionary regime should give way to either an authoritarian regime, in which those that accumulated the new assets control the state, or perhaps a democratic regime.[9]

Economic Reform and the Possibility of Democracy

According to the discussion developed in the previous chapters, we know that the likelihood that a democracy will be introduced and will then survive is related to the existing level of income inequality, the specificity of assets and the degree of political mobilization of the less well-off. These results in turn open up the question of whether the underlying structural conditions can be actively changed, and if so, how, to foster democratization. What we need to answer is whether the state can push through a set of structural reforms, such as land reform, that reduce the level of social tensions to the point where democracy is peacefully accepted by all contending sides.

The answer to the question is, generally speaking, rather pessimistic. An enlightened tyrant can seldom pass policy reforms to equalize conditions and hence make democracy possible. If he had been able to overcome resistance to change, then a democratic arrangement would have been possible in the first place and the reform unnecessary to start with. Those who oppose democracy oppose it for its distributional consequences and have the

---

[8] It is highly unlikely that economic development induced by individual investment decisions could take place in a postrevolutionary state because, even if the new ruler were not to control all the assets or were to allow for wages from which individuals could direct a portion to savings and investment, there would be a permanent threat of expropriation that would annihilate any incentives to invest.

[9] The solution adopted may be contingent on the type of political transition that takes place after the fall of the communist dictatorship. For an analysis of the divergent paths of Eastern Europe and most former Soviet republics, see Hellman (1998) and Frye (2002).

same incentives to block any reformist program directed to create the social preconditions for a successful democracy.

Notice that a similar conclusion must follow for a democratically elected government. Although a stable democracy requires the appropriate economic structures, we can think of cases in which, for various reasons (such as war or economic depression), dictatorships collapse and elections are held. If inequality and asset specificity are high, the odds are clearly stacked against the survival of democracy. According to the estimates in Chapter 2, a democracy lasts for only a handful of years in highly unequal countries. A good example would be Spain in 1931 or, for that matter, any Southern European or Eastern European country after World War I. If the democratic government attempts to reform the distribution of property or even to raise taxes to satisfy popular demands, it risks a reactionary backlash. But not meeting social demands may lead either to electoral episodes in which candidates who are more radical would outbid the elected government or to violent outbursts in the street.

A democracy that operates against the statistical odds has only one way forward. It should raise taxes modestly (less than the wealthy's repression cost ρ) and then apply them to generate a progressive shift, through human-capital formation, in the structure and distribution of assets across the population. In other words, direct redistributive programs should be kept at a minimum. Naturally, for this strategy of reform to succeed two conditions must be met. First, the flow of public investment (denoted in Chapter 5 as $\lambda\tau$, with $\lambda \to 1$ here) must have a positive impact on the productivity of individuals and hence on growth rates. Otherwise, those who are taxed would simply be taking a loss and those receiving the investment would not be adding any new, more valuable capital. Second, the government must be capable of imposing discipline on the electorate – we already pointed to this condition in Chapter 4 when discussing the need for a credible commitment from the poor.

Clearly, the chances that, in conditions of medium to high inequality, a democracy can survive and stabilize seem slim. Peaceful agrarian reforms in developing countries are generally a failure – either because they do not lead to an equitable land distribution or because they are interrupted by the current landowners. Hence the most efficient way to reform the economy quickly must be through foreign intervention. This explains in part why the Axis powers made the transition to democracy so smoothly after World War II. Foreign occupation turned out to be key in securing the success of democracy in Japan and Germany (and probably in Eastern

Europe after 1990) because it was the only way to overcome the very strong resistance developed by the prewar domestic elites to any program of reform. With the separation of West Germany from Prussia, where land was heavily concentrated in the hands of Junkers, democracy could flourish in the Federal Republic. The reunification of Germany in 1990 did not jeopardize democracy given the radical transformation that the Eastern part suffered at the hands of the Communist party. After World War II, the United States promoted a radical land reform in Japan that reduced the percentage of tenants from 43.5 to 11.7 percent (Huntington 1968: 386). Similar reforms in Korea and in Taiwan (the latter by the Kuomintang, with its expropriatory phase of 1953 developed after substantial American pressure [Powelson and Stock 1990]) and in Eastern Europe also explain the reduction of past revolutionary pressures and established the basis for the rapid transition to democracy after the collapse of the Berlin Wall.

Public Goods and the Possibility of Reform   In discussing the strategies open to a democratic government in a highly unequal country, I have emphasized the need to invest in capital-formation, productivity enhancing expenditures. This brings up a question that deserves a brief discussion here. In Chapters 1 and 4, taxes were modeled as distorting growth. However, I have introduced here the possibility that taxes may foster growth, provided that they are channeled into capital formation and the provision of public goods.[10] If this is the case (and if, in so doing, the taxes also contribute to equalizing social conditions), then the zero-sum game that pits capital owners against nonasset owners declines in intensity. Capital may be interested in bearing some taxes to finance public goods whose provision it cannot secure on its own, while workers benefit from infrastructure or education that raises their wages.[11]

Two additional points follow. In the first place, the demand for public goods from capital probably mitigates but does not suppress class conflict. As seen in Chapter 5, the size of the public sector rises with development – probably because the latter triggers demands for public programs that in turn sustain and foster the process of economic modernization. But transfers, that is, the purest redistributive part of public spending, are boosted only by democracy. To put it the other way around, demands for democracy

[10] See Alesina and Rodrik (1994) for a political-economic model in which taxes may be channeled into public investment and then generate growth.
[11] The idea that different types of capital holders may have different preferences about the size of the state is taken from Mares (2001).

persist even after the state has provided the needed amount of public goods to maximize growth.

In the second place, the demand for public goods is related to the type of productive structures dominant in each country. For certain types of capital, an efficient bureaucracy, a good patent-registration agency and the provision of skills to workers are extremely beneficial – as in the chemical, machine-tools and software industries. But for other types of capitalists, such as landowners, mining companies and even low-value-added textile firms, the provision of human capital is not a priority: it only costs money without boosting their firms' productivity. In short, the intervention of the state, and, as a result, the gradual transformation of assets across the population, requires certain types of capital to start with. And so we are again confronted with the question of how those types of industries, which may be more sympathetic to state activities and even to democracy, emerged in the first place.

The Sources of Inequality and Capital Mobility

If rapid domestic reforms are likely to founder and if the demand for growth-enhancing public spending requires certain, relatively sophisticated, types of capital, we should turn at this point to explore the processes through which different levels of economic inequality and asset specificity take root among countries.

Distribution of Assets

Assume a starting world where the only productive activity is agriculture – that is, a world where asset specificity is complete ($\sigma = 1$). (This naturally excludes hunting or preagrarian societies where there is only one factor, labor, which is completely mobile. In that world, of little interest for our purposes, social groups are structured around extended families and political hierarchies are virtually nonexistent. As the level of population density given the rate of productivity starts to go up, some violent competition should appear among individuals, and, in response to an emerging "security dilemma," we should observe the formation of tribes or confederations of families.)

In an agrarian world, where both land and labor are the factors of production and there is some technological exploitation of land, the distribution of assets and the type of political structure would vary as a function of

222

population density and military technology. Whenever the land/labor ratio is high and the military technology is primitive, the distribution of assets is generally equal and state structures are weak. If land is abundant, it is cheaper to move to new lands to avoid clashes with either neighbors or relatives than to invest in political arrangements to solve those conflicts – that is why frontier societies tend to be equal and prone to democratic governance. Because military technology is very simple, that is, the production of violence is labor intensive and does not rely on sophisticated weaponry (swords, chariots, horses, and so on), self-defense is possible. As a result, would-be predators – individuals who would use violence to extract rents from others – would not be troublesome since they could subject very few peasants at a time.

This equal and "stateless" world collapses after land becomes scarce or weapons grow more sophisticated. Political conflict arises in regions in which, with growing population density, the land/labor ratio declines. As less land is available, competition among farmers increases: moving to new lands becomes more costly. In addition, the costs of invading and expropriating from the neighbor, who is now geographically closer than in a sparsely populated world, diminish dramatically.

The constraints imposed by higher population density are exacerbated by the gradual sophistication of military technology. As weapons become more complex and expensive, previously independent farmers are faced with what may be called a "security dilemma." The production of violence becomes now a very specialized activity. Those individuals that decide to engage in predatory activities invest a substantial time and effort in mastering weapons. They become "professional" bandits, that is, agents that move around looting and razing peasant communities in a systematic manner. Producers, who, by definition, specialize in nonviolent activities to make a living, cannot oppose them – unless they turn as well into bandits.[12] As pointed out by Olson (1993, 2000), in the presence of "rovit" bandits that systematically raid farming communities and rob their crops, farmers eventually turn to those bandits that are willing to offer them protection on a permanent basis against other external predators. "Rovit" bandits now become "stationary" bandits: they seize a given territory, pacify it internally and exclude from it any other external (mobile) bandit. In so doing,

[12] As indicated by Hirschman (1981: 250–51), here following Nieboer, if highly sophisticated weapons are available, a low land/labor ratio may increase the incentives of those bandits to impose a slavery system precisely to curtail the exit options of the peasantry.

previously pirates and brigands become kings, feudal lords and nobles – "specialized agents" monopolizing violence and hence ensuring peace and order for the inhabitants of the area under their respective control.

The emergence of a political structure, that is, of rulers or states capable of protecting producers, has two consequences: an economic one, which has been well explored by North (1981, 1990) and Olson (2000), and a political one, which interests us more in this context. On the one hand, the now "stationary" bandits have a longer-term interest than do "rovit" bandits in maintaining the sources of (agricultural) production. As a result, the level of taxation under a state declines in comparison to the degree of plunder that takes place in stateless societies. Farmers now have an incentive to invest in the production of crops. As noted by North (1981), without military protection, that is, without states, the intensive practice of agriculture could not have taken place. On the other hand, the emergence of "stationary" bandits has fundamental political consequences. As part of the deal by which kings and nobles protect agricultural producers, they appropriate lands and accumulate assets, leading to a progressively more unequal society. And, as modeled in this book, it is to preserve this inequality that rulers rule in an authoritarian fashion.

The development of sophisticated weaponry and the growth of population do often, but not always, result in the creation of unequal political societies. Under certain conditions, farming communities may be able to preserve some equality of conditions (and therefore democratic arrangements). In regions that are protected by geographical barriers, such as seas or mountain chains, the cost of invasion by external bandits is high and the "security dilemma" faced by natives remains low. This may explain why areas such as the Swiss high valleys, Norway and Iceland sustained rather equal agrarian societies. Moreover, if farming involves a type of production strategy requiring cooperative practices that make farmers interdependent, the incentives to become a "bandit" are low: the existence of communal activities implies, first, that collective-action problems are sparse and that farmers can coordinate to defend the status quo against an internal enemy; and second, that by destroying many intercommunal ties, a strategy of expropriation may end up ruining the basis of production in the region.

So far I have sketched out how changes in population density and military technology affect the distribution of assets in the transition from preagrarian to agrarian economies – or within eminently agrarian economies. The main conclusion is, to put it briefly, that the unequal distribution of land resulted not from the workings of markets (due to, say, the presence of economies of scale) but from widespread use of political violence followed by expropriation.[13]

A similar logic can be applied to most state-building or foundational episodes happening in more recent times across the world. The history of nineteenth-century South America and postcolonial Africa is basically one in which state elites (*as well as* their challengers) employed their political resources to define the extent of their property claims, that is, to shape the distribution of economic resources to their advantage.[14] Likewise, as hinted by Frye (2002), different types of political transitions and institutions influenced the varying levels of inequality that emerged among countries in the post-Soviet world. In all those cases, "horizontal" or sectoral conflict over income distribution existed and thus mattered in the choice of political regimes. But it was subsumed in the strategies developed by "state builders" to appropriate rents and then secure them through the control of the state apparatus.

The Nature of Assets

To understand next how nonspecific assets emerge and transform the nature of agrarian economies (and how they affect the distribution of assets, that is, the parameter of inequality), we need to develop a theory of growth. Here I rely on the insights of North and Thomas (1973) and North (1981, 1990) while introducing some amendments to solve several empirical and theoretical gaps in that work.

Nonspecific assets result from the continuous generation of new products, such as wheels, alphabets, double-bookkeeping or aspirins. Inventions probably occur in an almost random manner, that is, unrelated to the property rights that may protect their authors. After all, even though Mozart was not paid as he had been promised for a concert for violin and harp that he composed about 1778 for a French count, he continued to write music at a frantic pace. However, the invention of new products leads to growth (and the multiplication of nonspecific assets) only if there is a certain institutional

---

[13] The extent to which landlords appropriate assets will be determined by, first, the balance of power with the population and, second, the production technology. Even if warlords have overwhelming military advantage, they will confiscate only to the point where they optimize profits.

[14] Thus, the history of late twentieth-century Africa should be properly compared to the emergence of states in Europe in the late medieval and early modern periods rather than to the politics of today's advanced world. I owe this point to Daniel Posner.

arrangement that protects inventors and investors from the expropriatory temptations of either the state elite *or* other private individuals and that therefore encourages them to invest in their new activities or technologies in a systematic manner.

As discussed earlier, in the subsection on rent appropriation in authoritarian regimes, protection against the threat of expropriation or excessive taxation may derive from having a particular (pluralistic or parliamentarian) type of state. As North and Weingast (1989) have suggested, the post-1688 English Parliament, in placing a check on the powers of the Crown, assured investors against the risk of arbitrary confiscation by the state. Or, in broader terms, the Parliament, acting as a committee of wealthy individuals, protected the rich from each other as well as from all other social classes. (Notice that in several Swiss cantons the industrial revolution progressed as fast as it did in England without their having a system of institutional checks and balances. However, they had a "committee-like" type of government and, as I consider later, a very fragmented system of sovereignty from a territorial point of view.)

Although having a pluralistic constitution may well have accounted for growth in England, this theory begs two questions.[15] First, the origins of parliamentary power are left unexplained – we know only that the forces of the royal and nonroyal parties were balanced in a way that led to the triumph of constitutionalism.[16] Second, and more importantly, it does not explain why Parliament did not expropriate from those investors who had no representation in Parliament. It may be that only those who were wealthy invested and hence were automatically protected by their participation in the decision-making process. It is difficult to argue, however, that investment, although in small quantities, did not take place among commercial and financial sectors that had no representation in Parliament. In short, in the same way that neoinstitutionalists have concluded that in absolutist monarchies the king can act arbitrarily, we should presume that parliamentary committees would be similarly tempted vis-à-vis nonparliamentary actors.

---

[15] Here I set aside any empirical concerns about the theory of Parliament as a credible commitment device. According to Rosenthal (2001), the size and sophistication of financial markets in France between the mid-seventeenth century until the French Revolution resembled those of financial markets in England despite the absolutist structure of the French monarchy.

[16] For a fresh exploration of the sources of parliamentarism, see Boucoyannis (2003) and Ertman (1997).

A simpler point of departure (which would not require introducing a distinction between crown and parliament) would be as follows. No sovereign has any incentive and means to make an entirely credible commitment not to expropriate. Like the king (the name of a stationary bandit in an agrarian world), parliament has the temptation to confiscate from all other actors. Any assembly of aristocrats has the incentive to tax the commercial class and the peasantry very heavily. Likewise, the incentive not to expropriate cannot come from any estimations about the potential rewards of letting some individuals invest in nonspecific assets. In the purely agrarian world that I posited at the beginning of this section, no sovereign has information about the possibilities of nonagrarian investment before it happens and changes the structure of the economy.[17] (In fact, because of their mobility, the creation of nonfixed assets is politically dangerous to the sovereign since the emergence of mobile assets may deprive the ruler from resources, thus reducing his bargaining power.[18])

If the factors that could check the state did not have a domestic foundation and could not spring from the rational calculations of a long-term and enlightened monarch, then the basis of the sovereign's credible commitment must have resided outside the ruler's territory. The first condition for a secure system of property rights in the Modern Age lay in the political fragmentation of Europe. If only one king had controlled the continent (broadly defined as an area where the costs of moving things outside it become close to infinite), no investment would have occurred because there could be no firm commitment against expropriation by the sovereign. By contrast, with several monarchs, each one controlling a region of the continent, and all of them living in the framework of an international balance of power, would-be investors had a chance to exercise an exit option against an expropriation move by one state. Thus, it was the territorial fragmentation of the international system that led to a game structure in which a "tacit" commitment to property rights was possible.

The difference between a unified empire and a divided continent, and therefore, between a kingdom where no capital-induced growth can occur

---

[17] Naturally, once other states see the economic expansion of nations that house nonagrarian activities, they will probably be interested in fostering such activities as well.

[18] The fact that Montesquieu and Turgot hailed mobile capital as a way of curbing the sovereign's power (Hirschman 1981) must mean, in turn, that all eighteenth-century monarchs were aware of the threat posed by these new forms of wealth. See also North (1981: 28–29).

and a region where new forms of (nonspecific) capital may be created, matches the different trajectories of China and Europe. In China, the ruling elite, threatened by the possibility of new emergent social sectors, blocked all plans for naval and commercial expansion after 1430. In Europe, in response to the confiscatory strategies of the Spanish kings in 1492 and of the French monarchs in the sixteenth and seventeenth centuries, both Jews and French Huguenots escaped to the Netherlands and Switzerland. It is also hard to believe that those who supported the English revolt of 1688 with Dutch capital would have done so without having the fallback option of taking refuge in the Netherlands had they failed. The cantonal fragmentation of Switzerland may have operated in the same direction: as a commitment device that by giving a cheap exit option secured the assets of capitalists and merchants against the temptations of their compatriots, it harbored a rapid economic take-off at the turn of the nineteenth century. To return to a previous example, Mozart's overall productivity may have been related to his capacity to travel across different states until he met, at least temporarily, the enlightened sovereign that understood his music and supported his living.[19]

Within Europe, that is, within a continent with a territorially fragmented sovereignty, investment in new activities and growth did not occur uniformly. For investment to take place, a general condition had to apply across all countries: basically, nations had to exist in a situation of a balance of power in which some relative peace prevailed. If, on the contrary, all countries had been in constant war with each other, then all the princes would have dissipated their national wealth and no productive activities could have been established. This may explain why financial markets and eventually industrial activity flourished in the eighteenth century after the Treaties of Westphalia in 1648 and Utrecht in 1714 settled key territorial claims on the continent.

Within that general condition of systemic peace, two factors may explain why investment rates differed across European nations. First, the degree of political stability, which, as emphasized by Olson (2000), affects their temporal perspectives and therefore monarchs' incentive to expropriate, varied across countries. In more stable regimes, monarchs discount more

---

[19] Although territorial fragmentation may have been a key cause of economic change, I am not claiming that it was the only one. As explored by Jones (1981), the European miracle was generated by such other factors as the demographic and consumption/saving decisions of families.

slowly and investment must be higher.[20] Second, incentives to confiscate new types of wealth differed across the continent. Assume that the revenue demands of the state are determined by both domestic consumption (to build palaces, fund artists and so on) and the level of external threat. Even the most conspicuous levels of consumption by the king must have had a similar ceiling: the construction of El Escorial, Versailles and the Hermitage or the purchase of Boscos, Rembrandts and Goyas must have absorbed equivalent sums of money in each country. By contrast, the level of external threat varied temporally and geographically. Tax pressures and the volume of loans were positively related to exposure to foreign invasions. In France, which was directly enmeshed in Central Europe's war, and in Spain, which had large swaths of territory in Germany and the Low Countries since the early sixteenth century, the monarchy absorbed large amounts of money and was repeatedly forced to default on its financial commitments. By contrast, the likelihood of being invaded was much smaller for islands, such as Britain, and for mountainous terrains, like Switzerland. Similarly, the Netherlands, with its capacity to flood itself and its invaders, may have also been a cheaper place to protect than neighboring areas of Northern Germany. The sparks of sustained growth, followed by a rapid takeoff around the turn of the nineteenth century, coincide with those areas.[21]

(The positive effect of territorial fragmentation on growth may as well be the result of a pure random mechanism rather than the existence of differential rates of military threat. Assume that any monarch has the same probability [for example, 1 in 6] of adopting the right set of policies to produce economic development. If there is only one country, the chances of choosing the right set are much lower [1/6 in the example] than if there are several countries and each one picks its policy independently: with 6 countries, at least 1 country will choose the right growth strategy. In short, in this explanation, a system of fragmented sovereignties is enough to trigger growth without having to investigate the country-specific factors that pushed each ruler to choose particular economic policies.)

[20] Again, a central component of political stability must be related to the weight of natural resources. The more abundant these resources are, the higher the incentive to stage a coup must be and hence the lower the rate of investment on patents that generate nonspecific assets.

[21] Once new types of assets appear, with productivity rates above the productivity rate of fixed assets, other countries, which do not match the conditions that facilitate the economic breakthroughs I describe, would have an incentive to develop political institutions to catch up with the early industrializers.

Equality Within an Increasingly Nonspecific Economy

To complete this section on the sources of the economic transformation of the world, we need to answer one final question: How does the emergence of nonspecific assets change the distribution of income across the population? The process of investment that leads from invention to new commercial and industrial activities takes place, to start with, among certain entrepreneurs who postpone some consumption to invest in new assets. As those new assets generate higher returns than more traditional activities generate, there is a growing disparity of incomes between the new investors and the rest of society and thus more inequality.

In due time, however, higher earnings in nonagrarian sectors gradually attract more individuals to those new activities. A growing proportion of the population decides to invest in the acquisition of those new types of assets, such as human capital, that grant higher salaries. Moreover, the higher returns in manufacturing industries spread to larger segments of the population and, with an increasing supply of educated workers, the wage gaps between skilled and unskilled workers that widened at the beginning of the industrial revolution narrow again. Thus, the progression from agrarian to modernized economies treads the path of Kuznets's inequality curve – inequality first grows with a shift in the structure of the economy and then declines progressively.[22]

The shift in the type of assets and in their distribution has then the political consequences described in the book. Political institutions liberalize with the growth of capital mobility in previously unequal societies. As both assets become more mobile and their distribution more equal, universal suffrage is introduced. Unless some exogenous shocks reverse the existing type and distribution of capital, democracy becomes a self-sustaining equilibrium: it fosters higher levels of equality (through extensive education and redistribution) and it blocks the expropriatory temptations of policy makers.

Conclusions

A theory of political transitions would be incomplete if we did not model the independent strategies of politicians and states vis-à-vis the rest of society in the political arena. Accordingly, this chapter draws on the recent

---

[22] For an excellent discussion of Kuznets's theory about the (curvilinear) relationship between development and inequality, see Williamson (1991).

literature on political accountability to explore how state elites may shift the distribution of assets to their advantage, hence changing the foundations of different political regimes, or even shaping the decisions of investors and hence the rate at which different types of assets are produced. In the first part of the chapter, I brought up fresh empirical material to show how the ability of politicians to exploit the public varies with political regime and the dominant type of wealth. Whereas in well-functioning democracies, that is, those with competent and well-informed electorates, corruption and confiscatory strategies are limited, in dictatorships rent-appropriation activities are much more pervasive. Moreover, the extent to which corruption takes place in authoritarian regimes varies with the internal pluralism within the elite – tyrannies exhibit much higher degrees of exploitation than do "committee-like" authoritarian regimes.

The introduction of a model of "vertical" conflict between rulers and citizens not only gives us a better, more well-rounded picture of the redistributive consequences of different political regimes – a topic that I started exploring in Chapter 5. It also allows us to map more extendedly the dynamics of political development and regime change. In Chapters 1 and 4 I focused mostly on the economic forces that underpin the choice of political constitutions – although I considered too the distribution of political and organizational resources. In this chapter I reversed the focus of attention to theorize about the political foundations of wealth distribution. I concluded that quick domestic reforms to create pro-democratic conditions are difficult to implement. Achieving moderate levels of inequality and substantially mobile assets is almost always a long-run enterprise.

The chapter closes with a discussion on these processes of development. In a world of specific assets, inequality arises as a result of the expropriatory actions of bandits, be they the Bourbons, the Sauds or the Somozas. In exchange for the protection they offer against similar warlords, they exact a heavy price in the form of wealth accumulation at the expense of vassals and peasants. To sustain their political and economic advantage, they invest thoroughly in repressing their contenders and crushing any popular revolts. Equality of conditions and hence democratic procedures can be sustained only in frontier societies and in farmers' communities that, for geographical reasons or perhaps due to the nature of their production endeavors, forestall the emergence of predators.

Since the Neolithic revolution, ninety-nine percent of the history of humanity has been grounded in the economic exploitation (and military expropriation) of fixed assets. In the last centuries, however, the nature and distribution of economic assets has been gradually reshaped by systematic investment in new inventions. The creation of new sources of wealth was bolstered by a politically fragmented international system, and perhaps by the existence of some institutionalized balance of power among landowners at the domestic level, which assured would-be investors against the risk of outright confiscation by the ruling clique. The mobility of these new assets in turn made their holders more sanguine about the consequences of democracy. Moreover, by fostering the spread of wealth to new social segments, mostly through the growing value of human capital, these new types of assets facilitated the transition to democracy even further. A new and relatively stable equilibrium around democratic institutions eventually evolved. By engendering political competition and policy transparency, representative institutions reduced the ability of politicians to expropriate assets from other political actors. Excluding any exogenous shocks, this should make democracy a self-sustaining political equilibrium.

7

Conclusions

Almost half a century ago, modern comparative politics was founded under the aegis of modernization theory. Although the scholars working in that tradition were a diverse lot in the opinions they spoused, they coincided in emphasizing the key role that economic and social development played in the evolution of political institutions. Political stability, the formation of liberal political attitudes and the emergence and consolidation of democratic regimes were all identified as the final destination in the process of political development. Their achievement was seen as part and parcel of the transition of all political societies from a pre-modern stage to full modernity.

It did not take long for comparativists, however, to dismiss the literature of political modernization altogether. The simple concept of political development could not encompass the multiplicity of ways in which underdeveloped societies were structured. It could not account either for the very distinctive regimes, democracy, fascism and communism, into which different developed nations organized by the end of the first third of the twentieth century. It was insufficient to explain the cyclical nature of violence and constitutional breakdowns that plagued many regions of the world. Finally, its theoretical implications were difficult to test. This was in part because it addressed *longue-durée* historical events. But it had mainly to do with the concept's lack of precise causal mechanisms. The cultural and political factors that generate institutional change and development remained ambiguous under modernization theory. As Inkeles put it in a seminal article, the process of change was "in a sense, strictly spontaneous; yet . . . in some ways the most strictly determined process history has yet known" (1966: 149).

After abandoning the theoretical shell of modernization theory, democratization scholars split into various strands. A few emphasized the

233

need to trace the divergent historical paths that different nations had taken in the contemporary period. The authoritarian spell of Latin America and the solid redemocratization of Southern Europe in the 1970s pushed most researchers, however, to emphasize the autonomy of political elites. Accordingly, the democratization literature focused on examining the negotiating skills of politicians as well as the ways in which different constitutional structures may contribute to the stability of democracies.

The fall of dictatorial regimes in Latin America and East Asia in the 1980s and the collapse of the Soviet system in the 1990s shifted again the terms of the intellectual debate. At the end of the twentieth century, the story of the last two hundred years emerged again as one of economic and political modernization. Prior to 1700, no economy enjoyed any significant growth in living standards and all countries had approximately the same level of income. The contemporary period started with the successive economic takeoff of a growing number of nations and their final transformation into relatively developed, well-educated and complex societies. All of these nations eventually became democratic. By contrast, those countries that either have remained poor and unequal or are rich only in natural resources have yet to democratize. The crises of the mid-twentieth century proved to be just growth crises – similar in nature to those often suffered by teenagers on their way to adulthood. In hindsight, the scholarly literature has had to conclude that development matters – and that it matters heavily.

Strikingly, the reassertion of development as a key factor behind political liberalization has not been accompanied by a systematic theoretical effort to trace the mechanisms that link wealth to democracy. In all matters that relate to the consolidation and the quality of democracy, the articulation of a complex civil society, the formation of a public sector and the delivery of good governance, the discipline of comparative politics has done a poor job in extricating the causes and effects of economic and political development. Even when using the sophisticated terminology of game theory, its results sound extremely similar to the rudimentary concepts of modernization scholars. In the most successful scholarly works of the last decade, the emphasis has been put on the idea that different political outcomes (in either regime type, level of civic engagement or quality of governance) should be thought of as distinctive equilibria resulting from path-dependent processes. In a sense, and to put it rather crudely, the only thing researchers have told us is that virtuous economies are virtuous polities too. But they have hardly defined the ways in which the latter come into life.

Conclusions

Understanding how the processes of economic and political modernization interact is a difficult goal – precisely because they are tightly interwoven phenomena. The purpose of this book has been to offer, so to speak, a surgical knife that lets us dissect the bones, nerves and flesh of the process of political development. To do so, that is, to understand the dynamics of political transitions and, more specifically, to overcome the correlational nature of most of the literature on political development and democratization, I have followed a two-pronged strategy. On the one hand, I have borrowed heavily from the insights and tools of analytical political science. Accordingly, I have posited a world populated with multiple political actors, endowed with different types and quantities of assets, and intent on maximizing their income both through standard economic means (the production and exchange of goods) and through the choice of political institutions that define their rights as well as their obligations toward others. In such a model, political institutions emerge from the strategic interaction of those agents, shaped by the nature of their organizational and military resources as well as by the information they have about the interests and capabilities of opposing parties. On the other hand, I have accumulated several layers of empirical evidence to strengthen the case for the model. I have exploited cross-national statistical data spanning the mid-nineteenth century to the late twentieth century. I have examined the evolution of representative institutions among the cantons of Switzerland and across the states of the United States during several centuries. I have also engaged in a more informal discussion of political processes that stretch from as far back as classical Greece and republican Rome to modern Europe.

The results of the inquiry have been discussed at length in the book. Political deals among elites may in some situations foster the democratization of a polity – particularly when the parties entering the constitutional pact have the incentives and organizational credibility to bank on the future. Certain constitutional designs may tip the balance in favor of democracy. Presidential systems carry more risk of an authoritarian takeover in an asset-specific country. Political decentralization defuses redistributive conflict – the cantonalization of Switzerland into minuscule polities and the Westphalian system of sovereign states are excellent examples. Nonetheless, the probability of democratic transitions, the stability of authoritarian institutions and the occurrence of revolutionary explosions ultimately hinge on the distribution and nature of assets among individuals and on the political resources people bring to bear in the solution of domestic conflicts. Successful democratic transitions take place whenever inequality is low or wealth is not country specific. Excessive differences between the wealthy and the poor push the former to restrict the franchise to avoid the redistributive consequences of a fully democratic system, unless capital mobility restrains the ability of the poor to expropriate from the wealthy. Revolutionary movements and civil wars take place when both inequality and country specificity are high, as long as there exists a sufficient degree of uncertainty about the balance of power among the contending parties.

The same building blocks employed to predict regime shifts have also been used with profit to explore the internal dynamics of democracies and authoritarian regimes and, even more broadly, to consider the forces that created certain economic structures. Democracies have the internal mechanisms to restrain their policy makers and hence maintain the conditions that propelled the process of political liberalization – that is, democracies are, broadly speaking, self-sustaining political equilibria. By contrast, authoritarian regimes are established to consolidate and even expand a process of asset expropriation. The extent to which expropriation takes place varies with the internal structure of power: tyrannies succumb to an ever-growing process of wealth accumulation in the hands of the dictator; pluralistic dictatorships, instead, may give some space for the creation of new wealth and the ultimate transformation of their basis of support. Putting together those insights about the incentives of state elites and social groups, I have then described the ways in which property has been distributed and its distribution politically enforced and on the sources of asset mobility throughout history.

Predicting the future may be the best way to change it. But, if we are to believe the model and the evidence gathered in this book, the world will look in the next decades as follows. Most of Europe, North America, Oceania and North East Asia will remain democratic for at least two reasons: first, their income distribution and the predominance of highly mobile assets will continue to make them specially suited to democracy; second, democratic institutions sustain, through the provision of human capital and other public goods and by constraining the rent-seeking inclinations of politicians, the conditions that make them possible to start with. There is only one threat to democracy in those areas. With current fertility rates, and in the absence of immigration, the population in Western Europe will halve in about fifty years. To compensate for this demographic collapse, Europe will have to open its frontiers widely. If the new migrants are too poor and, particularly, if their descendants are ghettoized outside the mainstream educational and political institutions, there could be unprecedented levels of economic inequality and considerable political strife. This will put democracy at risk. Two things should make this threat unlikely, however. First, the American experience shows that it is possible to integrate vast numbers of immigrants in a permanent manner. Second, given their interest in having skilled employees to maintain their production processes, European businesses will be most likely to lobby for the inclusion of foreigners in the existing economic and social networks (probably against the natural inclinations of European labor).

Sub-Saharan Africa, the Middle East and Central Asia constitute the mirror image of the Western and East Asian experience. Growth rates, which are abysmal in Africa and terribly low for the immense majority of the Islamic world, show little evidence of picking up. More importantly, the internal composition of the economy is not conducive to representative institutions. Natural resources are abundant in both areas. Once we exclude oil production, total output in the Middle East is similar to that of Finland. Devoid of complementary industries, and without sophisticated financial markets, state elites have no incentive to loosen their political grip on the national sources of wealth. Moreover, they have little interest in either investing in other economic activities or in generating the conditions, such as capital formation or institutional stability, that could spur growth – hence locking those countries in the trap of underdevelopment. Authoritarian regimes and fratricidal wars will be likely to alternate in a cyclical and devastating manner in the near future. Some tiny Arab states flush with oil may extend the franchise to their native population. But this will come at the cost of excluding from politics a substantial foreign population, who is employed in all productive sectors. For example, only one fourth of Qatar's population is today a national of the country. Just 19 percent of the population in the United Arab Emirates are Emiri. In some nations, such as Iran, with a more diversified economy and a more complex social structure, or Tunisia, which is successfully building a tourist industry, democracy may fall into place. But in both regions, and particularly in Africa, democracy will be sparse. A successful exit from such a dramatic equilibrium of repression and revolution is difficult to envision. A possible solution could come from abroad, through the intervention of a multinational force or an international institution that would put the management of fixed assets, such as oil and mines, under an international board controlled by democratic regimes.

Between the two political poles represented by the advanced world and the African and Middle Eastern regions, there is a vast stretch of lands whose political institutions will live in an uneasy equilibrium. The political futures of Latin America and South Asia will depend on the capacity of their governments to generate growth and to spread its fruits fairly. In the southern tip of America and in Mexico, democracy may persist, although for different reasons. The Southern Cone has a somewhat diversified (if not very productive) economy and a balanced distribution of political resources. Mexico is likely to witness a declining wage gap and manageable levels of political conflict as migration continues to flow to the North and firms keep moving southward. In the Caribbean region, democracies will prevail on small islands, which are relatively equal and grounded in tourism. Once the Castro regime falls, Cuba stands a good chance of democratizing: its population is well educated, the distribution of assets is equal and there is a large pool of mobile capital in Miami ready to move to La Havana. In the Andine countries and Central America, by contrast, the theory predicts considerable regime instability unless there are comprehensive land reforms or the urban economy moves from being based on an informal, thin network of entrepreneurs to a system of modern industrial enclaves. The weight of oil production in Colombia, Venezuela and Ecuador, the expansion of the exploitation of coca, also a fixed asset, and the continued reliance on certain agrarian products, such as bananas and coffee, in the context of a highly skewed distribution of land, will breed authoritarian solutions. In sum, many of the democracies established in the 1990s look short-lived or at least easily corruptible.

In Asia, predictions vary with each nation. India has been the big stumbling block of modernization theory – it should be a dictatorship according to models that employ per capita income as a predictor. Barrington Moore hinted that since India had not modernized, it had not yet experienced the authoritarian convulsions other nations went through. Although this book does not solve the Indian "paradox" completely, its insights approximate the case much better. Income and land inequality in India is mild and certainly much lower than in sub-Saharan Africa or Central America. Moreover, India's potential redistributive tensions have been softened by the use of federal structures. Kerala implemented a thorough land reform. By contrast, certain areas of northeast India have suffered from endemic violence related to land issues. But those conflicts have not spilled over into other areas of the country.

Some argue that China will democratize through a peaceful, "Korean"-style political transition, provided it experiences a steady rate of economic growth over the next generation. In this rosy scenario, China will continue to industrialize and urbanize at the pace of the last decade to the point that it will end up looking like its neighbors did in the early 1980s, that is, endowed with a relatively well-educated workforce and a substantial share of non-specific assets. A slight change in the international context or in the overall domestic levels of political mobilization will then trigger a swift yet bloodless change in regime. This optimistic forecast overlooks, however, China's fundamental problem: its massive internal differences, now exacerbated by growing income disparities between the coastal areas and the interior. In 1994, per capita income in the richest province, Shanghai, was four times higher than the national average and ten times the level of income in the poorest province, Guizhou. For the sake of comparison, per capita income in the richest American state is just twice as large as per capita income in the poorest one. China's substantial regional inequalities may well lead to territorial conflicts and to the country's ultimate fragmentation in the following way. Unless capital were sufficiently mobile to escape taxation, the coastal regions would resist the introduction of a democratic regime for purely redistributive reasons, that is, to prevent massive interregional transfers. But since it is unclear whether an authoritarian regime could ultimately protect them from the regulatory and expropriatory practices of the national political elite – or even from a confiscatory move by the interior provinces – the rich areas may be tempted to push for radical decentralization or even complete separation. As a matter of fact, a similar risk may threaten India if the process of economic liberalization it has recently embraced benefits certain states only. It is possible, however, that the presence of federal institutions may make it easier for India to accommodate growing territorial disparities by granting more autonomy to the richest states.

The extension of civil peace and democratic institutions will also hinge on the evolution of the international political and economic context. In the Greece of Thucydides the fate of small cities was related to the strength of the dominant political faction in Athens and to that city's balance of power with Sparta. In the same way, contemporary domestic elites of many countries continue to rely on the military and financial resources of big nations. Changes in the internal constitution and in the military strength of the great powers directly affect the resources and expectations of victory of the parties in contention on many continents: the democratization waves and reversals of the last one hundred years partially track the ascendancy of Britain and the United States, the stalemate of the Cold War and the collapse of the Soviet Union. A renewed period of unchallenged pax Americana in the next decades should bode well for democracy. This may change, however, if the United States meets a durable threat, similar in magnitude to the one posed by the Soviet Union. In that event, Washington may be tempted, for strict security reasons, to ally with the authoritarian elites of those countries directly threatened by the new ascending power. That would delay even more the possibility of a democratic transition in Africa, parts of Asia and the Middle East.

From an economic point of view, the globalization of international markets has contradictory effects on the evolution of political regimes across the world. The process of capital liberalization (in a politically fragmented world) fosters the exit option of asset holders in a way that speeds up the introduction of democracy. However, trade expansion has a double-edged effect. On the one hand, economic openness may suffocate the introduction of representative institutions if it reinforces an international division of labor in which some continents specialize in the exploitation of their natural resources. Moreover, if trade integration leads to the increasing regional concentration and specialization of certain industries, then cross-regional and cross-national differences and redistributive tensions should rise and democratic stability may suffer. On the other hand, trade can be beneficial to the cause of democracy. In countries in which labor is relatively abundant, wage compression will go up and democracy will be established. Similarly, a world of open borders could lead, in the twenty-first century, to the type of migration flows that took place in the nineteenth century and that compressed wage differentials within and across North Atlantic economies very rapidly. Trade liberalization and factor mobility may be in that sense the best tools we have to expand democracy across the globe.

In exploring the causes of political change, democratization and revolutions, this book has built a theory grounded on long-run phenomena. The truth in politics is that almost all of us live in preordained collective structures and witness historical events over which we have little control. There are few quick fixes to the problems that still afflict a considerable part of mankind. Pacifying countries, establishing viable democracies and imposing clean political institutions are, so it seems, as desirable as they are hard to come by. Our only hope is that all domestic elites will eventually embrace the institutions – markets and human capital formation – that generate durable growth and pluralistic societies. In the meanwhile, we should strive for the introduction of worldwide mechanisms that force politicians to conduct business in a transparent manner. And we should push for a liberal international order that fosters the gradual spillover of capital from rich to poor nations and facilitates human migration to the virtuous, free political economies.

References

Acemoglu, Daron, and James Robinson. 2000. "Why Did the West Extend the Franchise? Democracy, Inequality and Growth in Historical Perspective." *Quarterly Journal of Economics* 115 (November): 1167–99.

Acemoglu, Daron, and James Robinson. 2001. "A Theory of Political Transitions." *American Economic Review* 91 (September): 938–63.

Adserà, Alícia, and Carles Boix. 2002. "Trade, Democracy and the Size of the Public Sector." *International Organization* 56 (Spring): 229–62.

Adserà, Alícia, Carles Boix and Mark Payne. 2001. "Are You Being Served? Political Accountability and Government Performance." Inter-American Development Bank, Working Paper no. 438. Washington: IADB.

Alesina, Alberto, and Dani Rodrik. 1994. "Distributive Politics and Economic Growth." *Quarterly Journal of Economics* 109 (May): 465–90.

Alesina, Alberto, and Howard Rosenthal. 1995. *Political Parties, Divided Government, and the Economy.* Cambridge: Cambridge University Press.

Alesina, Alberto, and Enrico Spolaore. 1997. "On the Number and Size of Nations." *Quarterly Journal of Economics* 112 (November): 1027–56.

Alexander, Gerard. 2002. *The Sources of Democratic Consolidation.* Ithaca: Cornell University Press.

Alston, Lee J., and Joseph P. Ferrie. 1985. "Labor Costs, Paternalism, and Loyalty in Southern Agriculture: A Constraint on the Growth of the Welfare State." *Journal of Economic History* 45 (March): 95–117.

Alt, James E., and Michael Gilligan. 1994. "The Political Economy of Trading States: Factor Specificity, Collective Action Problems and Domestic Political Institutions." *Journal of Political Philosophy* 2(2): 165–92.

Amemiya, Takeshi. 1985. *Advanced Econometrics.* Cambridge, Mass.: Harvard University Press.

Andrey, Georges. 1986. "La quête d'un Etat national (1798–1848)." In *Nouvelle Histoire de la Suisse et des Suisses.* Editions Payot Lausanne. 2d ed. Chap. 6, pp. 497–598.

Aristotle. [1988]. *The Politics.* Edited by Stephen Everson. New York: Cambridge University Press.

Bairoch, Paul. 1990. "La Suisse dans le contexte internationale aux XIXe et XXe siècles." In Paul Bairoch and Martin Körner, eds., *La Suisse dans l'économie mondiale*. Geneva: Librairie Droz, pp. 103–40.

Baldwin, Peter. 1990. *The Politics of Social Solidarity*. Cambridge: Cambridge University Press.

Barro, Robert. 1973. "The Control of Politicians: An Economic Model." *Public Choice* 14: 19–42.

Barro, Robert. 1997. *Determinants of Economic Growth*. Cambridge, Mass.: MIT Press.

Barro, Robert J., and Jong-Wha Lee. 1993. "International Comparisons of Educational Attainment." NBER Working Paper no. 4349. April.

Bates, Robert H. 1999. "Ethnicity, Capital Formation and Conflict." Paper prepared for a conference sponsored by the Social Capital Initiative of the World Bank, June 15–16. Washington D.C.

Baumol, William J. 1967. "Macroeconomics of Unbalanced Growth: The Anatomy of the Urban Crisis." *American Economic Review* 57: 415–26.

Beck Nathaniel, and Jonathan N. Katz. 1995. "What to Do (and Not to Do) with Time-Series Cross-Section Data." *American Political Science Review* 89 (October): 634–47.

Bensel, Richard Franklin. 1984. *Sectionalism and American Political Development, 1880–1980*. Madison: University of Wisconsin Press.

Bergier, Jean-François. 1984. *Histoire Économique de la Suisse*. Zurich: Payot Laussane.

Biucchi., B. M. 1973. "Switzerland, 1700–1914." In Carlo M. Cipolla, ed., *The Fontana Economic History of Europe: The Emergence of Industrial Societies*. London: Fontana. Chap. 10, pp. 628–55.

Boix, Carles. 1998. *Political Parties, Growth and Equality*. Cambridge: Cambridge University Press.

Boix, Carles. 2000. "The Origins of Party Alignments: Electoral Mobilization in Belgium, Britain and Sweden from 1880 to 1940." Manuscript. University of Chicago.

Boix, Carles. 2001. "Development, Democracy, and the Public Sector." *American Journal of Political Science* 45 (January): 1–17.

Boix, Carles, and Sebastian Rosato. 2001. "A Complete Data Set of Political Regimes, 1800–1999." Manuscript. University of Chicago.

Boix, Carles, and Susan Stokes. 2002. "Endogenous Democratization: A Critique." Manuscript. University of Chicago.

Bollen, Kenneth A. 1979. "Political Democracy and the Timing of Development." *American Sociological Review* 44 (August): 572–87.

Bolton, Patrick, and Gérard Roland. 1997. "The Breakup of Nations: A Political Economy Analysis." *Quarterly Journal of Economics* 112 (November): 1057–90.

Bolton, Patrick, Gérard Roland and Enrico Spolaore. 1996. "Economic Theories of the Break-up and Integration of Nations." *European Economic Review* 40 (April): 697–705.

References

Bonjour, E. 1952. *A Short History of Switzerland*. Oxford: Oxford University Press.

Boucoyannis. Deborah. 2003. "The Hidden Sinews of Power. War and the Emergance of Constitutional Government in the Middle Ages." Ph.D. diss., University of Chicago.

Braudel, Fernand. 1984. *Civilization and Capitalism*, Fifteenth–Eighteenth Century. New York: Harper & Row.

Bresser Pereira, Luis Carlos, José María Maravall and Adam Przeworski. 1993. *Economic Reforms in New Democracies: A Social Democratic Approach*. New York: Cambridge University Press.

Burkhart, Ross E., and Michael S. Lewis-Beck. 1994. "Comparative Democracy: The Economic Development Thesis." *American Political Science Review* 88 (December): 903–10.

Cameron. David R. 1978. "The Expansion of the Public Economy: A Comparative Analysis." *American Political Science Review* 72 (December): 1243–61.

Capitani, François de. 1986. "Vie et mort de l'Ancien Régime." In *Nouvelle Histoire de la Suisse et des Suisses*. Editions Payot Lausanne. 2d ed. Chap. 5, pp. 423–96.

Collier, Paul, and Anke Hoeffler. 2001. "Greed and Grievance in Civil War." Manuscript. World Bank.

Cook, Thomas D., and Donald T. Campbell. 1979. *Quasi-experimentation: Design and Analysis Issues for Field Settings*. Chicago: Rand McNally College Publishing Company.

Cox, Gary. 1997. *Making Votes Count: Strategic Coordination in the World's Electoral Systems*. New York: Cambridge University Press.

Cutright, Phillips. 1965. "Political Structure, Economic Development and National Social Security Programs." *American Journal of Sociology* 70 (March): 537–50.

Dahl, Robert A. 1971. *Polyarchy: Participation and Opposition*. New Haven: Yale University Press.

Dahl, Robert A., and Edward R. Tufte. 1973. *Size and Democracy*. Stanford: Stanford University Press.

De Janvry, Alain. 1981. *The Agrarian Question and Reformism in Latin America*. Baltimore: John Hopkins University Press.

Deininger, Klaus, and Lyn Squire. 1996. "A New Data Set Measuring Income Inequality." *The World Bank Economic Review* 10(3): 565–91.

DeLong, J. Bradford, and Andrei Shleifer. 1993. "Princes and Merchants: European City Growth before the Industrial Revolution." *Journal of Law and Economics* 36 (October): 671–702.

Deutsch, Karl. 1961. "Social Mobilization and Political Development." *American Political Science Review* 55 (September): 493–514.

Diamond, Larry. 1999. *Developing Democracy: Toward Consolidation*. Baltimore: Johns Hopkins University Press.

Dinkin, Robert J. 1977. *Voting in Provincial America: A Study of Elections in the Thirteen Colonies, 1689–1776*. Westport, Conn.: Greenwood Press.

Downes, Alexander. 2000. "Federalism and Ethnic Conflict." University of Chicago. Mimeograph.

Easterly, William, and Levine, Ross. 1997. "Africa's Growth Tragedy: Policies and Ethnic Divisions." *Quarterly Journal of Economics* 112 (November): 1203–50.

Eichengreen, Barry. 1996a. *Globalizing Capital.* Princeton: Princeton University Press.

Eichengreen, Barry. 1996b. "Institutions and Economic Growth: Europe after World War II." In Nicholas Crafts and Gianni Toniolo, eds., *Economic Growth in Europe since 1945.* Cambridge: Cambridge University Press. Chap. 2.

Elliott, John Huxtable. 1986. *The Count-Duke of Olivares: The Statesman in an Age of Decline.* New Haven: Yale University Press.

Ertman, Thomas. 1997. *Birth of the Leviathan: Building States and Regimes in Medieval and Early Modern Europe.* Cambridge: Cambridge University Press.

Esping-Andersen, Gösta. 1990. *The Three Worlds of Welfare Capitalism.* Cambridge: Polity Press.

Evans, Peter B., Dietrich Rueschemeyer and Theda Skocpol, eds. 1985. *Bringing the State Back In.* Cambridge: Cambridge University Press.

Fearon, James D. 1995. "Rationalist Explanations for War." *International Organization* 49 (Summer): 379–414.

Ferejohn, John. 1986. "Incumbent Performance and Electoral Control." *Public Choice* 50: 5–25.

Fernandez, Raquel, and Dani Rodrik. 1991. "Resistance to Reform: Status Quo Bias in the Presence of Individual-Specific Uncertainty." *American Economic Review* 81 (December): 1146–55.

Flora, Peter, and Jan Alber. 1981. "Modernization, Democratization and the Development of Welfare States in Western Europe." In Peter Flora and Arnold J. Heidenheimer, eds., *The Development of Welfare States in Europe and America.* New Brunswick: Transaction Books. Chap. 2.

Franklin, Mark N. 1996. "Electoral Participation." In Lawrence LeDuc, Richard G. Niemi and Pippa Norris, eds., *Comparing Democracies: Elections and Voting in Global Perspective.* Thousand Oaks, Calif.: Sage.

Franscini, Stefano. 1827 [1991]. *Statistica della Svizzera.* Locarno: A. Dado.

Franscini, Stefano. 1855. *Statistique de la Suisse. La Suisse géographique, industrielle et agricole, par Franscini et par une société de géographes et de publicistes suisses.* Berne: Mathey.

Franzese, Robert. 1998. "Political Participation, Income Distribution, and Public Transfers in Developed Democracies." Paper presented at the annual meeting of the American Political Science Association. Boston, Mass.

Franzese, Robert. 2001. *Macroeconomic Policies of Developed Democracies.* New York: Cambridge University Press.

Frieden, Jeffrey A. 1991. *Debt, Development, and Democracy: Modern Political Economy and Latin America, 1965–1985.* Princeton: Princeton University Press.

Frye, Timothy. 2002. "The Perils of Polarization: Economic Performance in the Postcommunist World." *World Politics* 54 (April): 308–37.

Garrett, Geoffrey. 1998. "Governing in the Global Economy: Economic Policy and Market Integration Around the World." Manuscript. Yale University.

References

Garrett, Geoffrey. 2001. "The Distributive Consequences of Globalization." Manuscript. Yale University.

Gil Robles, José María. 1978. *No fué posible la paz*. Barcelona: Planeta.

Gourevitch, Peter. 1986. *Politics in Hard Times: Comparative Responses to International Economic Crises*. Ithaca: Cornell University Press.

Gruner, Erich. 1978. *Die Wahlen in den schweizerischen Nationalrat, 1848–1919: Wahlrecht, Wahlsystem, Wahlbeteiligung, Verhalten von Wählern und Parteien, Wahlthemen und Wahlkämpfe*. Vol. 3. Bern: A. Francke.

Gunther, Richard. 1992. "Spain: The Very Model of the Modern Elite Settlement." In John Higley and Richard Gunther, eds., *Elites and Democratic Consolidation in Latin America and Southern Europe*. Cambridge: Cambridge University Press. Chap. 2.

Haggard, Stephan. 1990. *Pathways from the Periphery*. Ithaca: Cornell University Press.

Hale, Henry. 2000. "The Parade of Sovereignties: Testing Theories of Secession in the Soviet Setting." *British Journal of Political Science* 30 (January): 31–56.

Hellman, Joel. 1998. "Winners Take All: The Politics of Partial Reform in Postcommunist Transitions." *World Politics* 50 (January): 203–34.

Hermens, Ferdinand A. 1941. *Democracy or Anarchy? A Study of Proportional Representation*. Notre Dame, Ind.: University of Notre Dame.

Hirschman, Albert O. 1981. "Exit, Voice, and the State." In Albert O. Hirschman, *Essays in Trespassing: Economics to Politics and Beyond*. Cambridge: Cambridge University Press. Chap. 11.

Hiscox, Michael J. 2001. Class Versus Industry Cleavages: Inter-Industry Factor Mobility and the Politics of Trade. *International Organization* 55 (Winter): 1–46.

Hiscox, Michael J., and David A. Lake. 2001. "Democracy and the Size of States." Manuscript. University of California at San Diego.

Holsey, Cheryl M., and Thomas E. Borcherding. 1997. "Why Does Government's Share of National Income Grow? An Assessment of the Recent Literature on the U.S. Experience. In Dennis C. Mueller, ed., *Perspectives on Public Choice: A Handbook*. New York: Cambridge, pp. 562–89.

Huber, John D., and G. Bingham Powell, Jr. 1994. "Congruence Between Citizens and Policymakers in Two Visions of Liberal Democracy." *World Politics* 46 (April): 291–326.

Huntington, Samuel. 1968. *Political Order in Changing Societies*. New Haven: Yale University Press.

Huntington, Samuel. 1991. *The Third Wave*. Norman: University of Oklahoma Press.

Huntington, Samuel, and Jorge Dominguez. 1975. "Political Development." In Fred Greenstein and Nelson Polsby, eds., *Handbook of Political Science*. Reading, Mass.: Addison-Wesley Publishing Company. Vol. 3, pp. 1–98.

IDEA (International Institute for Democracy and Electoral Assistance). 1997. *Voter Turnout from 1945 to 1997: A Global Report on Political Participation*. Stockholm: IDEA.

Inglehart, Ronald. 1997. *Modernization and Postmodernization: Cultural, Economic, and Political Change in Forty-three Societies*. Princeton: Princeton University Press.

Inkeles, Alex. 1966. "The Modernization of Man." In Myron Weiner, ed., *Modernization*. New York: Basic Books. Chap. 10, pp.138–50.

Jackman, Robert W. 1973. "On the Relation of Economic Development to Democratic Performance." *American Journal of Political Science* 17 (August): 611–21.

Jaggers, Keith, and Ted Robert Gurr. 1996. "Polity III: Regime Type and Political Authority, 1800–1994." Ann Arbor, MI: Inter-University Consortium for Political and Social Research. Number 6695.

Jones, E. L. 1981. *The European Miracle: Environments, Economics and Geopolitics in the History of Europe and Asia*. Cambridge: Cambridge University Press. 2nd edition.

Katzenstein, Peter. 1985. *Small States in World Markets: Industrial Policy in Europe*. Ithaca: Cornell University Press.

Keyssar, Alexander. 2000. *The Right to Vote: The Contested History of Democracy in the United States*. New York: Basic Books.

King, Gary. 1997. *A Solution to the Ecological Inference Problem*. Princeton: Princeton University Press.

Kitschelt, Herbert. 1992. "Political Regime Change: Structure and Process-Driven Explanations?" *American Political Science Review* 86 (December): 1028–34.

Kleppner, Paul. 1982. *Who Voted?: The Dynamics of Electoral Turnout, 1870–1980*. New York: Praeger Publishers.

Kleppner, Paul. 1987. *Continuity and Change in Electoral Politics, 1893–1928*. New York: Greenwood Press.

Körner, Martin. 1986. "Réformes, ruptures, croissances (1515–1648)." In *Nouvelle Histoire de la Suisse et des Suisses*. Editions Payot Lausanne. 2d ed. Chap. 4, pp. 333–422.

Kousser, J. Morgan. 1974. *The Shaping of Southern Politics: Suffrage Restriction and the Establishment of the One-Party South, 1880–1910*. New Haven: Yale University Press.

Kousser, J. Morgan. 1980. "Progressivism – For Middle-Class Whites Only: North Carolina Education, 1880–1910." *Journal of Southern History* 56: 169–94.

Kraus, Franz. 1981. "The Historical Development of Income Inequality in Western Europe and the USA." In Peter Flora and Arnold J. Heidenheimer, eds., *The Development of Welfare States in Europe and America*. New Brunswick: Transaction Books. Chap. 6, pp. 187–236.

Kuran, Timur. 1991. "Now Out of Never: The Element of Surprise in the East European Revolution of 1989 (in Liberalization and Democratization in the Soviet Union and Eastern Europe)." *World Politics* 44 (October): 7–48.

Landa, Dimitri, and Ethan B. Kapstein. 2001. "Inequality, Growth, and Democracy." *World Politics* 53 (January): 264–96.

Landes, David. 1969. *The Unbound Prometheus: Technological Change and Industrial Development in Western Europe from 1750 to the Present*. New York: Cambridge University Press.

References

LaPorta, Rafael, Florencio Lopez de Silanes, Andrei Shleifer and Robert Vishny. 1998. "The Quality of Government." NBER Working Paper no. 6727. September.

Laver, Michael, and Norman Schofield. 1990. *Multiparty Government: The Politics of Coalition in Europe*. Oxford: Oxford University Press.

Lerner, Daniel. 1958. *The Passing of Traditional Society: Modernizing the Middle East*. New York: Free Press.

Leven, Maurice. 1925. *Income in the Various States: Its Sources and Distribution, 1919, 1920, and 1921*. New York: National Bureau of Economic Research.

Lewin, Leif. 1989. *Ideology and Strategy: A Century of Swedish Politics*. New York: Cambridge University Press.

Lindert, Peter H. 1991. "Toward a Comparative History of Income and Wealth Inequality." In Y. S. Brenner, Hartmut Kaelble and Mark Thomas, eds., *Income Distribution in Historical Perspective*. New York: Cambridge University Press. 212–31.

Linz, Juan J. 1993. "Innovative Leadership in the Transition to Democracy and a New Democracy." In Gabriel Sheffer, ed., *Innovative Leadership in International Politics*. Albany: State University of New York Press. Chap. 7.

Linz, Juan J. 1994. "Presidential or Parliamentary Democracy: Does It Make a Difference?" In Juan J. Linz and Arturo Valenzuela, eds., *The Failure of Presidential Democracy: Comparative Prespectives*. Baltimore: John Hopkins University Press. Chap. 1, pp. 3–87.

Linz, Juan J., and Arturo Valenzuela, eds. 1994. *The Failure of Presidential Democracy: Comparative Prespectives*. Baltimore: John Hopkins University Press.

Lipset, Seymour M. 1959. "Some Social Requisites of Democracy: Economic Development and Political Legitimacy." *American Political Science Review* 53 (March): 69–105.

Lipset, Seymour M., and Stein Rokkan. 1967. *Party Systems and Voter Alignments*. New York: Free Press.

Londregan, John, and Keith Poole. 1990. "Poverty, the Coup Trap, and the Seizure of Executive Power." *World Politics* 42 (January): 151–83.

Luebbert, Gregory M. 1991. *Liberalism, Fascism, or Social Democracy: Social Classes and the Political Origins of Regimes in Interwar Europe*. New York: Oxford University Press.

Maddison, Angus. 1995. *Monitoring the World Economy, 1820–1992*. Paris: Organisation for Economic Co-operation and Development.

Mainwaring, Scott. 1993. "Presidentialism, Multipartism, and Democracy: The Difficult Combination." *Comparative Political Studies* 26(2): 198–228.

Mares, Isabela. 2001. "Firms and the Welfare State: When, Why and How Does Social Policy Matter to Employers?" In Peter Hall and David Soskice, eds., *Varieties of Capitalism*. Oxford University Press. Chap. 5.

Margo, Robert A., and Georgia C. Villaflor. 1987. "The Growth of Wages in Antebellum America: New Evidence." *Journal of Economic History* 54 (December): 873–95.

Meltzer, A. H., and S. F. Richards. 1981. "A Rational Theory of the Size of Government." *Journal of Political Economy* 89 (October): 914–27.

247

Milanovic, Branko. 1999. "True World Income Distribution, 1988 and 1993: First Calculation Based on Household Surveys Alone." World Bank Policy Research Working Paper no. 2244. November.

Montesquieu. Charles de Secondat. 1995. *De l'esprit des lois*. Paris: Gallimard.

Moene, Karl Ove, and Michael Wallerstein. 2001. "Inequality, Social Insurance, and Redistribution." *American Political Science Review* 95 (December): 859–74.

Moore, Barrington. 1966. *Social Origins of Dictatorship and Democracy: Lord and Peasant in the Making of the Modern World*. Boston: Beacon Press.

Muller, Edward N. 1988. "Democracy, Economic Development, and Income Inequality." *American Sociological Review* 53 (February): 50–68.

Muller, Edward N. 1995. "Economic Determinants of Democracy." *American Sociological Review* 60 (December): 966–82.

Nordlinger, Eric A. 1988. "The Return to the State: Critiques." *American Political Science Review* 82 (September): 875–85.

North, Douglass C. 1981. *Structure and Change in Economic History*. New York: Norton.

North, Douglass C. 1990. *Institutions, Institutional Change and Economic Performance*. Cambridge: Cambridge University Press.

North, Douglass C., and Robert P. Thomas. 1973. *The Rise of the Western World: A New Economic History*. Cambridge: Cambridge University Press.

North, Douglass C., and Barry R. Weingast. 1989. "Constitutions and Commitment: The Evolution of Institutions Governing Public Choice in Seventeenth-Century England." *Journal of Economic History* 49 (December): 803–32.

O'Donnell, Guillermo, and Philippe C. Schmitter, 1986. *Tentative Conclusions and Uncertain Democracies*. In Guillermo O'Donnell, Philippe C. Schmitter and Laurence Whitehead, eds., *Transitions from Authoritarian Rule: Comparative Perspectives*. Vol. 4. Baltimore: Johns Hopkins University Press.

Olson, Mancur. 1965. *The Logic of Collective Action*. Cambridge, Mass.: Harvard University Press.

Olson, Mancur. 1993. "Dictatorship, Democracy, and Development." *American Political Science Review* 87 (September): 567–76.

Olson, Mancur. 2000. *Power and Prosperity: Outgrowing Communist and Capitalist Dictatorships*. New York: Basic Books.

O'Rourke, Kevin H., and Jeffrey G. Williamson. 1999. *Globalization and History: The Evolution of a Nineteenth-Century Atlantic Economy*. Cambridge, Mass: MIT Press.

Paige, Jeffery M. 1997. *Coffee and Power: Revolution and the Rise of Democracy in Central America*. Cambridge, Mass.: Harvard University Press.

Pérez, Francisco et al. 1996. *Capitalización y crecimiento en España y sus regiones, 1955–1995*. Bilbao: Fundación BBV.

Persson, Torsten, and Guido Tabellini. 1998. "The Size and Scope of Government: Comparative Politics with Rational Politicians." Mimeograph.

Persson, Torsten, and Guido E. Tabellini. 2000. *Political Economics: Explaining Economic Policy*. MIT Press.

References

Piven, Frances Fox, and Richard A. Cloward. 1988. *Why Americans Don't Vote*. New York: Pantheon Books.

Powell, G. Bingham. 1973. "Incremental Democratization: The British Reform Act of 1832." In Gabriel A. Almond, Scott C. Flanagan and Robert J. Mundt, eds., *Crisis, Choice, and Change: Historical Studies of Political Development*. Boston: Little, Brown and Company. Chap. 3, pp. 103–51.

Powelson, John P., and Richard Stock. 1990. *The Peasant Betrayed: Agriculture and Land Reform in the Third World*. Washington, D.C.: Cato Institute.

Przeworski, Adam. 1985. *Capitalism and Social Democracy*. Cambridge: Cambridge University Press.

Przeworski, Adam. 1991. *Democracy and the Market*. Cambridge: Cambridge University Press.

Przeworski, Adam, Michael Alvaret, José Antonio Cheibub and Fernando Limongi. 2000. *Democracy and Development*. New York: Cambridge University Press.

Przeworski, Adam, and Fernando Limongi. 1993. "Political Regimes and Economic Growth." *Journal of Economic Perspectives* 7 (Summer): 51–69.

Przeworski, Adam, and Fernando Limongi. 1997. "Modernization: Theories and Facts." *World Politics* 49 (January): 155–83.

Przeworski, Adam, and Michael Wallerstein. 1982. "Democratic Capitalism at the Crossroads." In *Democracy*, Vol. 2, pp. 52–68. Reprinted in A. Przeworski. 1985. *Capitalism and Social Democracy*. Cambridge: Cambridge University Press, pp. 205–21.

Przeworski, Adam, Susan C. Stokes and Bernard Manin, eds. 1999. *Democracy, Accountability, and Representation*. New York: Cambridge University Press.

Quadagno, Jill. 1988. "From Old-Age Assistance to Supplemental Security Income: The Political Economy of Relief in the South, 1935–1972." In Margaret Weir, Ann Shola Orloff and Theda Skocpol, eds., *The Politics of Social Policy in the United States*. Princeton: Princeton University Press.

Rappard, William E. 1912. *Le facteur économique dans l'avènement de la démocratie moderne en Suisse*. Genève: Georg & Co.

Rappard, William E. 1914. *La révolution industrielle et les origines de la protection légale du travail en Suisse*. Berne: Staempfli.

Rappard, William E. 1942. *L'avènement de la démocratie moderne à Genève (1814–1847)*. Genève: A. Jullien.

Robertson, David. 1989. "The Bias of American Federalism: The Limits of Welfare-State Development in the Progressive Era." *Journal of Policy History* 1:261–91.

Rodrik, Dani. 1998. "Why Do Open Economies Have Bigger Governments?" *Journal of Political Economy* 106: 997–1032.

Rogowski, Ronald. 1989. *Commerce and Coalitions: How Trade Affects Domestic Political Alignments*. Princeton: Princeton University Press.

Rogowski, Ronald. 1998. "Democracy, Capital Skill, and Country Size: Effects of Asset Mobility and Regime Monopoly on the Odds of Democratic Rule." In Paul W. Drake and Mathew D. McCubbins, eds., *The Origins of Liberty*. Princeton: Princeton University Press. Chap. 4, pp. 48–69.

Rosenstone, Steven J., and John Mark Hansen. 1993. *Mobilization, Participation, and Democracy in America*. New York: Macmillan.

Ross, Michael. 2001. "Does Oil Hinder Democracy?" *World Politics* 53 (April): 325–61.

Rothstein, Bo. 1989. "Labor Market Institutions and Working Class Strength." University of Uppsala. Manuscript.

Rueschemeyer, Dietrich, Evelyne Huber Stephens and John D. Stephens. 1992. *Capitalist Development and Democracy*. Chicago: University of Chicago Press.

Sambanis, Nicholas. 2000. "Partition as a Solution to Ethnic War: An Empirical Critique of the Theoretical Literature." *World Politics* 52 (July): 437–83.

Scase, Richard. 1977. *Social Democracy in Capitalist Society: Working Class Politics in Britain and Sweden*. London: Croom Helm.

Shepsle, Kenneth. 1979. "Institutional Arrangements and Equilibrium in Multi-dimensional Voting Models." *American Journal of Political Science* 23 (February): 27–59.

Shepsle, Kenneth. 1991. *Models of Multiparty Electoral Competition*. Chur; New York: Harwood Academic Publishers.

Shugart, Matthew S., and John Carey. 1992. *Presidents and Assemblies: Constitutional Design and Electoral Dynamics*. New York: Cambridge University Press.

Singer, J. David, and Melvin Small. 1993. *Correlates of War Project: International and Civil War Data, 1816–1992* [computer file]. Ann Arbor: J. David Singer and Melvin Small [producers], 1993. Ann Arbor: Inter-university Consortium for Political and Social Research [distributor], 1994.

Skocpol, Theda. 1979. *States and Social Revolutions: A Comparative Analysis of France, Russia, and China*. Cambridge: Cambridge University Press.

Smith, Adam. [1981]. *An Inquiry into the Nature and Causes of the Wealth of Nations*. Indianapolis: Liberty Fund.

Steinberg, Jonathan. 1996. *Why Switzerland?* 2d ed. New York: Cambridge University Press.

Stepan, Alfred, and Cindy Skach. 1994. "Presidentialism and Parliamentarism in Comparative Perspective." In Juan J. Linz and Arturo Valenzuela, eds., *The Failure of Presidential Democracy: Comparative Prespectives*. Baltimore: John Hopkins University Press. Chap. 4, pp. 119–36.

Stokes, Susan. 1999. "What Do Policy Switches Tell Us about Democracy?" In Adam Przeworski, Susan C. Stokes and Bernard Manin, eds., *Democracy, Accountability, and Representation*. New York: Cambridge University Press.

Strikwerda, Carl. 1997. *A House Divided: Catholics, Socialists, and Flemish Nationalists in Nineteenth-Century Belgium*. New York: Rowman & Littlefield.

Tarrow, Sidney G. 1994. *Power in Movement: Social Movements, Collective Action and Politics*. New York: Cambridge University Press.

Tiebout, Charles M. 1956. "A Pure Theory of Local Expenditures." *Journal of Political Economy* 64 (October): 416–24.

Tilly, Charles. 1978. *From Mobilization to Revolution*. Reading, Mass.: Addison-Wesley.

References

Tilly, Charles. 1990. *Coercion, Capital, and European States, A.D. 990–1990.* Cambridge, Mass.: B. Blackwell.

Treisman, Daniel. 1997. "Russia's 'Ethnic Revival': The Separatist Activism of Regional Leaders in a Postcommunist Order." *World Politics* 49 (January): 212–49.

UNU-WIDER. 2000. *World Income Inequality Database.* The United Nations University – World Institute for Development Economics Research.

Vanhanen, Tatu. 1997. *Prospects of Democracy: A Study of 172 Countries.* London: Routledge.

Van Muyden, Berthold. 1899. *Histoire de la nation suisse.* Vol. 3. Lausanne: H. Mignot.

Vilar, Pierre. 1976. *A History of Gold and Money, 1450–1920.* London: NLB.

Wagner, A. 1883. *Finanzwissenschaft.* Translated and reprinted as "Three Extracts on Public Finance," in *Classics on the Theory of Public Finance,* edited by R. A. Musgrave and A. T. Peacock. London: Macmillan, 1962.

Walker, Mack. 1998. *German Home Towns: Community, State, and General Estate, 1648–1871.* Ithaca: Cornell University Press.

Weingast, Barry R. 1997. "The Political Foundations of Democracy and the Rule of Law." *American Political Science Review* 91 (June): 245–63.

Wilensky, Harold L. 1975. *The Welfare State and Equality.* Berkeley and Los Angeles: University of California Press.

Williamson, Chilton. 1960. *American Suffrage: From Property to Democracy, 1760–1860.* Princeton: Princeton University Press.

Williamson, Jeffrey G. 1985. *Did British Capitalism Breed Inequality?* London: Allen & Unwin.

Williamson, Jeffrey G.. 1991. "British Inequality During the Industrial Revolution: Accounting for the Kuznets Curve." In Y. S. Brenner, Hartmut Kaelble and Mark Thomas, eds., *Income Distribution in Historical Perspective.* New York: Cambridge University Press. 57–75.

Williamson, Jeffrey G., and P. H. Lindert. 1980. *American Inequality: A Macroeconomic History.* New York: Academic Press.

Wolf, Eric R. 1969. *Peasant Wars in the Twentieth Century.* New York: Harper.

Wood, Elisabeth. 2000. *Forging Democracy from Below: Insurgent Transitions in South Africa and El Salvador.* New York: Cambridge University Press.

World Bank. 1999. *World Development Report 2000.* New York: Oxford University Press.

Name Index

Acemoglu, Daron, 11, 11n12, 28n10
Adserà, Alícia, 63, 182, 182n8, 209
Afganistan, 107
Africa, 18, 94, 218, 225, 225n14, 234, 240; sub-Saharan, 28, 35, 184, 155, 237, 238
Alabama, 122
Albany, 103
Alber, Jan, 175n3
Alesina, Alberto, 131, 147, 165n23, 221n10
Alexander, Gerard, 9
Algeria, 106, 216
Alston, Lee J., 123
Alt, James, 54
Amemiya, Takeshi, 74, 75n6
America: Central, 30, 35, 37, 143n16, 184, 218, 238; Latin, 18, 71, 92, 94, 143, 155, 234, 238; North, 159, 236; South, 225. *See also countries and cities by name*
Andorra, 104
Andrey, Georges, 117, 118
Angola, 14
Antigua, 100
Appenzell, 112
Argentina, 28, 30, 68n4, 100, 179
Aristotle, 1, 11, 37
Armenia, 104

Asia: East, 13, 33, 234, 236, 238, 240; Central, 237; South, 238. *See also countries and cities by name*
Asturias, 46
Athens, 20, 29, 42, 239. *See also* Greece, ancient
Augsburg, 113
Australia, 109
Austria, 46, 71, 102, 111, 138
Azerbaijan, 104

Baden, 102
Bahamas, 100
Bahrain, 107
Bairock, Paul, 118n7
Baldwin, Peter, 54, 178n6
Bangladesh, 108
Barbados, 100
Barro, Robert, 41, 77, 207
Basel, 111, 113, 115, 118
Bates, Robert H., 94
Baumol, William J., 175n3
Bavaria, 101
Beck, Nathaniel, 182
Beijing, 218n7
Belarus, 104
Belgium, 46, 101, 117
Belize, 100
Benin, 105
Bensel, Richard Franklin, 123

Bergier, Jean-François, 112, 115n3, 116, 117, 118
Berlin, 222
Berne, 111, 113, 117, 118
Biucchi, B. M., 113, 118
Boix, Carles, 38n20, 43n30, 68, 78n10, 128n16, 176n4, 182, 182n8, 189, 209
Bolivia, 99, 216n4, 218
Bollen, Kenneth A., 4, 5n4, 68n4
Bolton, Patrick, 165n23
Bonjour, E., 112
Borcherding, Thomas E., 175n2
Bosco, 229
Botswana, 106
Boucoyannis, Deborah, 226n16
Bourbons, 231
Braudel, Fernand, 116
Brazil, 99
Bresser Pereira, Luis Carlos, 138
Britain. *See* United Kingdom
Brunei, 109
Buckhart, Ross E., 4
Burkina Faso, 105
Burundi, 105
Buthan, 108

Cambodia, 35
Cameron, David R., 182
Cameroon, 105
Campbell, Donald, 110
Canada, 98
Cape Verde Islands, 106
Capitani, François de, 112, 115, 115n3, 116
Carey, John, 143, 161, 181
Castile, 42, 212
Castro, Fidel 238
Catalonia, 42, 167, 213
Central African Republic, 105
Chad, 105
Chile, 30, 100, 216n4
China, 14, 35, 44, 107, 184n10, 228, 235, 239
Cloward, Richard A., 126
Collier, Paul, 35, 94n17, 218n6

Colombia, 99, 216n4, 238
Comoros, 106
Congo, Republic of, 105
Connecticut, 119, 121
Cook, Thomas D., 110
Costa Rica, 99
Cote D'Ivoire, 105
Cox, Gary, 161, 181
Croatia, 103
Cuba, 35, 98, 216, 238
Cutright, Phillips, 5
Cyprus, 103
Czech Republic, 102
Czechoslovakia, 46, 102

Dahl, Robert A., 2n1, 5nn4,5, 7n7,8, 44n31, 77
De Janvry, Alain, 216n4
Deininger, Klaus, 11, 65, 76, 76nn6,7, 79, 90, 156
Delhi, 218n7
DeLong, J. Bradford, 212
Denmark, 38, 57, 104, 143
Deutsch, Karl, 77
Diamond, Larry, 44n31
Dinkin, Robert J., 119
Djibouti, 106
Domínguez, Jorge, 139
Dominica, 100
Dominican Republic, 98
Downes, Alexander, 161, 181
Duverger, Maurice, 1

Easterly, William, 78
Ecuador, 99, 216n4, 238
Egypt, 207, 216
Eichengreen, Barry, 41, 138, 139n7
El Salvador, 41n27, 99
Elliot, John Huxtable, 42n28, 212
Equatorial Guinea, 105
Eritrea, 106
Ertman, Thomas, 226n16
Esping-Andersen, Gösta, 175n3
Estonia, 104
Ethiopia, 106

Name Index

Europe, 20, 21, 29, 44, 45, 46, 110, 119, 138, 139, 143, 148, 149, 159, 168, 225n14, 227, 228, 229, 235, 236; Eastern, 46, 71, 82, 184n10, 219n9, 220, 221; Southern, 71, 220, 234; Western, 13, 159, 213, 236. *See also countries and cities by name*
Evans, Peter B., 206n1

Fearon, James D., 14, 28n10
Ferejohn, John, 207
Fernandez, Raquel, 142
Ferrie, Joseph P., 123
Finland, 104, 237
Flanders, 42
Flora, Peter, 175n3
Florida, 122
France, 39n24, 40, 66, 68, 101, 113, 115, 117, 225, 226n15, 228
Franklin, Mark N., 180n7, 189n14
Franscini, Stefano, 115nn2,3, 116n4, 118n8
Franzese, Robert, 131, 138n4, 189n12
Fribourg, 111, 113, 117, 118
Frieden, Jeffrey A., 54
Frye, Timothy, 219n9, 225

Gabon, 105
Gambia, 105
Garicano, Luis, 21n1
Garrett, Geoffrey, 182, 217n4
Geneva, 111, 115, 117, 117n6, 118
Georgia, 104, 119, 121, 122
Germany, 29, 40, 44, 46, 68, 71, 101, 111, 113, 118n7, 148, 184n10, 218n7, 220, 221, 239
Ghana, 105
Gil Robles, José María, 9
Gilligan, Michael, 54
Glaris, 112
Gourevitch, Peter, 57
Goya, 229

Greece, 103; ancient, 7, 20, 29, 37, 42, 142, 235, 239
Grenada, 100
Grissons, 112n1
Gruner, Erich, 118, 118n8
Guatemala, 98, 216n4
Guinea, 105
Guinea-Bissau, 105
Guizhou, 239
Gunther, Richard, 9n10, 118, 118n8
Gurr, Ted Robert, 98
Guyana, 99

Haggard, Stephan, 142
Haiti, 98, 218
Hale, Henry, 168
Hansen, J. Mark, 180n7
Hellman, Joel, 219n9
Herfindhal, 77, 78, 214
Hermens, Ferdinand, 143
Heston, Alan, 182n8
Hirsch, 77, 78, 214
Hirschman, Albert O., 38n21, 39n22, 223n12, 227n18
Hiscox, Michael J., 44n31, 54
Hoeffler, Anke, 35, 94n17, 218n6
Holsey, Cheryl M., 175n2
Honduras, 99
Huber, John D., 145
Hungary, 46, 71, 102, 184n10
Huntington, Samuel, 2, 2n1, 29, 78, 139, 221

Iceland, 7, 104, 224
Illinois, 122
India, 108, 179, 184, 216, 218n7, 235, 239. *See also states and cities by name*
Indonesia, 29
Inglehart, Ronald, 5n4
Inkeles, Alex, 5n5, 233
Iran, 106, 237
Iraq, 107, 217
Ireland, 100

255

Name Index

Miami, 238
Michigan, 122
Micronesia, Federated States of, 109
Middle East, 18, 77, 217, 237, 240
Milanovic, Branko, 156, 159
Modena, 102
Moene, Karl Ove, 178n6
Monaco, 105
Mongolia, 107
Montesquieu, Charles de Secondat, 12n13, 38n21, 227n18
Moore, Barrington, 7, 11, 35, 37, 39, 40, 40n25, 58, 211
Morocco, 106
Mozambique, 106
Mozart, W. A., 225, 228
Muller, Edward N., 11
Mussolini, Benito, 46

Namibia, 106
Napoleon, 117
Nepal, 108
Netherlands, 46, 68n3, 101, 118n7, 228, 229
New Hampshire, 119
New Jersey, 122
New York, 119, 119n9, 119, 121, 122
New Zealand, 109
Newchatel, 115, 116n4
Nicaragua, 99, 211, 216
Nieboer, 223n12
Niger, 105
Nigeria, 105
Nordlinger, Eric A., 206, 206n1
North Carolina, 122
North, Douglas C., 211, 224, 225, 226, 227n18
Norway, 7, 20, 38, 46, 68, 86, 92, 104, 128, 143, 168, 209, 224
Nuremberg, 113

Oceania, 159, 236
O'Donnell, Guillermo, 8, 29, 29n11
Ohio, 122

Olivares, Count-duke of 42
Olson, Mancur, 26n6, 177n5, 223, 224, 228
Oman, 107
Orange Free State, 106
Oregon, 121
O'Rourke, Kevin H., 40, 123, 143

Paige, Jeffrey M., 37
Pakistan, 108, 216n4
Panama, 99
Papal States, 102
Papua New Guinea, 109
Paraguay, 99, 216n4
Paris, 29, 117
Parma, 102
Payne, Mark, 209
Pennsylvania, 119
Penya, Feliu de la, 212
Pérez, Francisco, 38
Persson, Torsten, 21n1, 23, 189, 189n15
Peru, 99, 216
Philadelphia, 118, 119
Philip V, 212
Philippines, 109, 187
Pincus, Steve, 39n24
Piven, Frances Fox, 126
Poland, 102, 184n10
Poole, Keith, 9n10
Portugal, 46, 101, 167
Posner, Daniel, 225n14
Powell, G. Bingham, 145, 210
Powelson, John P., 216, 221
Primo de Rivera, Miguel, 46
Providence, 121n10
Prussia, 37, 40, 111, 115, 221
Przeworski, Adam, 1, 4, 6, 8, 9n9, 29, 29n12, 41, 43, 53n30, 66, 66n1, 68, 68n4, 75n6, 78, 132n2, 138, 139n6, 153, 153n19, 177n5, 196, 202n17, 207, 211, 213

Qatar, 107, 237
Quadragno, Jill, 123

Name Index

Switzerland, 7, 12, 17, 20, 37, 30n23, 57, 65, 68, 101, 110, 111, 112–8, 118n7, 122, 128, 129, 189, 224, 226, 228, 229, 235. *See also cantons and cities by name*
Syria, 107, 217

Tabellini, Guido E., 21n1, 23, 189, 189n15
Taiwan, 108, 216, 221
Tajikistan, 107
Tanzania, 105, 216
Tarrow, Sidney G., 26n6
Texas, 122
Thailand, 108
Thomas, Robert P., 225
Thucydides, 29, 239
Tiebout, Charles M., 38n21
Tilly, Charles, 26n6, 42
Togo, 105
Treisman, Daniel, 168
Trinidad and Tobago, 86, 98
Tufte, Edward R., 44n31
Tunisia, 106, 237
Turgot, Jacques, 227n18
Turkey, 106
Turkmenistan, 107

Uganda, 105
Ukraine, 104
Union of Socialist Soviet Republics, 104, 184n10, 218n7, 239, 240. *See also* Russia
United Arab Emirates, 107, 237
United Kingdom, 37, 38, 38n20, 39, 46, 57, 66, 68, 68n2, 100, 113, 117, 118n7, 120, 142, 143, 210, 212, 226, 226n15, 229, 239
United States of America, 7,12, 17, 20, 33, 37, 39n23, 42, 57, 65, 68, 98, 110, 111, 118–29, 139n7, 143, 143n10, 155, 179, 189, 216, 222, 235, 239. *See also states and cities by name*

Unterwald, 112
Uri, 112
Uruguay, 100
Utrecht, 228
Uzbekistan, 107

Valais, 112n1, 113
Valenzuela, Arturo, 9n10, 29n11, 143, 161, 181
Van Muyden, Berthold, 113, 115
Vanhanen, Tatu, 89, 89n14, 90, 90n15
Vanuatu, 109
Vaud, 113
Venezuela, 86, 99, 216n4, 218, 235
Vienna, 111, 117
Viet Nam, 35, 109
Vilar, Pierre, 212
Villaflor, Georgia C., 120
Virginia, 119n9, 119, 122

Wagner, A. 175n3
Walker, Mack, 111
Wallerstein, Michael, 138, 178n6
Washington, 240
Weber, Max, 1, 116, 206
Weingast, Barry R., 8, 211, 226
Westphalia, 228, 235
Wilensky, Harold L., 175n3
Williamson, Jeffrey G., 47, 39, 40, 119, 120, 123, 143, 230n22
Wolf, Eric R., 35
Wood, Elizabeth, 12, 12n4, 41n27
Wuttenberg, 102

Yemen, 107
Yugoslavia, 103, 184n10

Zaire, 218
Zambia, 106, 216
Zimbabwe, 82, 106
Zug, 112
Zurich, 111, 112, 113, 115, 117, 118

Subject Index

accountability, 148; literature on, 206–19

Afrikaners, 12, 12n4

agency, political, 6, 7–8, 16–17, 16n15. *See also* political elites *and agents by name*

agriculture: agrarian reform, 18, 216; and cooperative practices, 224; distribution of property, 6, 89–90, 162, 224; land/labor ratio, 223; and political violence, 94–7; and public sector size, 190, 193, 196; rural-urban cleavage, 21, 57; share of GDP, 76, 84, 181. *See also* farmer economies; land

asset specificity. *See* capital mobility

asset taxability, 23, 25, 39, 43. *See also* capital mobility

authoritarianism. *See* right-wing dictatorship

bandits, 214, 223–4, 231

Belle Epoque, 29

bourgeoisie, 7, 9n9, 40, 40n25, 54–7, 113, 117, 121

capital mobility, 12–13; and country size, 42, 44, 227–30; data on, 76; definition of, 22–3; and economic development, 12–13, 41; and globalization, 41, 240; and

inventions, 225; level of and democracy, 32–4, 38–44, 78–88, 90–2; and pre-contemporary democracies, 41–2; sources of, 222–30; and taxation 14, 25–6; and wealthy dictatorships, 42–3

case studies, and external validity, 17, 110

chain index, 78

communism. *See* left-wing dictatorship; communist parties

communist parties, 138, 221

conservative parties, 16, 148

corporatism, 139

corruption. *See* rent appropriation

country size, choice of, 165–7. *See also* capital mobility and country size

credible commitment. *See* taxes and credible commitment

decentralization, 16, 155–9, 162–9; and capital mobility 167–9. *See also* federalism; democracy and constitutional rules

decolonization movement, 20

democracy: and constitutional rules, 15, 143–4; and cross-class alliances, 47–53; and cross-sectoral alliances 53–57; data on, 66–71, 98–109, 180–1; definition of, 10, 23, 66; and economic development, 5, 12–3,

260

income inequality (*cont.*)
    economic development, 6; and
    economic reform, 220; Kutznets's
    inequality curve, 230; level of and
    democracy, 10–12, 32–4, 37–8,
    78–88, 220; and political violence,
    94; and public sector size, 171, 191;
    sources of, 222–30; and tax rate
    23–5
income volatility, 141–2, 173;
    communal arrangements and, 175,
    177–8. *See also* social mobility
information: data on, 208–9; and
    polarization, 151–2; and political
    violence, 14, 27–30, 33; and rent
    appropriation, 207
institutionalism, 1, 7–8, 15, 138, 143,
    234
institutions, 144. *See also institutions by
    name*
insurance programs, 123, 141–2, 173,
    177–8
investment, incentives for, 224, 228.
    See also economic growth
Islamic fundamentalism, 218

Junkers, 40, 221

Kayapó, 39n22
Know Nothing movement, 121
Kuomintang, 221

land, 23, 38, 54, 120. *See also* agriculture
landlords. *See* democracy and landlords
left-wing dictatorship: definition of, 23,
    27, 30–1, 45; and asset expropriation,
    205, 214–19
left-wing parties, 16, 20, 36. *See also*
    communist parties; social democratic
    parties; mass parties
liberal parties, 7, 148
lootable wealth, 218n6

market economy. *See* democracy and
    economic development

Marxist analysis, 40n25, 129, 211
mass-parties, 20
median voter: in democracy 23–4; in
    dictatorship, 26; endogeneity of,
    177, 191; and tax rate, 23–5, 36,
    172
modernization theory, 1–2, 4–7, 42–3,
    77, 233–4
money, 23, 41, 43, 54
middle class, 6, 47–57; and cross-class
    alliances, 21, 47–8; and
    cross-sectoral alliances, 53–7
migration, 111, 121, 143
military, 9n9, 16
mines, 38, 168, 217n5, 222

nationalistic movements, 169n26
neo-institutionalism. *See*
    institutionalism
newspapers, circulation of, 208–9

ocupational diversity, 90, 162
oil, 12, 20, 42–3, 59, 168; data on, 76;
    and democracy, 42, 85–6, 129; and
    economic development, 218; and
    lack of accountability, 77; and
    political violence, 94; and size
    of the public sector, 190,
    217n5

parliamentarism, 147, 210–12; origins
    of, 226–8. *See also* democracy and
    constitutional rules
pensions, 15, 176, 196
plantations, 38
pluralistic values, 5, 77
political elites: as rent seekers, 16–17,
    177n5, 204–5, 214, 225; as
    representatives, 16–17, 204; as utility
    maximizers, 8–9, 207
political parties, 9n9, 13, 26, 45–6, 120,
    137–8. *See also* communist parties;
    conservative parties; left-wing
    parties; liberal parties; mass-parties;
    social democratic parties

Subject Index

political polarization, 152
political regime, definition of, 10, 171;
    choice of, 30–1. *See also political
    regimes by name*
political violence, 23, 27–30, 34–6,
    47–50, 93–7: and collective action
    problems, 13–14; costs of, 26–7, 166;
    definition of, 23; origins of, 61–2,
    223; and uncertainty, 14, 27–30, 49
presidentialism, 15, 16n15, 147–55;
    data on, 180; and public sector size,
    189. *See also* democracy and
    constitutional rules
property rights, 173, 207, 211, 226
proportional representation. *See*
    electoral systems
public employment, 193, 200
public goods, provision of. *See* public
    investment
public investment, 176–7, 220–2;
    definition of, 173
public sector size, 4, 171–203; in
    authoritarian regimes, 171, 174; data
    on, 179–80; in democracy, 171–2;
    and economic development, 193,
    200; model of, 172–8. *See also* taxes

racial discrimination, 111, 121–2, 126
redistribution, under democracy, 23–5;
    redistributive spending, 173–6. *See
    also* democracy, redistributive impact
    of
religion: data on, 78, 116; and political
    violence, 94–7. *See also* democracy
    and religion
rent appropriation, 16–18, 148, 207,
    226; and asset concentration, 214;
    data on, 208; and revolutions, 214–20
revolutions, 27, 34–6, 93–7: Chinese,
    14, 216, 219; liberal, 29; soviet, 14,
    92, 216, 219. *See also* political
    violence; rent appropriation and
    revolutions
repression, costs of: and organizational
    resources and technical means, 13,

26, 44–7; and political violence,
    34–6; and regime choice 10, 32–4,
    135, 149. *See also* political
    violence
right-wing dictatorship: definition of,
    10, 23; and economic reform, 219;
    and rent appropriation, 205, 210–14;
    and social mobility, 141
rule of law, 173. *See also* property
    rights

schooling. *See* education; human capital
separation of powers. *See*
    presidentialism
slavery, 120, 156
social democratic parties, 7, 46, 138
social mobility: and democracy, 14,
    140–2; as an equalizing force, 14; and
    tax rate, 141–2. *See also* income
    volatility
sociological theories of democracy, 7,
    15
stateless societies, 39n22, 223
subsidies. *See* transfers; unemployment
    benefits

tariffs, 57
taxes: asset taxability, 25, 39; and
    credible commitment, 14, 131–9,
    220; and economic development, 14,
    130, 221; establishment of tax rate,
    23–5, 131–3, 141, 172–3; income
    sensitivity of, 25–6, 39, 63;
    Meltzer-Richards model, 23, 174,
    175n2; and political decentralization,
    155; and regime choice, 10; and
    stationary bandits, 224; and
    unidimensionality of politics, 144;
    welfare loses of, 23, 130–1. *See also*
    public sector size
toleration. *See* pluralistic values
trade, and democracy 14–15, 54,
    142, 240; and compensation
    programs 177–8, data on, 182; and
    economic development, 14–15, 182;

Mark Irving Lichbach and Alan S. Zuckerman, eds., *Comparative Politics: Rationality, Culture, and Structure*

Doug McAdam, John McCarthy, and Mayer Zald, eds., *Comparative Perspectives on Social Movements*

Scott Mainwaring and Matthew Soberg Shugart, eds., *Presidentialism and Democracy in Latin America*

Anthony W. Marx, *Making Race, Making Nations: A Comparison of South Africa, the United States, and Brazil*

Joel S. Migdal, Atul Kohli, and Vivienne Shue, eds., *State Power and Social Forces: Domination and Transformation in the Third World*

Scott Morgenstern and Benito Nacif, *Legislative Politics in Latin America*

Wolfgang C. Muller and Kaare Strom, *Policy, Office, or Votes?*

Ton Notermans, *Money, Markets, and the State: Social Democratic Economic Policies since 1918*

Paul Pierson, *Dismantling the Welfare State?: Reagan, Thatcher and the Politics of Retrenchment*

Marino Regini, *Uncertain Boundaries: The Social and Political Construction of European Economies*

Jefferey M. Sellers, *Governing from Below: Urban Regions and the Global Economy*

Yossi Shain and Juan Linz, eds., *Interim Governments and Democratic Transitions*

Theda Skocpol, *Social Revolutions in the Modern World*

Richard Snyder, *Politics after Neoliberalism: Reregulation in Mexico*

David Stark and László Bruszt, *Postsocialist Pathways: Transformming Politics and Property in East Central Europe*

Sven Steinmo, Katheleen Thelan, and Frank Longstreth, eds., *Structuring Politics: Historical Institutionalism in Comparative Analysis*

Duane Swank, *Global Capital, Political Institutions, and Policy Change in Developed Welfare States*

Sidney Tarrow, *Power in Movement: Social Movements and Contentious Politics*

Ashutosh Varshney, *Democracy, Development, and the Countryside*

Elisabeth Jean Wood, *Forging Democracy from Below: Insurgent Transitions in South Africa and El Salvador*